Blanche of Castile

By Régine Pernoud
HELOISE AND ABELARD

ELEANOR OF AQUITAINE

BLANCHE OF CASTILE

BLANCHE
OF
CASTILE

RÉGINE PERNOUD

Translated by Henry Noel

Coward, McCann & Geoghegan, Inc.
New York

First American Edition 1975

First published in France under the title *La Reine Blanche*
Copyright © 1972 by Editions Albin Michel
English translation copyright © 1975 by Wm. Collins Sons & Co., Ltd.

SBN: 698-10595-8
Library of Congress Catalog Card Number: 74-79678
PRINTED IN THE UNITED STATES OF AMERICA

For Madou

CONTENTS

Illustrations follow pages 128 and 224.

PROLOGUE

Blanche of Castile is one of those figures in history whom the textbooks have irrevocably typed. Her name provokes comments as automatic as conditioned reflexes. 'She was a domineering mother,' is the most frequent. She is also called a 'shrew', a 'diehard', an 'old battle-axe', a 'cantankerous mother-in-law', and so on. Even when the general impression is not wholly unsympathetic, it is monolithic: a hard woman, cold and unfeeling.

Blanche belongs in those thousand years of history which are still persistently called the 'Middle Ages', despite the strictures of scientific method and common sense alike. Almost all the personages in that period have been stereotyped. We may count ourselves lucky that Blanche even has a place in that dreary portrait gallery which is all that the official histories allow to remain of those thousand years. From the professional historian's point of view, Blanche's reign and that of her son, St Louis, are the least-known in all French history. Complete catalogues have been made of the records of the kings preceding and following them, but nothing has yet been done for the period of half a century in which they reigned.

And what a period it was! The cathedrals and the castles, the great fairs, the *Summa Theologiae* of Thomas Aquinas, the founding of the University of Paris, and the start of the Inquisition – all came then. Yet only one systematic study of Blanche has been made, Élie Berger's biography, published in 1895, and it is far from complete. As for Louis, all we have is the biography written by Le Nain de Tillemont in the latter part of the 17th century and published only in 1847. Nothing further exists, except for accounts of the 'Lives of the Saints' type, designed for popular consumption. Our knowledge of the period still depends on the inevitably biased chronicles of the time, chief among which is Joinville's *History of St Louis*. Even this has never appeared in a critical edition.

Thus, from the point of view of scholarship, almost everything remains to be done. A systematic study of the period will no doubt yield some surprises.*

As it happens, the first picture of Blanche to appear in the records is radically different from the time-worn image.

It is the picture of a little girl crying as one can only cry at the age of twelve, with those around her vainly endeavouring to comfort her.

The incident is found in a biography considered to be a model of its kind: *The Life of St Hugh*, Bishop of Lincoln, by his contemporary, Adam, Abbot of Eynsham. It is a work unique in its accuracy and in the wealth of detail that brings every scene alive, with a flavour like that of *The Golden Legend*.

Hugh of Lincoln (like many Englishmen of the period, he was pure French, born at Avalon in Dauphiné) was on his way through Paris. A famous scholar and theologian, he had come from Saint-Denis, where the Parisian students came out in a body to greet him. He was first welcomed by the Bishop of Paris, then visited by the King's son and heir, young Louis of France. The prince, thirteen years old, asked him to come and see his little bride, Blanche of Castile. They had been married a month before, and now, for several days, Blanche had been crying over some unknown grief. Hugh went at once to the palace of the Cité, which was not far from where he was staying. He found Blanche and talked with her alone. The girl dried her tears, quieted her sobbing, and smiled again; her

---

* There is no dearth of records. In the French national archives the collection of *Trésors des Chartes* alone contains more than 4000 original documents: administrative records, treaties, bills of sale, donations, etc., half of which deal with the period of Blanche's reign. There are abundant materials for an exhaustive study of that reign.

grief had vanished. 'From then on,' says the chronicle, 'her looks and heart were of the happiest.'

The *Life of St Hugh* is full of stories like that, worthy of the 'Little Flowers' of St Francis of Assisi. They tell of children spontaneously smiling when his glance fell on them – even the babes in arms held out for his blessing. Animals also fell under his sway. No story of St Hugh is complete without the tame swan that followed him everywhere when he was in Lincoln, and would take food only from his hand.

It is tempting to try to imagine what these two may have said to each other: the Bishop in his sixties, and the little girl. Yet is it quite right to call Blanche a 'little girl'? She was twelve, the age at which girls were then considered adults and able to order their own lives.* Hugh, having spent his life in the abbey of the Grande-Chartreuse, near Grenoble, then at Witham, in England, where he was called to found an abbey, and finally at Lincoln as bishop, could not have known very much about feminine psychology, apart from what his own intuition may have taught him. But we may be sure of one thing: he would not have spoken to Blanche as to a child; he would not have tried to comfort her with empty words.

Blanche was to be Queen, and at that time being a queen was no mere decorative function. It meant a lifelong dedication to an exacting task. It meant assuming an important part of the government of the country, sometimes the entire responsibility. Blanche, having just made the trip from the banks of the Ebro in her native Castile to those of the Loire in the company of her grandmother, Eleanor of Aquitaine, may have drawn some useful instruction from the old queen's reminiscences. In the course of a long life, Eleanor had stood up to the Emperor, defied the Pope, wrested her son from prison, and evaded all the snares laid for her by the King of France. Blanche's own mother, Eleanor of Castile, had as energetically stood by her husband on the battlements of their castles of

* Boys only attained their majority at fourteen. The law took into account the fact that physical maturity came sooner in girls than in boys.

Palencia and Burgos, where the look-outs were ever on watch for the approach of the victorious Moors.

Blanche had learned of many queens in the history they had taught her: queens long dead and others still alive; haughty queens and frivolous; queens imprisoned or sent into exile; well-beloved queens and detested ones; happy queens and lonely queens. Not one of them had chosen her own lot, yet each had had the power to choose or refuse greatness.

A queen's destiny is set when she is born. Blanche had not chosen to be the wife of Louis – any more than Louis had chosen to be her spouse. But now a great role awaited her. She had been brought to France as a pledge of peace between two kingdoms. It would not be easy, and if fears, homesickness and apprehension overwhelmed her, it was understandable. Also, neither her uncle John, King of England, nor her father-in-law Philip, King of France, could have had a very reassuring look to a little girl. The palace of the Cité during that rainy spring must have seemed grim after the sparkling towers of Palencia, bathed in sunlight. The court of France was more austere than that of Castile, where every wandering troubadour was given a warm welcome and a place at table.

Yet this was to be Blanche's life and she must accept it, even if later she might gradually make things more to her own liking. For the moment there were too many others who depended on her, who looked to her for their happiness – her husband and his people, for a start. First and foremost she must think of them. A queen can only become great by forgetting herself. Was she not in any case committed to a cause far greater than herself? Her task was to bring an end to quarrels. For kings establish justice, but it is queens who establish peace.

I

A FOURSOME OF QUEENS

At the turn of the 13th century women were making history, and much history was being made. Throughout the feudal period, from the reign of Hugh Capet to that of Philip the Fair and his sons, it would be hard to find a more troubled time than the first years of Queen Blanche at the court of France, years that turned her from a girl into a woman.

Her whole life was to be shaped by the dramatic events that occurred between her twelfth and twentieth birthdays. Her whole reign was to be devoted to pacifying and ending struggles brought about, often unintentionally, by those whom we know as Eleanor, Isabella, Constance and Ingeborg.

At the time of her meeting with Hugh of Lincoln,[1] Blanche was still only a child with no problems to speak of. She had been born twelve years earlier, on March 4, 1188, in the castle of Palencia, in Castile, and had spent most of her childhood there. Her mother, Eleanor of Castile, must often have told her how she herself had left her childhood haunts in Poitiers England and Normandy, her birthplace, to come to Castile and marry King Alfonso VIII, whom they called Alfonso the Noble. She had been accompanied on that trip by her own mother, Eleanor of Aquitaine. Blanche could scarcely guess that one day that same grandmother Eleanor, now Queen of England, would come to fetch her too, and take her on her own life's pilgrimage, back along the way her mother had come.

The lively court of Castile was visited by all the greatest troubadours of the time. As a child, Blanche had heard the singing of Giraut de Borneil, Uc de Saint-Circ, and of Folquet de Marseille before he became a monk at the abbey of Le

Thoronet. Blanche and her two sisters had laughed when they learned that Guilhem de Berguedan was lovesick for their mother and had written poem after poem to her. The three girls had applauded Guiraut de Calanson, Perdigon, and the celebrated Peire Vidal. Blanche was one of the *donzelas*, noble ladies at the court of Alfonso, who had been at pains to learn by heart the song *Castia-gilos* by Raimon Vidal de Bezalu, about that King of Castile who

> Was crowned with many laurels,
> With wisdom and with mirth,
> And deeds of derring-do

– her own father; and about her mother, that gentle queen, gorgeously arrayed in her vermilion silk mantle edged with silver and embroidered with gold.[2]

Alfonso and Eleanor were a happy couple. Their court was the most cultivated in Europe, specially now that the court at Poitiers had ceased to exist. Theirs would also have been the gayest court but for the constant Saracen menace that hung over Castile. Blanche had learned about that very early in life. She was only seven when her father's armies were defeated on the battlefield of Alarcos.

Two years later her elder sister, Berengaria, had left them to marry King Alfonso of León. All three girls had been destined for illustrious matches, and Blanche was not surprised when, in the first days of the year 1200, she had learned that her sister Urraca was to wed the heir of France, the young Louis. In the middle of winter, with the wind blowing at the sparkling white stones of their Castilian castles and churches, Queen Eleanor of England had arrived. She was eighty years old, but still looked like an Amazon riding into the storm. She reached Palencia accompanied by Élie de Malemort, Archbishop of Bordeaux, and a whole retinue of knights, bowmen, and clerics. Blanche had watched her arrival with intense curiosity. So this was the great lady whose renown echoed throughout the West; who had been Queen first of France, then of England;

who had ridden into battle against the infidel in the East. Had not all the greatest troubadours sung her praises, and the Holy Roman Emperor himself bowed before her when she had gone in person to ask freedom for her son Richard?

And now here was the old queen at the court of Castile. She prolonged her stay for several weeks. She had just lost her beloved Richard and was sombre, devoured by cares which would have broken any lesser spirit. She dreaded to see her youngest son, John Lackland, ascend the throne. Little by little she relaxed in the presence of her daughter and her grandchildren in the friendly atmosphere of the Castilian court. She often talked with her granddaughters, and seemed specially friendly towards Blanche. One day the girl learned with amazement that it was she and not her sister whom they wanted to go to France and wed the young Louis. Why? Those close to Queen Eleanor claimed that the French could not get used to the name 'Urraca', while 'Blanca' would very naturally become 'Blanche'. A mere pretext, as everyone realized. To make things easier, Urraca was promptly affianced to the heir to the Portuguese throne.

Not long after Easter, and scarcely recovered from her surprise, Blanche found herself riding along the highroads, close to Queen Eleanor's litter. At the halts her grandmother talked readily with her and taught her how she must act. She described the girl's future husband, who was a boy scarcely older than Blanche herself. Eleanor had caught a glimpse of him when she had gone to swear fealty to his father, King Philip. Louis was blond and slender, perhaps a little frail, but with fine features and a clear gaze that he must have inherited from his mother, the gentle Isabella of Hainault. Maybe he also resembled his grandfather, King Louis VII of France, who had been Eleanor's first husband.

The young prince was said to be studious and devoted to literature. His father had given him excellent tutors, who could now help Blanche to complete her own education. One of them, Amaury of Bène, specially assigned to watch over the prince's studies, was a master from the schools of Paris, which were famous for their learning.

The Queen became less communicative when Blanche asked about her future father-in-law, King Philip of France, known as Philip Augustus. She did not answer at all when asked about her own son, King John of England, though she often spoke of Richard, whom all Christendom called Lionheart, telling Blanche of his great deeds in the East, at Acre and Joppa. She recited poems he had written, and told of his musical ear, so keen that he could not bear to hear people sing off key. Once, in a monastery, he had tried to get the monks to sing in unison by stamping up and down the choir in time to the music. She told of how, when he was only twelve – Blanche's age – he had received the fealty of the Limousin barons, and had had the ring of St Valeria, a precious relic of the beheaded martyr, slipped on to his finger in the cathedral of Limoges. She described the splendid tunic of rose-coloured silk, embroidered with silver crescents, which she herself had had made for his wedding to Queen Berengaria, on the island of Cyprus.

When Eleanor and Blanche made a halt at Bordeaux, the old queen recalled her own marriage in that town, at the cathedral of St Andrew, and the festivities which had followed at the Ombrière palace, the very place where they were now resting. Suddenly, while they were talking, messengers burst into the room. One of them whispered a few words to the old queen. Blanche saw her grandmother sway and grow pale at the news that a certain Mercadier, the leader of an armed band who were at times mercenary bowmen, at others mere plunderers, had for some unknown reason quarrelled with a similar band led by one Brandin, and had been killed in the brawl. Mercadier had often led his men faithfully in the service of King Richard, and had constituted Eleanor's own escort on her trip into Castile only a few weeks earlier. A rascal like all his breed, gallows-birds born, who made war their trade and booty their glory, Mercadier had none the less served Richard loyally and well. He had been at the King's side below the ramparts of the castle of Châlus when Richard had been struck by the fatal arrow. Mercadier's death, coming just after Eleanor's arrival with the heiress for the realm of France whom she herself had chosen, was sad news and must have seemed an evil omen to the Queen.

At Richard's death Eleanor had left the convent of Font-evrault, where she had intended to spend her last days, to throw herself with renewed energy into saving what might still be saved of the Plantagenet possessions. She was under no illusions about the ability of her son John. The Queen had had five sons by her second husband, Henry II Plantagenet. Through misfortune the first four had all died, leaving to the youngest the weighty inheritance of England, the possessions in Normandy, Poitou and Guienne in the west of France, which together made the Plantagenet dynasty the most far-flung and the richest in Europe.

But John Lackland did not have the makings of a King. He was intelligent, like all Eleanor's children, but he had – and to excess – the same instability that had so marred his father. He was incapable either of keeping his promise to others or of maintaining his own resolve. This was a major fault in an age when the whole cohesion of society rested on the pledged word, man to man, and a king's strength lay not in his ministers, or his army, or his treasury, but solely in the loyalty of the other lords within his realm. Moreover, John's personal be-haviour was disturbing even for his mother, despite all the deference he showed her. Since the age of seven he had refused Holy Communion. He was to be the only English king in history who did not receive the sacraments at the time of his coronation. On the other hand, like many unbelievers, he was superstitious.

When Bishop Hugh of Lincoln urged him to be worthy of his predecessors on the throne of England, John pointed to his amulet, a precious stone which he wore about his neck. 'This stone comes from my ancestors,' he replied, 'and he who possesses it also possesses the kingdom.' When the Bishop exhorted him to place his faith not in a lifeless stone, but in the living rock that was Jesus, the appeal proved useless. A few days later, at Easter High Mass, the chamberlain handed him the twelve gold coins which, traditionally, the King gave to the offering on that occasion. Instead of going to place them before the Bishop, John fingered and gloated over the gold, as if he could not bring himself to part with it. He raised his eyes towards the Bishop and sighed: 'Only a few days ago, rather than give them to you, I would have put them into my own pocket! Well, take them while they're going.' The Bishop, red with anger, had turned away, and in the end the King had tossed the coins into the collection plate.[3] A thousand similar stories, sordid and unbecoming, were told of him, and it was also said that in the cathedral of Rouen, on the day he was invested with the dukedom of Normandy, as the Archbishop placed in his hand the lance that symbolized that office, John let it drop to the ground – a bad omen for the future of the province.

Eleanor had exercised all her ingenuity in finding ways to help preserve the Plantagenet realm. First she had gone to Tours in July and sworn fealty to the King of France as suzerain with respect to England's continental possessions. By this gesture the dutiful liege made the suzerain bound to protect him. At the same time she had shown herself aware of the gains in power of the towns during the past century. They were now strongly asserting themselves. She had toured all the main towns of western France, granting everywhere the charters eagerly petitioned for by the burghers, and binding them in turn to supply troops should her son need them.

She had looked further still and, always acting in person, had done all that was in her power to safeguard the future of the kingdom. That was why she had crossed the Pyrenees in order to bring back to France the heiress she herself had chosen. For John Lackland's rather dull wife, Hawisa of Gloucester, had given him no children. But now, even if John should lose his French possessions, these would not entirely slip away from the Plantagenets. Someone of their blood would still be on the throne, and might even accomplish what had once been Eleanor's fondest dream: the union under one crown of France and England.

Thus it was that on May 23, 1200, Blanche was solemnly wed to Louis, prince and heir of France. One senses in the language of the chroniclers of the time something of the popular enthusiasm that must have greeted the girl on her arrival in France. She was the pledge of peace between rival kings. She was also beautiful, with a straight clear gaze. Her contemporaries did not leave a detailed description of her, saying only that she was renowned for her beauty. And they made a pun on her name, which, they attest, perfectly suited her: '*Candida candescens candore et cordis et oris*'[3] – translated loosely as, 'Frank in frankness, white in heart as in head.'

Queen Eleanor was not present at the wedding. She had left the party when they reached the Loire and returned to her retreat at Fontevrault, entrusting to the Archbishop of Bordeaux the duty of leading Blanche to her royal destiny. But in the course of many talks with her grandmother Blanche had already become fully aware of what she represented to those who welcomed her. She knew of all the bad blood between the Plantagenets and the kings of France, of the quarrels which wanted only a pretext to break out again. Philip of France had never concealed his designs on the English dukedom of Normandy; he had attempted to seize the Norman fortresses while King Richard was in captivity in Germany. Blanche's own dowry, the town of Evreux with its surrounding land, was a bone of contention between the two kingdoms. Philip had taken it the year before, and no better compromise had been found than for him to give it to his new daughter-in-law, while at the same time John Lackland, her uncle, gave her the fiefs of Issoudun and Grapay in Berry.

The wedding ceremony took place amid suitable pomp, but not without a certain embarrassment. King John, who had gone to place himself voluntarily in hostage on French soil, was not present. The ceremony itself was held at the Abbey of Port-Mort in Normandy – on English soil – because (and it had been a delicate matter to explain this to Blanche) the kingdom of France was under an interdict.

The word takes us back to a time quite different from our own, and deserves some explanation. It was an age of faith. When persons sinned notoriously against universally accepted practices, the Church had two weapons against them: excommunication and interdiction. Excommunication deprived such sinners of the right to receive the communion of the faithful, the Holy Eucharist. When they were excommunicated, an interdict struck further at those holding power. It forbade, throughout all their lands, the functioning of any kind of church offices, even to the giving of sacraments and the ringing of church bells.

On January 13 of that same year, 1200, the Pope's legate had placed the kingdom of France under an interdict. The reason was a woman.

The court of France had been in turmoil. Philip, left a widower by his first wife, Isabella, had requested and been granted the hand of Ingeborg, sister of King Canute VI of Denmark. Their union had been solemnized on August 15, 1193, at Paris. To this day no one knows what happened on the wedding night. But the following morning, upon seeing his bride again – whom, it should be noted, everyone agreed was a lovely girl – King Philip had fallen into a cold sweat and nervous tremors and had that very instant declared that he would have none of her. It is one of the riddles of French history.*

---

* Only one man might have sympathized with the King in this matter, though for quite different reasons, and reasons, again, of which we know nothing. It is that Carthusian monk, a very holy man, of whom the biographer of Hugh of Lincoln tells us that his prior gave him the mission of founding a convent in Denmark. He refused point-blank, and went up and down the corridors and cloisters of the monastery, shouting: 'Lord, save me from Denmark!'

Whatever may have been the physical peculiarities of the Danish princess, the King's treatment of her was inexcusable. He not only refused to consider Ingeborg his wife, but, in order to facilitate finding another wife, he decided to have her imprisoned. Then, seeking a pretext for divorce, he discovered that Ingeborg was a relative of his first wife, Isabella of Hainault. He thereupon, without delay, married Agnes of Meran, daughter of a prince of the Holy Roman Empire, even though she was so closely related to him that their union was automatically forbidden by canon law. He had found obliging churchmen to annul the first marriage and solemnize the second, on May 7, 1196. But Ingeborg had appealed to the Pope, who had no choice but to uphold her. Pope Celestine III did no more than issue appeals and warnings. But when Innocent III became Pope in 1198 the affair had been dragging on for two years, and Rome's condemnation became much more forceful. When Philip simply would not yield, the kingdom was placed under an interdict.

Too late, King Philip tried to fight back. But he was caught. At that time an interdict was a formidable disciplinary measure. The whole population was deprived of the sacraments. The mere fact that the church-bells could no longer be rung had all kinds of unpleasant consequences, for it was the bells that marked the whole tempo of daily life, calling to and from work and prayer, signalling feast-days, and announcing to the people all the many occasions of public rejoicing and bereavement. In an attempt to keep the bishop of Paris, Odo of Sully, a great hereditary lord in his own right, in his interdicted diocese, Philip confiscated all his horses. Undismayed, the Bishop walked out of Paris.

No bells rang out the news when Louis and Blanche crossed the Seine to Paris, and took up their quarters in the palace of the Cité. The interdict remained in force until the following September, when Philip at last agreed to be separated from Agnes, and the Pope raised the ban. Blanche thus gained first-hand experience of the meaning of ecclesiastical penalties. The incident came at a turning-point in history, for the Church was shortly to start misusing its considerable weapon.

Blanche's first months in that realm of France, whose queen she knew she would some day be, were spent in the Ile-de-France, for the most part in the palace of the Cité of Paris. The Archbishop of Bordeaux, who had escorted her all the way from Castile, had taken leave of her after blessing her marriage. Then she had gone to Paris and Fontainebleau with her young husband and the kings of both France and England. Her father-in-law, ordinarily parsimonious, had ordered splendid wedding celebrations. Philip and John seemed to be on good terms. They had amicably settled the question of Blanche's dowry, which she was probably too young to take much interest in. She could not assess the value of the castellanies of Hesdin, Bapaume, and Lens, given her on behalf of her spouse, any more accurately than that of the possessions in Normandy and Berry given by her uncle.

On the other hand Louis, her companion in studies and games until they should really become man and wife, had immediately won her affection. Born on September 5, 1187, he was only a few months older than she. He was of medium stature, blond, with handsome features – the image of his mother, Isabella of Hainault, everyone said. But he had scarcely known that gracious and beautiful princess:

> . . . Queen Isabeau,
> Of lovesome form and eyes aglow.

She was only sixteen when Louis was born, and she had died two years later, leaving fond memories of her goodness, also a precious relic of history: her silver seal, found in her tomb.

Louis was 'a child of happy disposition',[4] but his health was delicate. At the age of two, just after his mother's death, he himself had almost died of dysentery. At nineteen his life would again be in danger. There was a striking contrast between the fragile son and his father, King Philip, whom Blanche,

little by little, was getting to know better. Though Philip was
    Well-made, well-wrought, and straight and tall,
    His whiskers russet-tinged, withal,
there was little of the courtly hero about him. He had strongly
practical instincts, and huge ambitions held in check only by a
fox-like cunning. He was temperamental, say the chroniclers,
'easily roused and easily appeased'. Yet beneath the look of a
free-for-all wrestler he hid some tenderer feelings. He dearly
loved his son, and also his bastards: Philip and Mary, the
children of Agnes of Meran; and Peter Charles, whom he had
had by 'a demoiselle of Arras'.

The gardens of the palace rang with the shouts and games of
children, but they were too young for Blanche to look upon
them as companions. On the other hand, several noble young
ladies of her own country had accompanied her and were living
in the palace. Among them may have been the Spanish girl
Amincia, called by the diminutive Mincia, who is often mentioned in the records. Blanche's mother and father, and her
sister Berengaria, affectionately nicknamed Berenguela, sent
her letters and messengers regularly. Blanche remained faithful
to that correspondence all her life. Mention is often found in
the court ledgers of a Rodriguez or a Garcia, to whom some
small present was made upon his arrival or departure.

Like most young persons of their day, Blanche and Louis
divided their time between studies and sports. From earliest
youth they had learned to ride, which was the only means of
travel other than walking. Louis had very early evinced a
passion for horses. About the age of ten he had written to his
godfather, Stephen, Bishop of Tournai, with the blunt request
that he send him a handsome palfrey. The good man had
hastened to do so, accompanying the gift with many exhorta-
tions to 'study your letters with utmost diligence, for they will
be useful to you and to your kingdom, and needful when in
council of state in your palace; for treating of the business of
your government; for concord in peace and for victory in
war.'[5] Louis was an obedient child and took this advice to

heart. Moreover King Philip, whose own education had been neglected in such matters, was very particular that his son should master them.

Blanche studied with Louis. She learned 'grammar', which we would now call 'literature', music, and also the more exacting sciences of geometry and astronomy. Queens were expected to know Holy Scripture, Latin, and to have some familiarity with legal terms. Clerks might actually pen the correspondence, but many ladies were able to compose letters of great individual elegance, at a time when stylistic perfection was highly important. And Blanche wrote not only prose, but verse.

> Love, who too late has captured me,
> Has taught me by his mastery,
> O Queen of Heaven, Sovereign Lady,
> That he who would your praises sing
> And hymn the joy that is lasting
> Must love and serve you above all thing,
> O Queen and maiden, fleur-de-lis.[6]

Prince Louis had also to learn the handling of sword and lance, and for this warlike training the King appointed Henry Clément, Marshal and faithful servant of the royal family. Finally, hunting was for both Louis and Blanche a combined pleasure and study. The treatises on venery show that it took a practised eye and long experience to know how to stalk game. At that time hunting, like dancing, was a favourite 'revel' of young people. From their earliest years Blanche and Louis had followed the hounds in the forests of Fontainebleau and Senlis, and even in Vincennes wood, where Henry Plantagenet, elder brother of King John, had released a herd of stags and does as a present to King Philip upon his accession.

Studies in common, and habits acquired together, softened somewhat the harshness of these arranged marriages which were the rule in all titled families at the time. One did not first love and then marry; one learned to love through being married. Living through the last years of childhood together created a bond between the two young persons pledged to each other. With Louis and Blanche the pledge was clearly confirmed by personal affinity.

There was no lack of companions for study and games. The children of the leading barons were all brought to live at court, beginning with the orphans, who were the king's wards. Thus young Theobald, the future Count of Champagne, had been at court since the age of four or five. He plainly worshipped his cousin Blanche, ten years his senior. There were also Johanna and Margaret, the two daughters of the Countess of Flanders. Their father, Baldwin, had been proclaimed Emperor while in the East, but had soon after been killed in battle. All these became closely associated with Blanche and Louis. In particular, Arthur, the young Count of Brittany, and his sister Eleanor, were their intimates, even if not for long. Their father, Geoffrey Plantagenet, an elder brother of John Lackland, had died young, and John had reason to fear their eventual claims to the throne of England – claims which King Philip encouraged on the sly. Philip was only too pleased that Arthur's mother, Constance, had given the boy into his care, for Constance loathed the Plantagenets. The whole matter was left in deliberate ambiguity at the court of France. No one had any inkling of the drama that would end it. For that matter, the main subject of gossip at court a few months after Blanche's arrival was the romantic circumstances surrounding another young woman who had just come on to the stage of History.

Isabella, daughter of the Count of Angoulême, was fourteen years old. It was the age of Shakespeare's Juliet and, according to her contemporaries, she was as beautiful. She was betrothed to Hugh of Lusignan, Count of La Marche. Her father and her fiancé were both vassals of King John, since Poitou, along with most of western France, formed part of the Plantagenet domain. John, having bid King Philip farewell after Blanche's wedding, had set out to visit his continental possessions. He was welcomed with great pomp at the château of Lusignan, where Isabella was presented to him by her fiancé.

A few weeks later, news came that King John himself had wedded Isabella, in the presence of her father, and hence with his complicity. It was little less than an abduction; the rightful fiancé had not even been notified. At one fell swoop King John had robbed a powerful vassal of both his bride-to-be and the Angoulême heritage which she brought with her. Fearing possible reprisals, John cut short his visit to France and returned precipitately to England, where he had had Isabella crowned queen in Westminster on October 8, 1200.

To say that Europe was thunderstruck is to put it mildly. John's French vassals in Poitou, Saintonge and Aquitaine, were so taken aback by the suddenness of the affair that they did not even react. At one stroke the King of England had broken all the rules of feudal law. No suzerain had ever treated his vassal in such a way. Presently Hugh of Lusignan pulled himself together and protested at the double outrage, claiming compensation.

It is easy to guess the interest all this aroused at the court of France. Philip had never concealed his designs on the Plantagenet continental possessions. He linked them to Arthur of Brittany's own ambitions, which were easily whetted. Since John had outraged feudal honour, was this not the occasion for both Philip and Arthur to act?

The winter passed in an atmosphere of calm before the storm. Everyone seemed aware of the impending crisis except John himself, who was wholly taken up with dalliance. Isabella showed a talent for making the best of things; she loved merry-making, and the banquets and balls followed one after another at Westminster.

For Blanche and Louis it was mainly a winter of bereavement. The sad news had reached them that Bishop Hugh of Lincoln had died on Martinmas Day, November 11, 1200. The saintly man who had so cheered and encouraged Blanche had been taken ill in France while on a last pilgrimage to his native Dauphiné and the abbey of the Grande-Chartreuse, where as a youth he had felt the call to be a monk. He had scarcely managed to return to Lincoln before succumbing. His funeral there drew huge crowds, for everyone had loved him. The long procession was headed by two kings, John of England and William of Scotland, helping to carry the coffin, followed by a score of archbishops and bishops, a hundred priests and as many barons, and a great multitude of commoners.

Around Easter 1201, King Philip decided that it was time for him to assume his role of arbiter, for John was after all his vassal with respect to his continental fiefs. All the barons connected with the family of Lusignan, kinsmen of the Count of La Marche, were up in arms, led by Hugh's brother, Ralph of Exoudun, Count of Eu. Philip, who wished to exhaust all means of conciliation, invited John to come with his bride and stop long enough in the Ile-de-France for the Lusignan complaints to be carefully considered. Thus Blanche and Isabella met in Paris in June 1201. Isabella proved to be a most liberated young princess, who liked above all to dance late into the night and then 'to sleep until noon of the following day', as a scandalized chronicler reports.[7] This girl who had not balked at breaking her plighted troth without even consulting her fiancé was clearly a headstrong individual.

Philip spared neither expense nor courtesy in his hospitality to the royal couple and to their English barons and squires. The wine flowed in abundance, though it should be recalled that 'French wine' then meant wine from the Ile-de-France, the slopes around Paris, whose vintages were then considered excellent. The superior quality was rather lost on the English, however, who were indiscriminate, if heavy, drinkers. 'There was much mirth among the King of France and those of his court,' noted a chronicler, 'to see how the English King's people drank all the bad wines and left the good ones![8]'

As for King John, he was ecstatic, for he reasoned that if he were so sumptuously feasted, it must mean that Philip was afraid of him. And Philip, who was always on the look-out for an extra acre here or there, had Blanche ask John if he would, simply as a personal favour, cede the bit of land between the

Evreux district (which was Blanche's own dowry) and the river Andelle – a favour which she easily obtained in the generally festive and accommodating atmosphere.

However, the agenda did require that Philip bring up the matter of the Lusignan complaints. John produced a bright but rather antiquated idea: a judicial combat. Let Hugh of La Marche designate a champion. He, John, would do the same, and the two men chosen would fight it out in the lists. Whichever man won would be deemed to be in the right. But the assembled French barons rejected this primitive solution. John and Isabella returned to England with the problem unresolved.

With great patience, Philip then sent negotiators to Le Goulet in Normandy, where the terms of Blanche's betrothal to Louis had been agreed upon. But this time the French envoys could not reach agreement with those from England. The custom of the time required that all possible means of settlement be exhausted before resorting to force, so John was now summoned to be tried by a court composed of the barons, his peers. He had returned to the continent and was staying at Les Andelys. When the summons reached him, he complacently disdained to answer. The court of barons none the less sat on April 28, 1202, and judged that 'the King of England shall be deprived of all the lands which hitherto he and his ancestors have held from the King of France,' which was to say all the English continental possessions. John, by his truculence, had given Philip a better than hoped-for pretext to undertake the eagerly coveted reconquest of Normandy.

What followed was brief and dramatic, and left a strong impression on Blanche's fourteen-year-old mind, for the events that now took place involved many of those closest to her. First, Arthur of Brittany. The youth bade Blanche and Louis farewell early in July 1202, and rode out to the glorious destiny he had been assured awaited him. Philip was advancing him as one advances a gambit pawn in chess. Arthur was well-liked in Brittany, where his father Geoffrey, formerly Duke of Brittany, was vividly remembered. One can still find old votive stones in the chapels there, inscribed *Pro Gosfrido Deum orate* – 'Pray God for Geoffrey.'

So Philip had given young Arthur a large part of the western lands of which John had been stripped – not only Brittany, but also Anjou, Maine, Touraine, and Poitou – all to be his fiefs if he could conquer them. Philip, whose prime objective was Normandy, had begun by seizing a string of towns and fortresses between Eu and Lyons-la-Forêt (between Rouen and Beauvais). Arthur joined him at Gournay-en-Bray, where he was solemnly knighted and swore allegiance to the King of France for the promised fiefs. Then, very proud of his new knighthood, of the two hundred barons who were escorting him until the promised reinforcements from Poitou should arrive, and of the large sum of money his suzerain had just given him, the fifteen-year-old set out for the Loire. He was never again seen at the court of France.

How he fell into the hands of his uncle, John Lackland, was soon common knowledge. The details that reached Blanche must have been the same as those given in the biography of William Marshal, and she was undoubtedly upset to learn that her own grandmother, Eleanor of Aquitaine, had played a principal role. The old queen, in her retreat at Fontevrault, had learned of the preparations for war and had left to seek safety in Poitiers. But she had been overtaken by the sudden arrival of her grandson Arthur, and had sought refuge at Mirebeau.

When Arthur and those of Poitou were come before the castle, the town was thereupon surrendered to them, but the castle held out. Arthur did parley with his grandam, beseeching her that she might come out therefrom and go her way in good peace with all her chattels, whithersoever she should list, he intending against her person no dishonourable deed. The Queen answered that she should not come out, but he, of his courtesy, should go his way, for other likely castles were to be found, to which he might lay siege, than this one in which she was. And she ceased not to marvel that he should besiege that same castle wherein he knew her to be, forasmuch as he and those of Poitou were her liege men. Notwithstanding, neither Arthur nor those of Poitou inclined to leave off, and they laid siege to the castle, but took it not. And they lodged themselves in the town.[9]

An Angevin knight, William des Roches, who was to play an important part in what followed, left at once to warn John, who was then in the town of Le Mans. 'Sire,' he said, 'if you will faithfully swear, as King and my lord, that Arthur, your nephew, who is my lord and whose man I am against all others save yourself, shall be dealt with by you according as I counsel, I will bind myself to deliver him to you, together with all those of Poitou attendant on him.'

King John hurriedly promised, and ordered his own troops into action. He had learned of the siege of Mirebeau during the night of July 30–31. On August 1, at dawn, he came in sight of the castle. Through Arthur's youthful carelessness, and the over-confidence of those with him, they had not posted scouts. John's arrival became known only when the town watchmen gave the alarm.

When those on watch saw them coming they began to cry out: 'To arms! To arms!' And those of Poitou hastened to arms. Geoffrey of Lusignan, a valiant knight who had done many gallant deeds on this side the sea and beyond, was at table, awaiting a dish of pigeons. When the news came to him that many armed men were to be seen, and no one doubted they were those of John the King, he swore by the Devil he would not rise from the table until he had eaten his pigeons. Time failed him to say more. William des Roches had already forced the only gate left open in the town. Those of Poitou had thought to do well in walling up all gates save one alone, but through this they were taken as in a trap, for when that one was seized by the armies of John Lackland, they had no escape.[10]

Arthur was taken prisoner by a man whose name will be heard again in this narrative: William of Briouze. The whole incident may be summed up here as it was in the *Chronicle of the Dukes of Normandy*: 'What shall I tell you more? All those of Poitou were discomfited, and Arthur and they all were taken. Not one of those proud barons did escape.'

A monk, travelling day and night, brought the news to the Earl of Salisbury, who, with William Marshal and William of Warenne, Earl of Surrey, was defending the Norman fortresses threatened by King Philip.

This monk with all courtesy delivered to them his message and told of the capture of Arthur, of Geoffrey of Lusignan, of his nephew Hugh of Lusignan, Count of La Marche, of Savary of Mauléon, and the other great barons who had joined with Arthur. William Marshal rejoiced exceedingly and said to the monk: 'Carry this message to the Count of Eu with the army of the French at Arques, so that he too may take pleasure in it.' 'Sire,' answered the monk, 'I beg you to excuse me therefrom, for if I go thither, his anger will be such that he may kill me. Do you send another.' 'Not so. You shall go, sir monk. It is not the custom in this land to kill messengers. Go. You will find him with the army.' The monk hastened to Arques and brought the news of Poitou to the Count of Eu, brother of Hugh of La Marche. The Count had looked for a far different message. He grew white and kept his peace. Then he betook him to bed, greatly vexed, for he would tell none other what he had heard.[11]

It was to be the only victory won by King John during his entire reign. It is noteworthy that it was due, at least indirectly, to his mother, Eleanor of Aquitaine.

Blanche may have had cause to fear for Louis during the ensuing battles, but this is not certain. Philip seems to have wished to guard his heir's life and health, though he was in no hurry to make him a partner in affairs of state. He himself had been crowned while his father was still alive, but he had no such plan for his own son. 'He believed that one man alone sufficeth to rule the world,' asserts a contemporary.[12] Louis's first campaign appears to have been a brief and unimportant expedition into Brittany in 1206, a year Parisians were to remember because of the floods which, in December, brought the Seine up to their second storeys, forcing them to move about by rowboat. The Petit Pont collapsed and for several days at least the palace of the Cité became an islet.

Blanche and Louis lived, as did the King, in the nearby residences at Fontainebleau, Melun, Étampes and Orléans, but during their youth they spent most of their time in Paris, and it was the provost of that city who kept their accounts.

To our regret the records are very scant, and give more details of Louis's expenditures than of Blanche's. On the feast of St Andrew (November 30) in 1203, Louis bought a matching cape and hood of green wool, and a camelshair surcoat. At Christmas the same year he acquired 'a black robe and another of camelshair, and a pelisse', at a cost of fifteen *livres* and five *sols*. The green robe that Blanche wore on the same occasion cost thirteen *livres* less five *sols*. The following year in May Louis and Blanche received seven hundred livres for their expenses. The ledger provides details of the young prince's wardrobe. A week before the feast of St Mary Magdalene (July 22), he ordered a cloak and hat of sendal (a thin supple silk), and a green woollen tunic lined with satin. On the Saturday following the 15th August he bought a soberer outfit: a robe made of estanfort, a rich woollen cloth woven in the north of France. In September yet another camelshair robe and a fur-lined cape; then, for the feast of St Rémi, on October 1, two rain-capes. A fortnight later, another green woollen robe and camelshair hood, this one lined with vair. And then another camelshair robe for All Saints' Day, November 1.

The ledger tells far less about the purchases for Blanche's wardrobe. Perhaps she did not buy her clothes in Paris! In any case the records are so incomplete that we are fortunate to possess the list of Louis's purchases during most of a year. We find that on the Saturday following Ash Wednesday, 24 ells of linen* were bought in Paris, 'for the ladies' shifts'. These 'ladies' may have been Blanche herself and her followers. At the same time the unnamed 'ladies' bought twelve slips with silken laces, and two pairs of dresses for Pentecost.[13] On the whole, disappointingly little information, where we should have gladly learned much more.

Despite the alarums and excursions of that troubled period, and the proximity of the war in Normandy, Louis and Blanche probably enjoyed life. We may suppose that it was around the year 1204, when King Philip completed the conquest of Normandy, and a Fleming became Emperor of Constantinople, that their young love flowered. The chroniclers tell us that their marriage was consummated early in 1205. It was to be a perfect union.

> And never queen loved more her lord,
> Nor fondlier of him implored
> His children, that the same she bear,
> The King as well did find them fair . . .
> For each the other loved so well
> That all with them one mind befell.

Meanwhile society was waking up to the changes that had occurred during the preceding century. When Blanche and her grandmother Eleanor had come on their long journey from beyond the Loire, they had seen how many towns and large villages had sprung up in recent decades, with their brand-new

---

* The ell measured about 1.20 m. It would be nice to be able to give the equivalent values of the currency, but the records will not allow any precise estimate to be made. We know that there were 20 *sols* (or *sous*) to the French *livre*. The *livre* was worth one pound's weight of silver, but a pound's weight varied between 380 and 552 grams, according to where one was. It has been estimated that in 1200 the *livre* was worth about one gram of pure gold, at modern rates for the value of gold.

walls, their churches under construction, the houses pushing up like mushrooms. Where before, one castle meant one town, now innumerable new towns seemed to be growing up, on river-banks, at crossroads, at the sites of markets and fairs. Some of the lords, great and small, felt threatened. Others recognized that there was something irresistible in this upsurge of population, and also a promise of prosperity that could benefit them too. In Paris, King Philip had shown an exemplary interest in the townsfolk, doing all that he could for them. From the very start of his reign, when he was only nineteen years old, he had clearly understood the importance for his kingdom of having well-built towns, easy of access and pleasant to live in. He had had the streets of Paris paved – fine sandstone flags that were currently the pride of the city. Better still, with the population spreading to both banks of the Seine, he had built a powerful new city wall. It described a huge semi-circle on the Right Bank, starting (near the church of St-Germain-l'Auxerrois) with the new castle of the Louvre which the King was building. From her windows in the palace of the Cité Blanche could see its keep rising higher and higher.

Philip had realized that with the increase in population the communal bread-ovens were no longer justified, and had allowed each baker to maintain his own oven. This eliminated the endless bread-queues that had so complicated life for the Parisians. To encourage trade he had built a huge stonework enclosure, supported on pillars and called Les Halles, on the site of the new market which his father had established at the spot called Les Champeaux. Crowds of townspeople swarmed here, especially when the fair of St Lazare opened its gates. The King did not stop at assuring the merchants' safety within the enclosure of Les Halles. He also wished to make travelling easier by improving the approaches to Paris. He decreed that henceforth all roads leading to the city-wall must be at least 18 *pied-mains* wide,* for example the road leading to the

* A little over 7 metres, since the measure called a *pied-main* (literally a 'foot-hand') was 0.391 m.

Chaillot bridge, and that between the church of St-Honoré and the Roule bridge.

Philip was now planning to build a similar trading enclosure on the Left Bank. The Right Bank had the advantage of a landing-place for the numerous merchants arriving by boat – the Grève, now the square in front of the Hôtel-de-Ville, but the population of the Left Bank was also growing rapidly, since the schools of Paris were attracting throngs of students. Mont Sainte-Geneviève (today topped by the Panthéon), where thirty years before there had been only farmers tending their vines, was now entirely covered with houses full of teachers and students. The poorest students were sheltered in the 'colleges', private institutions the first of which had been founded about twenty years earlier. They offered bed and board to those entitled to enter them; more and more of them were being started. Latin was the commonest language in those streets of the Left Bank, for it was the *lingua franca* of the world of thought and letters, spoken by the scholars from all over Europe who mingled in the noisy cosmopolitan crowd in what became known as the 'Latin Quarter'.

Those students were a troublesome lot. Now and then rumours of their goings-on reached the palace. Masters and students spent their time arguing (in fact the *disputatio* was a genuine scholarly exercise when undertaken seriously). But they were not always content to deal in ideas. Some were as skilful with the sword as with their quotations from Aristotle.

Aristotle was virtually their Bible. Some of them, following in the footsteps of that Master Abelard whose teachings had been condemned more than eighty years before, even claimed that Holy Scripture – revealed truth – should be scrutinized by the methods of Aristotelian logic. As if faith could be subjected to reason! If only the students would stick to their logic! But they were also hard drinkers and hard fighters, and quarrelled not only among themselves but with the peace-loving towns-folk of Saint-Germain-des-Prés. When Blanche first came to the Cité in 1200, everyone was talking of the riots that had just shaken the Latin Quarter. Five persons had been killed, not only clerks but also laymen, persons who had no connection with the world of learning.

Philip's reaction had been disconcerting. Far from calling the students to account, he had disowned the heavy-handedness of his own soldiers, who had assumed that their main task was to restore order. More than that, the King had disregarded his own provost and decided that henceforth the teachers and students should be under the exclusive jurisdiction of the Church. A rioting student might no longer be chastised or imprisoned. The King's sergeants-at-arms were no longer empowered to arrest him, except to hand him over to the ecclesiastical court. This almost amounted to giving the student complete immunity, for now he would be judged by his peers. The King had thus granted an autonomous status to the world of learning. There was no lack of voices at court predicting that such freedom for a wild and noisy lot would turn into licence. But the King held firm, and was duly praised in the Latin Quarter.

There was a great thirst for knowledge at the time. There were no less than eleven 'little schools' governed directly or indirectly by the precentor of the cathedral. There was also a girls' school. In all of them the rudiments of learning were given, as well as in many other parishes throughout the land.

Philip, ordinarily so jealous of his authority, was following the example set by his father in being indulgent towards the students. Indeed, Louis VII had insisted on having the students be the first to learn of Philip's own birth, and now Philip also showered his royal benevolence on them. On the other hand the Archbishop of Paris, or more exactly his chancellor, who was traditionally the one empowered to grant the right to teach (called the *licence*, which promoted one from a student to a master), was more and more at odds with the professors on precisely this point. Strange rumours were going round. It was said that the masters and students intended to set themselves up as an autonomous body; that those of the Cité, particularly the ones living near the Petit Pont and on the Mont Sainte-Geneviève, had already met and delegated eight of their number to draw up the statute of their 'university', by which they meant the entire membership of the teacher-student body. In other words, they intended to free themselves completely from the Bishop's tutelage.

Public amazement reached its height when it was learned that the Pope had taken their side. Instead of supporting the Bishop, he had approved the regulations which the masters and students had drawn up for themselves. Thus the two supreme authorities of the kingdom and of Christendom were in agreement that the world of learning, of study and instruction should enjoy virtually total autonomy.

There was not the least doubt that, in Paris, the scholars were imbued with a genuine zeal for learning and that the standard of scholarship was very high. It was a period of transition; whatever was new was eagerly considered. Aristotle was being so zealously translated that some wondered if it foreshadowed a return to paganism. Great store was set by the modern arithmetical science of Leonardo da Pisa (better known today as Fibonacci, his real name), as he developed it in his *Liber Abaci* (The Book of the Abacus). He taught the use of certain special symbols (learned from the Arabs) for making calculations, instead of the Roman letters previously used. The Paris scholars adopted his method, which led them to make changes not only in Arithmetic, but also in the three other branches of the *Quadrivium*: Geometry, Music and Astronomy.

It was not only secular learning that was undergoing radical change. The sacred science, theology, was also being transformed. A whole new way of practising religion was arising. When Blanche arrived in Paris she had surely visited the new cathedral under construction, called Notre Dame de Paris. Only the nave and chancel were finished then, and the building must have reared up like some enormous ship, an astonishing sight to foreigners.

In her native Castile and the south of France Blanche had

seen nothing like this architecture which until now was to be found only in the Ile-de-France, Normandy and England. What was her impression when she entered by a side-door, since the foundations of the towers, the façade, and the first bay were all under construction in 1200? Was she impressed by the boldness of this 'French art'? 'If ever this edifice is completed,' the abbot of Mont Saint-Michel had cried upon entering Notre Dame, 'there will be nothing to compare it to but the mountains themselves!' And he had seen only the beginning. The man who had undertaken this noble work, Maurice of Sully, though only a peasant's son, had known how to 'think big'. So big that some people were indignant. 'It's a sin to build the kind of churches we do these days!' scolded Peter the Precentor (an important person in the cathedral chapter). 'What's the use of such height? It's simply a mania . . .'

Who was right? Those who claimed that the simple romanesque church, with its robust semi-circular arches, was best suited to the meetings and prayers of Christians? Or those who praised the new style of building with larger edifices more light-filled than before? Those who inveighed against what they considered needless expense, or those who strove to add more and more splendour to God's house? Not forgetting that it must also welcome God's people, and that the crowds were growing so huge that churches only fifty years old were already too small to accommodate them.

Even as a girl Blanche must have been aware of the disputes that such questions raised in the very core of Christendom. One above all was hotly debated: the wealth of the prelates and church dignitaries. The monasteries were flourishing, but their very opulence brought them under criticism. The donations had accumulated down the years, but no new St Bernard had arisen to exhort the abbeys to simplicity. True, some, like Cluny, and some orders, like the Carthusians, set excellent examples. But there were so many prelates and abbots sumptuously dressed, surrounded by armed escorts superbly mounted and riding at the head of lords of the realm! Many good

Christians were scandalized. Some clamoured for reform, others set out to preach by example.

There was much talk of those 'Poor Men of Lyons' who had formed round a certain Peter Waldo. He had been a rich merchant who, it was said, upon reading the legend of St Alexis, had forsaken his counting-house to live in voluntary poverty. He had attracted large numbers of disciples who went barefoot in pairs along the highways, sharing all they had. Many people admired them and followed their example, but some bishops accused them of preaching without a mandate, without sufficient knowledge of Holy Scripture, and confusedly. Most of them were in fact illiterate. Yet in the hamlets, and even more in the towns, their humble way of life was frequently contrasted with that of the canons, living comfortably on their prebends.

There was also much discussion in Blanche's day of the question of manual labour. When everyone else did useful work, was it right for churchmen to shirk it, on the pretext of tending the altar? Some bishops started working with their hands, like William of Marnès, Bishop of Cambrai, or Julian of Cuenca, who made wickerwork baskets. Peter Waldo's disciples, however, refused to work because it resulted in profit-making; they intended to live entirely on alms. Others seemed perfectly willing to accept the profit principle, but had moved away from the common faith of everyday Christian folk. They were called 'Bougres' or 'Patarins', but they called themselves 'Cathars', meaning 'The Pure'. The very year that Blanche was married, eight of them were convicted of heresy and burned at Troyes. But they continued to flourish, particularly in the towns of northern Italy, so that they came to be called the 'Lombards'; they were also numerous in the Languedoc region of south-western France.

The theologians were unable to agree on how to deal with the Cathars. Some, such as Alan of Lille, declared that one should be severe with heretics only in extreme cases. Others, like Peter the Precentor, in Paris, indignantly denied that they should ever have to suffer the death penalty, and called for its abolition. The people in general did not much like these strange folk who claimed that marriage was a sin and giving one's solemn oath an abomination and that all nature was the handiwork of an evil god. Yet sometimes the people themselves were won over to the heresy, as allegedly happened in the lands of the Count of Toulouse.

One man, however, kept a cool head in the midst of all these concerns: Philip the King. He had only one preoccupation, one well-defined goal: Normandy.

Since the setback at Mirebeau the news of the war told of nothing but French victories. The reconquest of the province was proceeding in the face of all opposition. Falaise was captured by the French; then Vaudreuil; then Château-Gaillard, the cherished fortress of Richard Lionheart, an impregnable stronghold on which his engineers had lavished all their expertise, all the refinements of the art of war. No one had dreamed that the King of France would attempt even to besiege it. King John, who had decided to go hunting in Normandy that spring, had sent a messenger to his constable of Château-Gaillard to go over his preserves and get horses and falcons in readiness. The messenger reached the fortress just in time to learn that King Philip of France was going to occupy it that same day. A surprise attack on March 6, 1204, had enabled some French forces to enter via the latrines tower. The defenders had not even had time to reach the safety of the keep before Château-Gaillard fell.

A few weeks later news had come of the death of Queen Eleanor at Fontevrault. She had passed away still cherishing her memories of the magnificent Plantagenet realm which she had known but which was not to survive her long.

Philip had all his own way. His adversary contented himself with witticisms and taunts, some of which seemed almost unhinged. 'Let him get on with it!' John would shout to the bearers of bad news who followed thick and fast at the court of England. 'One day I'll take it all back again!' When he learned that Vaudreuil castle, full of his silver, provisions, and military equipment, had fallen without a blow being struck, he sent a circular to all the English barons, declaring that he had ordered the surrender. And when messengers came from his constable Peter of Préaux, besieged in Rouen, John refused to interrupt a chess game to receive them. By June 23, 1204, the eve of the feast of St John the Baptist, Philip was master of Rouen.

But at the court of France the most urgent question had to do with Arthur of Brittany. Blanche and Louis became increasingly anxious over the unknown fate of the lad who had been their companion for several years. His sister Eleanor, called the 'Pearl of Brittany', was known to be languishing in some English fortress, probably Corfe Castle in Dorset. But what of Arthur? Some said that John had locked him up in the castle of Falaise and sent a henchman, Hubert de Burgh (later to be the King's justiciar), with orders to castrate him and put out his eyes, so that he should never be fit to rule. But Hubert had balked at such work, and it was thought that when John was obliged to leave Falaise he had had Arthur transferred to Rouen. When the French entered that city they did not suspect the evil deed its walls had witnessed; the young man's fate remained a mystery. The anxiety about him and the harsh treatment meted out by John to his other prisoners all aided Philip's cause. John had acted 'so unseemly' towards the Poitevin barons taken at Mirebeau, according to one contemporary chronicle, that 'those with him who saw such cruelty were ashamed.' One after another, mighty lords were seeking out the King of France and transferring their allegiance to him. John had held his Christmas court in 1202 at Caen. It was the last time any descendant of William the Conqueror ever held court in Normandy.

For the ordinary Christian at the beginning of the thirteenth century, the Crusades were virtually a fact of life. For over a hundred years he had regularly heard the call to 'journey over-sea'. Not a family, in town or country, but had listened to some itinerant preacher at markets and fairs, or given an alms to help someone departing 'oversea'. In an age when the whole idea of pilgrimage was strongly rooted, this pilgrimage in arms, though it meant added hardships and dangers, was no longer the unwonted experience that the First Crusade had been.

Jerusalem, the common fief of all Christendom, had fallen into the hands of the Moslems again in 1187, the year Louis was born. He and Blanche had grown up with the ever-present awareness of great things to be accomplished 'oversea'. Louis's father Philip was clearly not eager to talk of the expedition he had taken part in; it had brought him little glory. He had been unable to stand the climate, or the popularity of his rival, Richard Lionheart. Yet the old tales of battles in the East, and the new complaints coming in, kept the subject on all lips. Every wandering minstrel had in his repertory the *Chanson d'Antioche*, the *Chanson des Chétifs*, or some other epic from the saga of the great hero of the First Crusade, Godfrey of Bouillon. All this had a special meaning for Blanche, for she had spent her childhood listening to accounts of the great event of her time: the expulsion of the Moors from Castile.

The entire West had taken the loss of Jerusalem as a personal affront. Innocent III was scarcely on the papal throne before he sent out the call for Christians to take up arms again to free the Holy Land. The mere call of a preacher, Fulk, curé of Neuilly-sur-Marne, a new Peter the Hermit, was enough to cause the knights at a tourney to lay aside their dress helmets and take the cross.

The enthusiasm had an odd climax. The year 1204 became in the annals of Christendom the year in which the crusaders who had left to recapture Jerusalem seized Constantinople instead. When the news reached the West people at first did not believe it.

Had the imperial capital, city of cities, with its mighty

palaces, its churches, its incredible walls which had resisted all Arab assaults, been seized by a Christian army? As more and more reports confirmed it, dismay turned to indignation. Pope Innocent III excommunicated the crusaders guilty of using forces meant for liberating the Holy Land to seize a Christian city. Some of the crusaders returned to Europe, having refused to take part in such a doubtful venture. One of them, the mighty baron Simon de Montfort, had secretly deserted the crusaders' camp rather than act against his own conscience. The indignation grew with each report of looting and massacre of which these new-style crusaders had been guilty. The Pope, renewing his excommunications, proclaimed his horror at their deeds: 'These defenders of Christ, whose steel was meant only for the infidel, have waded in Christian blood. Not content with emptying treasuries and despoiling private persons, they have even seized the wealth of the churches . . . They have broken into cemeteries and carried off the icons, the crosses, the relics.'[14]

Gradually the furore died down as the crusaders' own accounts came in. According to them, they had had no option. The Venetian shipowners on whom they had relied had demanded such huge sums for taking them to their destination that they had ended by making the trip as an army at the disposition of Venice. Then young Alexius IV, whose father, Isaac II Angelus, had been dethroned in 1195 by Alexius III, brother of Isaac and uncle of Alexius IV, Emperor of Constantinople, had begged them to help him take the city and restore his father to the throne. But when the crusaders were in Constantinople they had been shabbily treated by the Greek population there; then Alexius IV had tricked them with promises of rewards he could not give. Finally the crusaders had been driven to seize the city themselves. And now a Latin prince, Count Baldwin of Flanders, reigned over the city of Constantine and the Byzantine Empire and had solemnly received the imperial crown at the church of St Sophia. Those obstinate and perfidious Byzantines, who time after time had hindered the crusaders and betrayed them to the Saracens, were now rendered harmless, and their city could be used as a staging area for new expeditions which really would be sent to Jerusalem.

These explanations gradually salved the conscience of the West. Besides, from now on good Flemish and Burgundian names would be heard up and down the Near East. Louis of Blois became Duke of Nicaea. Geoffrey of Villehardouin became Prince of Achaea. Thebes and Athens, renamed Estive and Satine, were now the dominions of the Dukes of La Roche. The Peloponnesus, renamed the Principality of Morea, became the stamping-ground of the Champlitte and Villehardouin families. Finally Pope Innocent III, still hoping that Jerusalem would some day fall into Christian hands again, annulled his excommunications. And the Venetian merchants, now masters of the Adriatic, ploughed the seas in their galleys, bringing back each year richer and richer cargoes from far-off trading stations to the counting-houses of the doges.

People did not celebrate their birthdays in the 13th century. No one worried about exactly how old he was. The only dates that mattered were those of the deaths of the saints, which is to say, their births into eternal life. In 1208 Blanche reached the age of twenty, her husband twenty-one. Though of little personal interest to them, that year was to remain etched in their memory and to affect their entire lives. For on January 14, 1208, an incident occurred on the banks of the Rhône which everyone realized would affect the whole kingdom profoundly and immediately. Peter of Castelnau, the papal legate, was murdered by an officer of Raymond of Saint-Giles, Count of Toulouse.

For Blanche it was primarily a family matter. The Count of Toulouse had married Blanche's aunt Joan, a very beautiful woman who had taken the vow of the religious of Fontevrault on her deathbed. She lay now next to her mother Eleanor of Aquitaine in that same convent. Her son by Raymond, the future Raymond VII of Toulouse, was Blanche's first cousin. Joan could not honestly have congratulated herself on her husband. She had been his fourth wife (he had repudiated two others in quick succession), and she had not been dead long when he took a fifth. However, she had given him his only legitimate heir, though he had fathered a horde of bastards. Indeed, Raymond IV was known as a shameless philanderer. They sang of him:

The Count of Saint-Giles
The Gospel reviles.

What had led him to murder? There was no doubt that he was the one behind it, just as Henry II of England had been behind that of Thomas Becket. The papal legate had visited him on behalf of Innocent III, calling on him to break publicly with the heretic Cathars who were swarming in his lands. The interview had reached an impasse. The Count had dismissed the legate with these threatening words: 'Wherever you go, by land or by sea, beware. I shall be watching you.' The very next day, as he was preparing to cross the Rhône, Peter of Castelnau had been attacked by a knight of Beaucaire, who had run him through with his lance.

Blanche was well placed to know what might come of such violence. The messengers who kept her in touch with her family travelled periodically through that very region, Languedoc. She must have been impressed by the changes being brought about there by her countryman, the scholar Dominic of Guzmán. He had been brought up, like Blanche, at Palencia, where her father, King Alfonso VIII, was thinking of founding a university on the model of Paris, and had revolutionized the style of preaching in Languedoc. Like many others, he had been dismayed at the decadence of the clergy in the south of France. In Venice the Bishop was living with a concubine. In Narbonne the Archbishop was brazenly selling church offices. Dominic was scandalized. These high-living churchmen were the persons supposedly sent to rescue the people from the pernicious Cathar doctrines. On one trip through Toulouse Dominic had posed the question prompted as much by his own common sense as by his missionary spirit: 'How can the people fail to be impressed when they see the Perfects fasting and abstaining, and travelling on foot, humbly clad, while you go about on horseback with splendid retinues?'

The Perfects, according to Cathar belief, were initiates who abstained from any and all action tending to perpetuate the created world, for that created world, in their view, was the work of an evil god. Only the spirit was the work of a benevolent god. The Perfects ate only fruit and vegetables. If one of them even accidentally touched a woman, he purified himself by fasting on bread and water for three days. On the other hand, among ordinary Cathars, only one thing was required: that when dying they receive absolution from one of the Perfects; this gave them access to eternal life. Thus the Perfects possessed tremendous prestige. The people never tired of contrasting their frugal way of life with that of the churchmen corrupted by their wealth.

So Dominic of Guzmán, with a few comrades inspired by his example, started trudging barefoot from one town to the next, wearing simple homespun and living entirely on alms. He preached tirelessly. He constantly sought out and debated with the heretics, and gained some converts. It was even said that the female Perfects whom he had brought back into the fold banded together and founded a convent at Prouille, where they led lives of poverty and prayer.

Here was the programme of reform that the Church needed: preaching, first of all, by personal example, converting the heretics by persuasion, by sound knowledge of the Gospel. But would such peaceful means be effective?

In Christian lands the papal legate was the direct representative of the faith's supreme authority. To murder him was to outrage universally accepted norms. Pope Innocent III had specifically declared that all government was within his jurisdiction, 'not only that of the Church, but all secular authority as well.' How would he react?

II

BLANCHE'S HERITAGE

Pentecost Sunday, May 17, 1209. A huge crowd, 'such as was never before seen', according to the chronicler William Le Breton, who was not inclined to exaggeration,[1] was swarming round the approaches to the palace of Compiègne. It was the baronial assembly, which periodically brought together all the lords of the realm. If it was the biggest ever, that was because, since the beginning of the Capetian dynasty, the realm itself had never been so vast. Many former vassals of the King of England now owed direct allegiance to the King of France. That Pentecost day would stick in the memories of all present if only for the fact that the honour of serving the first two dishes at the royal banquet had fallen to Guy of Thouars, Count of Brittany. Who would have believed, only a few years ago, that this vassal of John Lackland would be an honoured guest at the table of King Philip? In seizing Normandy the King of France had fulfilled the dream of his youth. One day, according to his contemporaries, upon seeing far off the stronghold of Gisors, with its sparkling new battlements, he had cried out: 'I would those walls were of gold, silver, and gems!' And when his companions expressed surprise, he had added: 'The more precious, when I shall seize them!'

But the festivities at Compiègne had not – officially – been ordered to proclaim the crushing of the King of England and the defection of his vassals, but rather to celebrate the knighting of Philip's eldest son and heir to the throne. That day Louis would receive a knight's sword and spurs from his father's hand. In accordance with custom he had spent the night in the palace chapel, praying with a hundred other young men who were to be knighted with him. That morning, having bathed and heard Mass, he would, in a ritual henceforth considered sacred, be attired in a shirt of white linen, a tunic of cloth of gold, and hose of silk. His father would gird about him the white baldric from which hung the sword that had lain all night on the altar, and the gold spurs that would be attached to his hose. Then would come the merrymaking, feasting and banqueting, but not before the new knight had given some display of his prowess. With his companions, Louis would have to make his horse prance, and show his skill at arms before the ladies' stand, where Blanche with her followers would be watching.

Blanche also must have been excited. Knighthood was a social as well as a religious matter. It meant that her husband, whom she loved dearly, was assuming the full rights and duties of manhood. But for Blanche the splendour and festivity of the occasion were mingled with another feeling, half hope, half fear. She was expecting a child in four months' time. Several years earlier, in 1205, at the age of seventeen, she had borne a daughter, who had not lived. The chroniclers do not even tell us if the child had a name; it was probably stillborn. Today, before the lists, Blanche must have been wondering if some day she and Louis would also have an heir to safeguard the future of their royal dynasty.

But what everyone that day most remembered and discussed was the oath that the King of France required of his heir upon his being knighted. Louis was in his twenty-second year, considerably older than most knights when they received their spurs. Knighthood was most often conferred at eighteen, though Arthur of Brittany had been fifteen when knighted, and Philip himself only fourteen. The King had drawn up a whole list of undertakings to be required of his son; they had been carefully inscribed in the chancellor's records. Louis promised never to take into his own service any knights or sergeants-at-arms who had not sworn allegiance to his father the King. He swore never to threaten the King's commoners and burghers, nor to demand any pecuniary assistance of them without the King's authorization.

Finally – and it was without doubt the most exorbitant demand a king had ever made of his heir – Louis had been required to swear that he would never take part in a tourney. Whenever the knights went to the lists he would attend only as a spectator. To make doubly sure that he should never yield to the temptation to participate, he would on those occasions wear only the habergeon, a light sleeveless jacket of mail, and a simple metal hat, attire that would automatically debar him from taking part in dangerous jousts for which the hauberk and helmet were required. It took a very obedient young man to make such exceptional promises. They were perhaps not merely a sign of Philip's headstrong nature. In his youth he had seen Count Geoffrey of Brittany killed at his side in a tourney, and had been deeply affected. As they had been in the act of burying Geoffrey in the newly-finished choir of Notre Dame of Paris, he had attempted to leap into the tomb, and had had to be restrained. Bluff and practical though he might be, Philip's nerves could crack. What he clearly wanted most was to safeguard an heir whose health had already given cause for alarm. Who would have guessed then that the docile youth so willingly giving his father his way would be known to posterity as Louis the Lion?

It was even more out of the question to let the heir to the throne of France go off with the crusaders, for whom the eve of the merrymaking had also been a vigil of arms. All the barons who had decided to answer Pope Innocent III's call were then met at Compiègne. He was pressing them to undertake a new crusade, even a new *kind* of crusade, for they would not have to cross the seas and face the infidel, but merely to ride to the Garonne and punish the heretics. Peter of Castelnau had been treated with violence; violence would be the reply. This easy way of being a crusader appealed to many knights, for at the beginning of the 13th century taking the cross was not only a kind of salvation insurance, it brought many earthly advantages as well. The Pope had called upon the King to 'take up the sword in defence of the Church, against a tyrant and an enemy of the faith.' But it had fallen on deaf ears. Philip had allowed the crusade to be preached within the kingdom but had both refused to take part in it himself and – more than ever the highhanded father – to allow Louis to do so.

There was one compensation for all this paternal domination. During the festivities at Compiègne the King made over to his heir, for Louis and Blanche's personal expenses, the revenues of several castles, among them Château-Landon, Lorris and Poissy.

In the year of Our Lord 1209, the ninth day of the month (September), at the hour of Prime, Blanche once more brought a child into the world, a son. His birth, so long hoped for, gives a lord to the French and to the English, and his name shall be Philip. May he, as successor to his grandfather also so called, prove as worthy of his valour as of his name.[2]

Blanche's child, a healthy boy this time, was the hope of a vigorously growing dynasty; he ensured the future of the French crown. The name Philip was not only a graceful gesture towards the child's grandfather; its Greek origins called forth images of glory and conquest. It was moreover a Capetian tradition. A hundred years earlier the first Philip of the line had been so named by his mother Anne, daughter of the Duke of Kiev, from whom Hugh Capet's descendants had acquired a little Slavic blood. King Philip had even given the name to one of his bastards, the one called 'Hurepel – bristlehead' because of his shock of hair.

'A lord to the French *and to the English*.' All the history of the ensuing years was in those few words. As Blanche's child was born, one thought was on everyone's mind: the raid on England planned by the King of France. And Blanche had become one of Philip's trump cards. It was all quite plain. King John had been ignominiously defeated on the continent.

He had been stripped of his privileges by a court of his peers; his authority was as much on the wane in England as in France. But John was not the only one holding legitimate claims to the Plantagenet realm. His nephews also had such claims. John was the youngest son of King Henry II. The children of his elder brothers and sisters might feel that their claims to the throne were better than his. One of his nephews, Otto of Brunswick, was known for his lofty ambitions, aiming above all at the throne of the Holy Roman Empire. The other nephew was Arthur of Brittany – but what had happened to him? Blanche's own claims, however, were as good as those of Otto and Arthur, for through her mother she was the grand-daughter of Henry II Plantagenet. It was perhaps time to put her claims forward.

If one is to believe his contemporaries, the idea came to Philip like a flash of lightning.

It happened that King Philip of France was sleeping one night in his bed, when of a sudden he leapt to his feet, all overwrought and shouting: 'By God! What am I waiting for, that I am not conquering England?' His chamberlains who slept near him marvelled greatly, but did not dare to speak. Forthwith the King ordered that they should bring Brother Guérin to him, a Hospitaller much esteemed in the King's counsels, also Bartholomew de Roye, well loved of the king, and Henry Le Maréchal, a humble knight who had served him well and whom the King loved and had much favoured. The chamberlains caused these three to come to the King, and others also of his counsellors. The King commanded that they send throughout the realm and to all ports on the sea, to order into the King's service all the ships they should so find, and that they make a multitude of new ships. For the King meant to betake himself to England, and conquer it.[3]

It was nothing extraordinary, on the face of it. For a hundred and fifty years now Angevin and Norman kings had reigned in England. They were the vassals of the King of France with respect to their continental fiefs. Now that those fiefs were in part conquered, why should their island fiefs not be conquered as well? The language, customs, and traditions at the court in London were the same as those in Paris. During the preceding reign it had been planned that an Angevin king, the elder son of Henry Plantagenet, should join the crown of France to that of England. The situation was reversed, but what more natural than to plan now to join the crown of England to that of France?

In any event, King Philip's intimates did not hide their hopes. 'The sceptre of England should be yours by Blanche's right!' one of them cried to Louis.[4] Now to make good that right.

One evening a strange individual came to beg refuge at the court of France. He seemed a beggar, exhausted and in rags. He claimed to have a message of the utmost importance for King Philip. When brought before the King, the news he divulged was terrifying.

He was called William of Briouze. He had been King John's favourite, his chosen companion at play and dalliance. It was he who, at Mirebeau, had seized Arthur of Brittany, and John had given the noble prisoner into his care.

William of Briouze told how King John had brooded alone for two whole days in the royal manor of Moulineux, outside Rouen. No one had been allowed to come near him. Then he had come to Rouen and been joined by Geoffrey Fitzpeter, his justiciar, a man said to be harsh and merciless. The two had dined together, and at the end of the meal King John had seemed 'drunken and possessed of the devil'. In the dead of night he had ordered William of Briouze to follow him. They had gone to the dungeon cell where Arthur was held prisoner. They had taken the lad, speechless and trembling, to a postern gate opening on to the Seine. John had leapt into the boat they found moored there, ordering William and Arthur to do like-wise. When he had cast off the painter from the mooring ring, William of Briouze had turned round to find Arthur lying lifeless in the bottom of the boat, his throat cut by his uncle. The King had ordered William to tie a stone round Arthur's neck and together they had heaved the body overboard. This had been done on Holy Thursday, April 3, 1203.

The whole business had taken place in utter silence: not a cry, not a sound, except the splash when the body went into the water. Thereafter William had kept the secret, but not well enough. Some months before coming to France, William, who had been losing favour with the King, had been so rash as to become his debtor. The King had required security, then had wanted his henchman's son as hostage. At this, Matilda of Briouze, William's wife, had unwisely said 'I will not deliver my child into the hands of Arthur's murderer.' She was disobeying a formal order, for all it was a tacit one: no one was allowed to utter the name of Arthur in the presence of the King.

William had been sent to Ireland, where he had learned that his wife and child had been imprisoned in the dungeon of Windsor castle, and left to die of hunger. He had managed to cross the Channel, disguised as a beggar, and had thus reached the court of France to provide hideous confirmation of the pre-vailing opinion of King John, of whom a contemporary wrote:

Right cruel was King John, too hard on men, too lustful after women. Many shameful wrongs did he work upon the lords of the realm, for which he was much hated. Never his true mind did he speak and set his barons one against the other whenever he might, delighting in the hatred among them. Himself hated all wise and prudent men, out of envy. He was ever displeased to see a good deed done.[5]

At any rate, Arthur's fate was known. In fact, the morning after the murder, the monks of a priory on the Seine had seen the body floating on the river. They had retrieved it and given it Christian burial. William of Briouze was well treated by the King of France. He retired to Saint-Laurent de Corbeil, where he died the following year.

Such a revelation could only stiffen Philip's resolve to claim Blanche's heritage for her. As time went on new reasons were revealed, almost always in the form of victims of John's cruelty, who arrived as fugitives at the court of France. The story of one of them, Robert Fitzwalter, was told by the chronicler as follows:

Sire, I come in great need, for the King has driven me from England and seized all my lands.' 'Why so?' said Philip the King. 'Sire, I shall tell you. He would by all means come into my daughter's bed, and when I would not suffer it he ruined me and drove me from my lands. I pray God you will take pity on me, for I am unjustly treated.' 'By Saint James's sword!' cried the King, 'your wrong comes in good season, for I mean to sail to England, and if I conquer that land you shall have full amends.'[6]

In addition to incurring the anger of his subjects, King John had been excommunicated. He had quarrelled with almost all the bishops in England, among them the famous Stephen Langton, the eminent prelate and theologian, who made the division of the Bible into chapters that we still use today. Though he also had taken refuge in France some years before, the monks of Canterbury had just elected him Archbishop, much to John's annoyance. The King was being deserted on all sides. The more things went against him, the more he seemed to take cruel pleasure in creating new grievances. When the Pope had placed England under an interdict, Geoffrey, archdeacon of Norwich, one of the lords of the Exchequer, decided to resign his functions. John had had him seized, thrown into a dungeon, and left to starve, clad in a leaden cope which slowly crushed him. When the Welsh became restless, John thought to forestall a rebellion by Llywelyn ab Iorwerth of North Wales (afterwards the first Prince of Wales) by hanging the 28 sons of noble Welshmen whom he had taken as hostages, in Nottingham. He maintained his reign wholly by terror. The English barons were thinking of offering the throne to Louis of France or to Simon of Montfort, who was Earl of Leicester through his mother's side. It was the talk of England. A man called Peter of Pontefract, who claimed to be a seer, began to predict early in 1213 that 'the King will be King no longer on Ascension Day.' When news of this reached John Lackland, 'much dread he felt,' said those around him. He summoned Peter of Pontefract before him, and swore he would have him hanged the morning after Ascension Day if his prophecy had not come true. Peter calmly went on repeating it.

Meanwhile King Philip had prepared his expedition with care. He had accumulated stocks of provisions and equipment, and had hastily built a fleet of fifteen hundred ships, most of which he held in readiness at Gravelines, next to Dunkirk. Everyone remembered William the Conqueror's exploit and thought to see it repeated. Philip, however, had chosen Flanders as his base of operations, not Normandy. He was planning to marshal his army at Boulogne.

We have no indication from contemporary documents that Blanche took any active part in all this. Yet she showed so much skill in operations of this kind several years later when she personally carried forward a similar enterprise, that it seems reasonable to conjecture that she was not without experience. The whole expedition was mounted in order to secure her claims. She would be crowned Queen of England at the same moment her husband was crowned King. It is not impossible that she took some part, directly or indirectly, in the preparations.

By Easter 1213 everything was ready. On the Monday following Palm Sunday Philip held court at Soissons, told his barons of the projected expedition, and asked their help. All but one of them rallied to the King: Ferdinand, Count of Flanders, who had not put in an appearance. Philip was annoyed and sent word summoning him to Boulogne on the eve of Ascension. But on that day, May 22, 1213, neither the Count nor his messengers were on hand.

This was a grave breach of the feudal oath. But it was nothing to what was in store for the King of France.

A few weeks earlier Philip's henchmen had escorted Pandulf, the legate of Pope Innocent III, to Wissant, next to Calais, where he had embarked for England. It was Pandulf who, in 1209, had brought the King of England news that in addition to the interdict on his kingdom he was personally excommunicated. Now Pandulf had gone to tell John that, because of his crimes, his perjuries, and his insubordination, the Pope had solemnly deposed him. The King of France, or rather, the latter's heir, would receive the crown that John Lackland no longer deserved.

A few days after Ascension a ship anchored off Gravelines, where Philip was marshalling his fleet. On it was Stephen Langton, Archbishop of Canterbury, escorted by several English bishops. Taken before King Philip, they told him the sensational development that had occurred three days before Ascension. John had given to the Pope, in the person of his legate Pandulf, *the kingdom of England*.

At one stroke all King Philip's plans crumbled. The entire situation was turned inside out. Where a week before England had been an interdicted realm with a king under excommunication, it was now an inviolable place and under the direct protection of the Holy See.

King John had drawn up in the presence of the papal legate a solemn charter and deed of assignment.

> We hereby freely give and concede to God, to his apostles Peter and Paul, to the Holy Roman Church, our mother, and to the lord Pope Innocent as well as all his successors, the entire realms of England and Ireland, with all their rights and appurtenances . . . We will render liege homage in the presence of the lord Pope if we are able to appear before him.

John had also promised to do penance.

In the prison at Cork, where the King had locked him up, Peter of Pontefract enjoyed his brief and bitter satisfaction: 'The King will command me to be hanged, I know it. But it will be unjustly done, for he had surrendered his kingdom to the Pope before Ascension Day. And forasmuch as he holds the kingdom now in vassalage to a mortal man, he himself is no longer King.' The chronicler reports that Peter was in fact hanged a few days later, by John's order.

As for King Philip, he managed to pull himself together and not lose face before those who had brought him the shattering news. 'It is my triumph,' he said, 'for it is thanks to me that Rome has subdued the kingdom of England.'[7]

But it was a harsh blow, all the more for the discovery that there were of traitors in the camp. First of all the man whose defection had been so disturbing, Ferdinand of Flanders. Ferdinand had every reason to show gratitude to the King of France. He was the brother-in-law of Blanche's sister Urraca, Queen of Portugal, thus Blanche's own kinsman. Though he was himself a landless younger son, he had been married to Johanna, heiress of the county of Flanders, a union that had put him at the head of one of the wealthiest domains of the realm. They had had a brilliant wedding in Paris, in January 1212. Now, scarcely more than a year later, the upstart was defying his suzerain! Philip avenged the slight forthwith by seizing the Flemish towns of Cassel, Ypres and Bruges, and by ordering his fleet to join him in the port of Damme, near Bruges.

Philip could not linger in Boulogne, for it was in territory which he had recently seized from Reynold of Dammartin, Count of Boulogne. Two years before Reynold, who nursed old grudges against the French dynasty, had refused to sit with the court of peers and had gone off to give his homage to the King of England. He was a traitor, but he had set a dangerous example. And in fact when Philip laid siege to the town of Ghent, Ferdinand of Flanders turned an attentive ear to the counsellors urging him likewise to make overtures to John. Ferdinand sent one of his knights, Baldwin of Nieuwport, to England.[8]

Thus, everything was turned upside down. King John, at the very end of his tether, deserted by all, and almost faced with a crusade launched against him by the Pope (there had been talk of it at Rome), now suddenly became the arbiter of the situation. Under the mantle of the highest moral authority in Christendom, he himself could throw his court open to disgruntled barons who were 'victims' of the King of France.

John's last word was yet to come. As early as Pentecost week an English fleet suddenly fell on the French ships at anchor. Led by William Longsword, Count of Salisbury and illegitimate brother of King John, Hugh of Boves, and Reynold of Dammartin in person, the English burned four hundred of the French ships and dispersed the others. Philip hurriedly abandoned the siege of Ghent and put the attackers to flight, but before returning to Paris he was obliged to scuttle or disperse what was left of his fleet. Meanwhile, on May 31, 1213, Ferdinand of Flanders did homage to the King of England in the person of the King's envoys. The Boulogne expedition had cost the King of France sixty thousand livres. It ended in the worst set-back he had ever suffered, and the desertion of two of his most important vassals.

To add to the general consternation, Blanche suffered a more personal affliction. On 26 January of that same year 1213, she had given birth to twins who had not lived.

In the midst of all this misfortune the news from Spain provided one bright note. Blanche's elder sister Berenguela, in a letter which we still have, wrote:

> I have pleasant news for you. By the grace of God, from whom is all might, the King our father has defeated Amiramomelin in open country. [She was referring to the Emir Mohammed-el-Nasser.] It is a signal honour, for it is unheard of that the King of Morocco be vanquished in open country. A man of our father's household had brought me the news, but I would not believe 'til I had seen letters written by our father's hand.[9]

And the letter goes on to give the details of the historic battle of Las Navas de Tolosa, which decided the fate of Spain.

For the first time the Saracens had been totally routed. Berenguela continued:

> Our father pursued them with his army until after sunset and into the night . . . He took so much booty from their camp, gold and silver, garments and animals, that it cannot be reckoned. Twenty thousand beasts of burden were scarcely able to carry the bolts and arrows alone . . . Tell that to the King of France.

Blanche did indeed spread the news without delay, telling not only the King but everyone, near and far, who might be interested. We have the letter in which she conveyed the news to her kinswoman Blanche of Navarre, daughter of King Sancho VI of Navarre, who had married Theobald III, Count of Champagne. Before writing she must have received another, more detailed, letter, for she tells the story with as much enthusiasm as Berenguela had shown in writing to her, and with more facts. 'The Christians started to go through the mountain pass the Thursday before the feast of the virgin martyrs Justa and Rufina [July 10, 1212]. When they were come to the top they perceived a multitude of Saracens.' They were in the famous Puerto de Despeñaperros ravine, in the Sierra Morena mountains, a wild, narrow place, well guarded by the enemy. 'On Saturday they found guides who knew the place well and led the army over the saddle of the mountains towards an easier passage, and there they came face to face with the army of King Amiramomelin.' This detour round the mountain-pass was to elicit many flights of imagination. One legend ascribed it to St Isidor, who had died half a century before, whose spirit was said to have miraculously guided the Spanish army by secret paths and allowed it to surprise the Saracen forces from an unsuspected direction.

The Spanish victory ended once and for all the threat to Blanche's homeland that had existed since the disaster at Alarcos in 1195. The Arabs of Spain and North Africa had been emboldened to the point of preparing a major offensive against

Castile. The whole Christian reconquest of the Iberian penin-
sula had been in the balance. The Archbishop of Toledo,
Rodrigo Jimenez de Rada, had sounded the alarm. He was a
remarkable man, a great builder and scholar, who gave us the
present cathedral of Toledo and did much to encourage the
university there by fostering the translation into Spanish of the
Arab philosophers. He had gone up and down Western Europe
alerting everyone to the imminent danger to the Christians of
Spain. His own city of Toledo was threatened with encircle-
ment; all Castile could be overrun by the new assault. His call
had been answered, for in the army of Blanche's father at
Las Navas de Tolosa had been crusaders from every part of
Europe. Among them was one Theobald of Blazon, a French
troubadour of whose prowess Berenguela had written warmly.

It is evident that Blanche and Berenguela had been very
close and still were, each in her own place doing the same sort
of thing and exerting the same kind of influence. All her contemporaries agree that Berenguela was 'a woman full of good
sense, able, prudent, a loyal counsellor and gifted in many
ways. Everyone came to her for help and was guided by her
advice.' Similar praise was showered on Blanche when she
became queen.

Castles and churches sprang up around Berenguela. It was
she who encouraged the rebuilding of the cathedral of León,
who started that of Burgos and, with Archbishop Rodrigo, that
of Toledo. She reformed the Benedictine abbey of Saint-
Vincent of Segovia according to the Cistercian observances,
and established the Templars in Guadalajara. She founded too
many churches to list, but mention should at least be made of
that of Osma, near Burgos, whose Bishop, Diego, was a close
friend of St Dominic, founder of the Dominican or Preaching
Order.

But Berenguela's tireless activity did not stop there. She
perceived that changes were taking place in her time. She
instituted more rights for the villagers and took their side
against the lords in their castles. With her husband, Alfonso IX

of León, she helped to found the University of Salamanca. Yet she had been obliged to separate from Alfonso. This blameless woman had paradoxically spent half her life in a state of excommunication, the reason being that she and Alfonso were too closely related. Her four children were only very belatedly declared legitimate by the Pope. The eldest, Ferdinand III, was destined for sainthood, as was Blanche's son Louis.

There is an unmistakable personal note in the sisters' letters, and none of the high-sounding phrases of the clerks in the chancelleries. Yet they were in Latin, for it was still the written language at the beginning of the 13th century, despite the fact that French and Castilian were coming to be spoken more and more generally, even at court. Everyone was still more or less bilingual, although the vernaculars had made great strides because the Bible, the common foundation of learning in both western and eastern Christendom, had now been translated into them. And while Latin was still the language of the liturgy, the sermons generally had been in French since the 11th or 12th century. There is an amusing story about a curate who had just given a sermon in polished Latin prose. That night an angel came to him in his dreams and said sternly: 'Thou shalt atone for that preaching in Purgatory!' But it was not until later, in fact during Blanche's own reign, that personal correspondence began to be written in French.

We do not possess the original of Berenguela's letter, but we know to some extent what it must have looked like. There are in the French national archives a number of letters from various Spanish grandees to Blanche and Louis, dated only a few years later.[10] They are of medium size, written in large characters, and – what is unique – they bear silver seals. In France and most other countries of the West, one made do with wax. Only the Holy Roman Emperor, the Byzantine Emperor, and the city of Venice sealed in gold. The Pope, as a token of humility, used lead. The silver-sealed Spanish letters were from noble Castilians with high-sounding names: Rodrigo Diaz de los Camberos, Gonsalve Pedro de Molina, Gonsalve d'Orvaneza, and others. They were dissatisfied with having a woman as regent, and wished to offer the throne of Castile to Louis and Blanche. The woman in question was Berenguela herself, who was acting as regent while her son Ferdinand was still a child.

No answer was forthcoming to the letters with silver seals. Blanche was too fond of her sister to become her rival. But such letters show how close were the ties between France and Castile at the time. They seemed like sister-kingdoms because of Blanche and Berenguela: and any true picture of Blanche must take into account the place of her Castilian family in her heart.

Like it or not, King Philip had been tricked by John Lackland. He was obliged to abandon his efforts on behalf of Blanche's heritage. Now there were two new enemies, Ferdinand of Flanders and Reynold of Dammartin, Count of Boulogne, and the outlook was bleak. It was time for the young heir of France, Louis, to prove his worth. There was war in Flanders during the winter of 1213–14. It was a busy thriving region, whose riches were often described in the chronicles of the time. There was Ghent, whose haughty burghers lived in houses topped with towers; Ypres, fond of display, whose people were expert wool-shearers; Bruges, rich in her orchards and meadows, and maker of fine boots for noblemen, with her neighbouring port of Damme; Arras, a very ancient and powerful city, full of money and avid of more, even through usury. Indeed, the whole of Flanders was a wealthy and warlike province, peopled with clear-skinned, rosy-cheeked people who were hard-working, thrifty and sober.[11]

The Flemish question monopolized attention at the court of France during the following years. The events of 1213–14 were particularly decisive ones, and Louis played the chief part in them. It would be more correct to say Louis and Blanche, for Flanders had become important not only as a threat to the kingdom of France, through Ferdinand's and Reynold's treachery, but also as the indispensable base of operations for the conquest of England. Blanche followed the course of the fighting closely. She was pregnant again during that winter of 1213–14, but it clearly did not prevent her from keeping in close touch with her husband's affairs, to judge by the promptness and resolve she showed later, when she herself took part in them.

Louis was not a rank beginner in warfare. Earlier in 1213 he had shown his mettle at Damme by putting Count Ferdinand to flight. Now he brought off a number of coups during the winter campaign. With his loyal marshal Henry Clément, 'small of body, great of heart', he had set up a strategic position at Lille, where he could keep an eye on all Flanders. When he learned that Ferdinand had ordered his troops to Courtrai, he made a swift but drastic raid there, so that when Ferdinand and Reynold reached the town they found it in flames. Louis had already returned to Lille with a sizeable booty.

After a quick trip to Paris to inform his father and Blanche of this success, he returned to Flanders and began a series of increasingly ferocious operations. There were massacres, pillaging, conflagrations. At Bailleul Louis was almost burned alive in a fire started by his own troops. 'There were none,' writes the anonymous chronicler who was an eye-witness, 'be he king's son or other, bolder or less afeared for his own life.' The torch was set to Steenvoorde, called Estanfort by the French; it was there that the rich cloth of that name was woven. As the town went up in flames Brother Guérin, the Hospitaller trusted by King Philip, shouted: 'See here, my lords! Was ever *estanfort* better scarlet-dyed?'

It was all great prowess, but it made war more cruel and the political situation more difficult: pillaging on one side led to pillaging on the other. Louis raided Nieuwport, Hazebrouck, and Cassel; Ferdinand raided Souchez, Houdain and Bouchain, and even looted the famous abbey of Saint-Omer. The people bore the brunt of it, and the fighting spread. Reynold of Dammartin was attempting to rally the barons of Northern

France, those of Holland and Germany, and even the Holy Roman Emperor, Otto of Brunswick, who was all the more favourably inclined for being himself a nephew of the King of England. But this would not have been enough in itself. The fact that Otto did intervene shows how severely the war had shaken all Europe.

Otto had scarcely been crowned in 1209 when he found himself embroiled with the Pope. The contest between Rome and the German rulers of the Holy Roman Empire was a long-standing one; but the Pope now on the throne of St Peter, Innocent III, was not the man to let an emperor over-reach himself. He had promptly sponsored a rival to Otto in the person of young Frederick of Hohenstaufen. The struggle going on at the same time between the Kings of England and France made them both eager for allies. Louis, while in Artois to claim the inheritance left him by his mother, had seized an envoy from John to his nephew Otto. This was enough to make Frederick of Hohenstaufen the logical ally of France. Louis had sought a meeting with Frederick. They had met at Vaucouleurs and reached an agreement. The terms were not made known, but it was clear that the two sets of alliances now in existence could decide the fate of the Holy Roman Empire.

At this moment, it was learned at the court of France that John Lackland himself had landed at La Rochelle, on February 15, 1214, at the head of an army of mercenaries which he had assembled at great expense to do battle with the man he called 'his capital foe, the King of France'.

So the kingdom was now under attack both from the north-east and the south-west. The Norman barons had only very recently become Philip's vassals, and most of them possessed fiefs in England which they were anxious not to jeopardize. It was uncertain how far their new loyalty to France would extend. Similarly, the barons of Poitou had no love for King John, but their country was the cradle of the Plantagenet dynasty. Could the King of France now count on them?

Never had descendants of Hugh Capet been in so ticklish

a situation. This time Philip could not leave it to his son; he set out in person towards the west. John Lackland had started towards the county of Marche, north of Limoges, intending to force the surrender of the Lusignans, the most powerful barons of Poitou. Philip and Louis boldly attempted to cut off his retreat towards the sea. They crossed the Loire and rode on towards La Rochelle, but John got wind of their coming and nimbly slipped away towards Saintes, south of La Rochelle, then much further still towards La Réole, halfway between Bordeaux and Agen. The French were beginning to wonder how far they would have to go to catch sight of their elusive foe, when bad news came from the north. The war had broken out again in Artois. Philip and Louis had to fight on two fronts.

Philip stopped at Châteauroux to lay his plans. He decided to return to Flanders at top speed, leaving Louis to deal with John Lackland.

When the anxiety was at its height, on April 25, 1214, Blanche gave birth to a son. She named him Louis, after her beloved husband now facing the King of England alone. It was the day of the so-called 'black crosses', the major Rogation processions imploring God to preserve the coming harvests. Blanche was at Poissy at the time. It was said that she was disturbed by the abbey bells. For her confinement she went to a farm belonging to the priory of Poissy, called La Grange-de-Poissy, but the child was baptized in the abbey church and given a wet-nurse named Mary of Picardy, with whom Blanche left him for the first few months.

As the theatre of war in the south was not far from Poissy, news must have reached Blanche regularly. She was familiar with the scenes of the fighting. Louis had his headquarters at the castle of Chinon, one of the favourite residences of the Plantagenets. His situation was becoming daily more perilous, for as soon as King John heard of Philip's departure he had returned in force. A lucky raid had made him master of Nantes. Then almost without striking a blow he had taken Ancenis and Oudon, on the Loire, and afterwards Angers, which did not yet have its ramparts. Finally his troops had taken the castle of Beaufort-en-Vallée, which dominated the lowland between Angers and Saumur. Was he going to take back at one stroke, as he had promised, all the lands wrenched from him one by one by Philip of France? Geoffrey of Lusignan, having lost his two castles of Mervent and Vouvant, had already gone over to the King of England. More and more emboldened, John was now laying siege to the castle of La Roche-aux-Moines, recently built by his foe – a former vassal – William des Roches. The castle commanded the approaches to Nantes, where one of Louis's closest cousins, Robert of Dreux, was held prisoner by John.

Should Louis draw back, or risk an encounter with John's mercenaries, who greatly outnumbered his own forces? Very conscious of what was at stake, he sent an urgent message to the King. The answer soon returned: 'His father sends word that he should ride against the King of England and compel him to raise the siege.'

Once more Louis behaved like an obedient son. He rode against the King of England and did indeed 'compel him to raise the siege'. In fact it was easier than he had expected. As feudal honour required, he sent his adversary a formal challenge. The garrison defending La Roche-aux-Moines was exhausted and ready to surrender. All the contemporary witnesses declare that Louis's forces were numerically far weaker than those of the King of England. Yet when John Lackland was told of Louis's approach, he abruptly raised the siege and 'shamefully took to flight'. Where a battle had been expected there was only a headlong pursuit. John abandoned all his tents, his military equipment, his perriers and mangonels with their piles of rocks, and rode off 'as fast as ever his horse would go'.

It was July 2. On the 4th he was already at Saint-Maixent, between Poitiers and La Rochelle, thirty leagues away, which gives some idea of the rapidity of his flight. The incident earned him the nickname 'Dollheart', a wry reminder of his brother

Richard, while Louis was dubbed 'Louis the Lion' by his contemporaries.

The young hero lost no time in sending word to his father that he had accomplished what he had been told to. Legend has it that the messenger, when he had reached the paved road at Villemétrie, near Senlis, met another courier coming from the opposite direction, sent by King Philip, to bring the news of the victory of Bouvines. The ruins of the abbey built to commemorate the double victory may still be seen at the very spot where the two messengers met.

The chronicler William Le Breton describes the victory celebrations:

What words could describe, what heart could contain, what writing or picture could show the exultant thanks, the pæans of triumph, the unnumbered crowds dancing with joy, the priests' melodious litanies and the sweet blending of trumpets in the processions that greeted this victory? No cranny was left undecked, be it in the churches with their solemn ornaments, both without as within, the villages, the streets of the towns, or the walled cities and fortresses. Everywhere were tapestries and silken hangings, heaps of flowers, greenery, and festive branches. Rich and poor, young and old, man and maid, all thronged out to hail the triumph. Peasants left their harvest and, hanging about them their scythes, rakes and pitchforks, pressed in crowds towards the roads, craning their necks to catch a glimpse of Ferdinand in his chains – Ferdinand whose armed might they had so feared before. They jested at his name [the French form, 'Ferrand', means a steel-grey horse] as for a wonder it was two such horses that drew him in his litter. They shouted to him that now that he was chained he would rear no more, that unruly 'Ferrand' who had before pridefully reared and lashed out at his master. Thus it went till the victorious army reached Paris, where everyone, students, priests and townsfolk, even more jubilantly than the peasants, crowded out to greet the

King with songs and hymns, shouting and displaying their hearts' joy. And the day was not enough for them, but their rejoicing went on into the night, and not for one night but seven, always with uncounted lights and torches, so that the night became brighter than the day. More than any, the students in their zeal were never done, never tired of planning banquets, choruses, dances and songs.[12]

The joy at the double victory, the relief, the sense of salvation now that the kingdom was no longer threatened – all this stirred up a jubilation among the people such as Blanche had never seen, such as doubtless had never before been seen in France. And not without reason. On the eve of the battle of Bouvines the enemy were said to outnumber the French by four to one. The realm of France had already been divided up. Otto of Brunswick had assigned the city of Paris to Ferdinand, Count of Flanders; Péronne (east of Amiens) and its lands to Reynold; Dreux to William Longsword, illegitimate brother of King John of England; the Gâtinais region (watered by the Loing river, south of Paris) to the Count of Nevers; and so on. Otto had also made plain that he intended to be 'crowned as suzerain over all these'. France was to become an adjunct to the Holy Roman Empire.

Count Ferdinand, full of his previous successes, had also set great store by an oracle that his mother-in-law, Matilda, Queen of Portugal, had unearthed for him. 'There will be war,' it said, 'and in the fighting the King of France will be thrown from his horse and trampled underfoot. And he will have no sepulchre. After triumphing, Ferdinand will be welcomed in Paris amid great acclamations.' The chronicler slyly adds that one can indeed consider the oracle to have been right, if one interprets it correctly.[13]

Louis and Blanche, still happy over the birth of their new son Louis, listened eagerly to the details of the pitched battle that King Philip had fought at Bouvines on July 27, 1214. It had been a Sunday. Otto, the Emperor, had sent a messenger to the King in the morning to inform him that he meant to give battle. Philip had asked that the Sunday truce be observed and the encounter put off until the next day. The result had been that each side suspected the other was balking. The standards had been set up among the enemy ranks. Otto's showed a dragon with wide-open jaws gaping towards France, 'as if to gobble up the whole kingdom'.[14] But the French, whether by chance or choice, were fighting with the sun at their backs. A small advantage, yet of some help at a time when the helmets, coats of mail, swords and shields all reflected a constant glitter and dazzle. So the King of France, with the sun as his ally, had won the day. He had been unhorsed and in great danger at one point, and would probably have been taken prisoner but for a prompt rescue by his attendants. Now it was he who held Ferdinand prisoner. From his tower in the Louvre castle the Count of Flanders could gaze out at that city of Paris which he had coveted. His ally, Reynold of Dammartin, was in a similar situation, while Otto of Brunswick had only saved himself by running away, as had King John a few weeks earlier. John had fallen back to Parthenay, west of Poitiers, where he now awaited developments with considerable trepidation.

King Philip himself rode to the west and at Loudun received the barons come to beg for mercy. John Lackland sent him a messenger, Ranulf of Chester, and the Pope sent a legate, Robert of Courçon, who being English-born was well-suited to plead John Lackland's cause. In any case the King of England was more than ready for peace after the alarums and excursions of the past few months. A truce was finally signed at Chinon on September 18, 1214, whereby the two kings swore to keep the peace for five years.

'None dared to go to war with him; thus lived he in great peace,'[15] a contemporary chronicler wrote of Philip, thereafter called Philip Augustus. But another chronicler, an Englishman, Matthew Paris, wrote: 'The French rejoiced less over the victory won at Bouvines than at the rout sustained by the

King of England at Louis's hands. For the French hoped that in Louis they might have a valiant sovereign, and one able to confound that same King of England.'[16] The victory at La Roche-aux-Moines had indeed been a decisive one, for if John Lackland had been able to link up his forces with those of his allies there is no doubt that France would have been defeated. Yet Bouvines and La Roche-aux-Moines were only a step towards the conquest of that other kingdom that Blanche and Louis hoped for.

However, the Kings of France and England had sworn a truce for the present, and no action could be taken until it was over. It was a time for waiting and building new strength. The general rejoicing may have helped Blanche during the dark days she was now living through. She was doubly in mourning. Her father had died on August 6, 1214, and on October 31, Blanche's mother had died of grief at the loss of her husband. As King and Queen of Castile, they had set the example of a perfect married couple, each drawing strength from the other's faultless love. Their example was not lost on Blanche, nor their last wish which was to be buried side by side in the monastery of Las Huelgas which they had themselves founded near their castle at Burgos. Blanche passed on this idea of a family place of burial within an abbey to her son, the subsequent King of France, and he created a royal mausoleum at Saint-Denis. To this day the nuns of Las Huelgas gather regularly in the fine chapter-house built by Alfonso and Eleanor. Hanging on the wall there is a framed cloth of scarlet silk, richly embroidered in gold – the personal standard of the Emir Mohammed-el-Nasser, captured by Alfonso at the battle of Las Navas de Tolosa.

As the victor of La Roche-aux-Moines Louis had been called 'the Lion'. But the name could not mean much so long as a tiresome truce kept him from the field. In 1213 he had wanted to ride against the heretics in the south of France, but his father had forbidden it. Now his only thought was to press Blanche's claims to the English throne.

Just then, however, at the beginning of 1215, the heretics became a more serious problem than ever. Guy, Bishop of Carcassonne, came to ask the help of the King of France in the struggle against them. The situation was not very clear, apart from the fact that Simon de Montfort, who had been named leader of the crusade, was complaining of a lack of men. The knights with him could return home with their men after serving the required forty days, and Simon received reinforcements only very sporadically. Louis did in fact set out with some of his suite, and reached the valley of the Rhône. His arrival caused some apprehension. What was 'the Lion' planning to do? The Pope had just sent a legate, Peter of Benevento, into the area, who was afraid that the heir of France 'might wish to occupy or destroy towns and castles that the Church of Rome had taken under its protection'. But when they met at Valence, the legate was completely reassured. Louis, he found, was very 'gentle and kind'.

Very kind indeed. Louis, going from town to town, granted everything that was asked of him. At Béziers, where there had been a frightful massacre at the beginning of the crusade, he assured the people that he would protect them. He did the same at Montpellier. At Simon de Montfort's request he made the inhabitants of Narbonne throw down their city walls. He confirmed Simon in his possession of Toulouse, a city the Pope had attempted to shield from the rapacious crusader. Then Louis rode back to the Ile-de-France, bearing a relic as a gift from Simon: the jawbone of St Vincent.

When Louis told his father of his visit to the south of France, and of how he had seen without comment all there was to see, including 'Simon de Montfort's self-seeking and self-enrichment', the King 'answered not a word and kept silent'.[17]

The Lion had momentarily become a lamb, but a piece of news arrived that soon had him back in fighting trim. It again had to do with Blanche's heritage. In September and October 1215 the comings and goings across the Channel became incessant. The conquest of England was no longer a questionable undertaking. The English barons themselves came and asked the King of France to become their suzerain and take them under his protection. They offered Blanche's heritage, the throne of England, to her husband.

England, in fact, was living through some of the great moments of her history. On June 12, 1215, the barons had openly revolted against John Lackland. With a boldness that astonished the world, they had summoned the King to appear before them in Runnymeade Meadow and compelled him to affix his seal to the Magna Carta, a solemn instrument listing the rights they intended to enjoy. Old William Marshal served as intermediary between the barons, led by Robert Fitzwalter, the erstwhile fugitive, and King John, who had only seven knights still at his side.

When John returned from Poitou, doubly discredited after the defeats at La Roche-aux-Moines and Bouvines, he had unwisely demanded fines from those barons who had not accompanied him to France. That was the limit. The English lords very opportunely remembered a charter that had been granted to the barons in 1100 by Henry I, in which he had promised to abide by the 'laws of Edward the Confessor' (the ancient Anglo-Saxon legal customs as they were reaffirmed around 1070 by William the Conqueror). Seconded by the burghers of London, the lords had opted for open defiance of the King. Their demands had been set down in writing and, like it or not, King John was obliged to sign the Magna Carta.

> The King of England remained alone . . . That night he withdrew to Windsor Castle, lying down to rest but finding no rest. In the morning, being very troubled in his mind, he fled by stealth to the Isle of Wight. There, in great anguish, he started to consider the arguments he might use and what revenge he might seek against his barons.[18]

The Magna Carta had gone so far as to require what the King may have felt was a kind of guardianship. Twenty-five barons had been appointed to oversee the enforcement of the

Charter. They were aware that they had the upper hand and now that they had the man they loathed at their mercy they spared him no insults.

One day the twenty-five barons came to the King's court to hold a trial. The King lay in his bed, so constrained by a malady in his feet that he could neither come nor go, and he sent word to them that they should come into his chamber to render the judgement, seeing that he could not go to them. They sent word to him in reply that they would not, for it would be contrary to their right, but that he, if he could not come, should rather cause himself to be carried. The King, who could naught else, caused himself to be carried before the twenty-five barons, where they sat. And they did not rise for him, for they were told it were against their own right, had they risen. And they heaped such boastfulness and insults upon him in great plenty.

The King of England still had one recourse: appeal to the Pope. In desperation, John now played his trump card: he took the crusader's oath – an act he well knew would bring him the Pope's good-will. It worked completely.

'So the barons of England would drive from his realm a king who has taken the cross and placed himself under the protection of the Holy See. They would deliver to another the domain belonging to Holy Mother Church. By St Peter, such an affront shall not go unpunished.'

The Magna Carta had received the King's seal in June 1215. By September the English barons were already excommunicated. They needed a spokesman, a leader, a king. Quite naturally they turned to Louis of France. One day there appeared before the King of France a whole solemn deputation led by the Earl of Winchester, Saher de Quincy, requesting that Louis be urged to press his wife's claims without delay. The talks with Philip got off to a sensational start. No sooner had the Earl declared that he came in his own name and in the name of his peers to do homage to Louis of France, than a messenger arrived and asked to be received by the King. To the amazement of all present he handed Philip a letter from King John announcing that he had just reached an agreement with his barons. Thank you all the same, but Louis need not trouble himself, and furthermore he would be reimbursed for any expenses he might have incurred in preparing to cross the Channel. This letter bore the signatures and seals of all the leading barons whom Saher de Quincy had just finished saying he represented. After a moment of astonishment, King Philip grew livid. What sort of ploy was this? Saher de Quincy got a grip on himself and asked to examine the letter and the seals. They were forgeries – faked by King John. It was learned later that he had sent similar forgeries to the barons in the north of England, claiming in Robert Fitzwalter's name that he had made peace with the barons.

Saher de Quincy and his party exchanged promises with Philip and took leave of him. However, the King judged it prudent to require hostages, and soon twenty-four youths, sons of the rebellious English barons, arrived at the castle of Compiègne as pledges of Louis's safety. Louis himself now made ready to cross the Channel.

Louis's and Blanche's claim to the English throne was undeniable. They had been deliberately sent for by the barons and also by the merchants and artisans of London, whose influence was steadily increasing. From the military point of view Louis seemed to have at least as much chance of success as William the Conqueror. 'Therefore did Louis summon throughout France all bachelor knights whom he could levy and betook him to Hesdin, his castle, where he did ask the barons upon his dominions to send him their knights, that he might go to England, and some barons did he ask to come in their own persons.'

This scion of France, eager for his own throne, was 'gentle' no longer. But some of his vassals had uneasy consciences because the English barons were excommunicated. Louis brushed that aside and overrode all obstacles. Duke Odo of Burgundy protested that he had vowed to leave for the Holy Land. Very well, let him leave, but let him first pay a thousand silver marks to help defray the expenses of the expedition to England. Countess Blanche of Champagne protested that she could not help to depose a crusader-king – John Lackland's ploy was working! Louis sent a company of armed knights to bully her, with such prompt results that she shut herself up in her chamber, terror-stricken, and promised all they asked. King Philip was shocked at such rough methods, and told his heir to show more restraint.

A first contingent of 140 French knights landed in Orwell Haven, near Harwich, early in December 1215, and made their way to London. 'There they were excellently welcomed and thereafter lived right merrily,' says the chronicler, adding 'but they suffered much for lack of wine, having to drink only barley-beer, with which they were little pleased.'[19] A second contingent, 120 strong, arrived early in January 1216, 'so lashed by the sea that they entered in at the mouth of the Thames and so reached London Bridge.'

> Louis, eldest son of Philip the King, to his followers and friends which are in London: greeting and true love. Know for sure that next Easter day we shall be in Calais, ready, God willing, to put to sea. For your zeal and bravery in all my business, I send you much thanks and do earnestly beg, and yet more earnestly request, that you shall continue to lend me the same zeal and bravery. It is in truth our purpose that you know for certain, in short, that our succour shall be forthcoming, and touching thereupon we do earnestly request that you trust no false counsel, nor letter, nor messenger. For we believe that herein you have received false letters and lying messengers. Farewell.[20]

Louis must have sent that letter towards the end of March or the beginning of April, 1216, for that year Easter Sunday fell on April 10. Those of his knights who had been in London three or four months already must have been finding the days long and the barley-beer watery, though the English barons and the citizens of London, with the agreement of their Lord Mayor, Serlo the Mercer, were doing all they could to make life pleasant for them. They held many tourneys, one of which ended tragically.

The knights had begun to joust to pass the time. Geoffrey of Mandeville, Earl of Essex, was there with the others. But he had donned neither doublet nor coat of mail. A French knight, whom they called 'Brambleberry', had at him. When the Earl saw him coming he called to him: 'Brambleberry! Wait! I have no doublet!' But the knight heeded him not and struck him in the belly so hardily that he died of it. The which caused much grief, but the youth was not punished for it.[21] [Geoffrey of Mandeville had particularly asked, as he lay dying, that the French knight be not troubled.]

But while the knights in London were jousting, John Lackland was, at last, fighting desperately for his life. He had called in Flemish and Welsh mercenaries and others at great expense. Some of his roving gang-leaders, like Savary of Mauléon from Poitou, and the Norman Fulk of Bréauté, were forerunners of the terrible freebooters of the Hundred Years' War in the 14th and 15th centuries. John still had the loyalty of a few men, such as Peter des Roches, Bishop of Winchester, also from Poitou, a man of sinister reputation, whom both the French and English accused of treachery. Also Hubert de Burgh, Philip of Aubigné, and William Marshal, all of whom – particularly the last – set examples of lifelong steadfastness to their lord, whatever the cost. The rebellious barons, on their side, had been able to conclude alliances with the Welsh chieftains and with King Alexander II of Scotland, but they hesitated to take the field until Louis, now their chosen leader, should be with them. King John, meanwhile, had promptly started ravaging the countryside. On both sides of the Channel impatience mounted, but new obstacles were delaying Louis's long-awaited landing in England.

Pope Innocent III had been observing all this with the closest attention. He once more found himself in one of those impasses which had been the bane of his pontificate.

If the King of England be defeated [he reasoned], we become confounded by his own confusion, for he is our vassal and we are bound to defend him. Yet if the lord Louis be defeated, which heaven forfend! the Church of Rome is struck by that same blow that strikes him, and his wound is ours. For we have always looked upon him as the right hand, the solace, and the refuge of the Church of Rome, in whatever circumstances, and amid all woes and persecution.

Innocent endeavoured to stop the course of events by sending his legate Cardinal Gualo of Beccaria, to France. The choice of Gualo was significant; he was known as a man who stood for no nonsense. It was he who, eight years before, had come to take Queen Ingeborg's side against King Philip. This did not prevent his being received at the court of France on this occasion with great pomp. A solemn assembly was called at Melun on April 24, 1216. Blanche was again with child – her son Robert, who was born in September – and we cannot be sure that she was present. But it was her interests that were at issue, and she was, in spirit at any rate, at the centre of the discussion.

The discussion lacked cordiality. The papal legate sat enthroned in the same vermilion robes as the Pope in Rome, for he represented him while on mission and wore the same badge of office. The King of France was surrounded by his barons. Louis strode in to take his place by his father, scowling, say the chroniclers, at the legate.[22] Gualo of Beccaria spoke first, repeating what the Pope had already asked by letter: 'That Louis give up his plan to land in England and seize the domain of the Church of Rome; that Louis's father not allow him to.'

'I have always been devout and faithful to the Lord Pope and the Church of Rome,' Philip answered, 'and in all concerns until now have done my best to further her interests. And even now it is not through my help or counsel that my son Louis would in any manner lay hands on what is the Church's. None the less, if Louis has claims to press touching the realm of England, let him be heard and let him be granted what is right.'

When he had finished, a knight chosen by Louis to be his proxy for the occasion rose and took the floor.

'Sire,' he said, ''tis known to all that John, calling himself King of England, was condemned to death for his treachery towards his nephew Arthur, whom he killed with his own hands, and that he was so condemned by his peers in your own court. Also that the barons of England have repudiated him for the many crimes and outrages of which he is guilty. They will not suffer him to rule over them and they are waging war to drive him from the realm once and for all. It is known that the said King, without asking his barons' leave, delivered his realm of England to the lord Pope and the Church of Rome, receiving it back from their hands, to hold in consideration of a yearly tribute of a thousand marks. But while he might not give the throne of England to another without the consent of his barons, he might relinquish the throne. So soon as he had done so he ceased to be King and the realm was without a king. But it could not remain thus without the consent of the barons. Therefore they have chosen the lord Louis, seeing that the mother of Louis's spouse, the Queen of Castile, was the only one left living among the brothers and sisters of the king of England.'

A brisk discussion followed, in which the papal legate argued that King John had taken the cross, and Louis's proxy responded by listing John's crimes. The legate brandished the threat of excommunication. Louis then turned to his father, saying:

'Sire, I am your liege man for the fief you have granted me in your lands on this side of the sea, but matters touching the realm of England are not yours to decide. Therefore I ask judgement in this of my peers: to wit, whether you should restrain me from seeking my right, for touching it you are not my suzerain. I ask you not to hinder me from seeking that right and even fighting to the death, if need be, for my spouse's heritage.'

With this, Louis left the assembly accompanied by his own retainers. The papal legate asked Philip for a safe-conduct to proceed to the sea. The King answered: 'In my own lands I will gladly give you safe-conduct. But if perchance you should fall into the hands of Eustace the Monk, or of some other of Louis's men who guard the sea-ways, do not hold me responsible for whatever misfortune might ensue to you.' Gualo stalked out furiously.[23]

Now Louis was only waiting for fair weather to cross the Channel. But that spring of 1216 was blustery, with storm following storm. A fleet that King John had sent against Calais had been dispersed by bad weather, much to the satisfaction of the French, 'for one of his ships was worth four of Louis's.'[24] English superiority on the seas was already becoming a reality. True, Louis possessed a trump-card in the person of Eustace the Monk, of whom Philip had spoken, an extraordinary character whose exploits made him appear something of a sorcerer. His reputation as seaman and pirate was such that he became the hero of an epic some time later, the *Roman d'Eustache le Moine.* He got his nickname from having been in orders at the monastery of Saint-Wulmar, at Samer, near Boulogne, before deciding to abandon the monastic life. Like many others, he had taken service under the King of England, but had been so shabbily treated that, as soon as he was able, he had come to offer his services to the heir of France.

The French cause was immensely helped by having seamen such as Eustace for allies. 'I much dread that the King lack the strength to withstand him, when he shall come,' wrote an English lord to a friend on January 7, 1216, referring to Louis. 'He comes with such might that I fear the land shall be ruined. He is giving out his enemies' domains as rewards, so I am told.'[25]

Thus any barons whom John had not yet succeeded in alienating may have rallied to the French side for fear of losing their lands. The citizens of London were already entirely in Louis's camp. As to the people in the towns and villages, they were pulled both ways. Two English chroniclers show us, each quite vehemently, the contradictory English feelings of the time. 'Those French varlets have guzzled many hogsheads full,' wrote Matthew Paris (not specifying whether it was wine or barley-beer!) The other, Giraldus Cambrensis, cries out enthusiastically: 'O happy English breed, upon whom Providence at last has glanced with favour! Let them rejoice and, bowing down with all due docility, learn to serve him whom they may thank for this prosperity.' Two things were certain: John Lackland was loathed by all, and the English were used to seeing a king come from across the Channel to rule them.

As for the clergy, their position was difficult. Almost at the same moment that Louis landed, the Pope's legate, Gualo of Beccaria, also arrived, and fought on grimly for John. He had excommunicated Louis. Stephen Langton, the Archbishop of Canterbury, had already been suspended by the Pope for helping the barons and playing an important part in the drawing up of Magna Carta. Many Englishmen must have wondered why these penalties were inflicted on a blameless churchman and a blameless prince, while a man like John Lackland, whose crimes were past counting, was upheld. London was divided into parishes 'where they sang' and parishes 'where they sang not', the latter being those that respected the papal interdict. Soon there were in all London only five parishes 'where they sang not'.

Meanwhile the weather seemed calmer and Louis fixed his departure for May 20, 1216, at nine o'clock in the evening. He 'ordered his trumpets to sound and the sails to be set.' During the night the bad weather returned. Some ships had to turn back, among them those of Enguerrand of Coucy and Harvey of Donzy, Count of Nevers. (This last was to play a rather equivocal role in the whole expedition. He had been John Lackland's ally at one time, and had been planning to marry his daughter Agnes to John's son.) Louis, bold as always, decided to carry on despite the bad weather, but only seven ships were still with him when he sighted the English coast next morning. Suspecting that Sandwich Bay would be guarded by John's men, he opted for Stonor, further north on the Isle of Thanet.

By this time John had wholly 'lost heart'. The author of the *History of the Dukes of Normandy*, probably a mercenary in John's pay, shows him utterly dejected at the moment of Louis's arrival.

He rode a little up and down the shore, and had his trumpets sound. But those with him were little roused and little comforted, so poor a show he made. Shortly he went off a little with his horse at a walk, then galloped at top speed towards Dover. He was a good league distant before his people noticed it . . . When they saw that the King was gone they were greatly vexed and dared not remain, but followed after him all in tears, for they were very downcast and wroth, and at Dover they found the King most disconsolate.[26]

The outcome seemed certain. Louis was as energetic as John was disinclined to do battle. He entered London on June 2, 1216, was received 'amid great joy' by the townspeople, and started campaigning on the 6th. On the 7th several castles in Sussex surrendered to him; on the 8th, Guildford in Surrey surrendered; on the 11th, Farnham. He then turned towards Winchester and obliged Savary of Mauléon to capitulate. All the remaining nobility of England rallied to him. He even received the homage of William Longsword, Earl of Salisbury and King John's own bastard brother, who had till then kept faith with the Plantagenets. Only two men still remained doggedly faithful to John: Ranulf de Blundeville, Earl of Chester, and William Marshal, Earl of Pembroke, whose own son had gone over to Louis. Young Alexander II, King of Scotland, also came to do homage to Louis.

Louis was virtually master of England by the beginning of July. Only three fortresses held out for John: Lincoln, Windsor and Dover. Lincoln was defended by a woman, Nicole de la Haie, who had stubbornly held out in a first attack. The siege of Windsor proved fruitless. The assailant, the Count of Nevers, had only half-heartedly espoused Louis's cause, and was suspected of having arranged with the defenders not to push matters too far. There remained Dover, which Louis besieged for two months without taking it. Finally a truce was arranged with the defender, Hubert de Burgh, who agreed to surrender if King John sent no help, and did so on October 14, 1216.

Five days later came sensational news. John had died at the Abbey of Swineshead, on October 19. Some said it was from indigestion caused by eating green peas, others that it was a dysentery brought on by too much cider.

Blanche's heritage at last seemed within reach. Confronting Louis now were only John's numerous bastards, and the three legitimate children he had had by Isabella of Angoulême. These three were very young, the eldest, Henry, barely nine years old. Before dying, John Lackland had given Henry into the care of the man who had placed John himself on the throne, William Marshal, then eighty years old. 'For God's sake, do you beg the Earl Marshal that he pardon me the wrongs I did him, for which I do repent me fully, for he always served me loyally and betrayed me never, whatever I might do or say in his spite. For God's sake, my lords, pray he may pardon me, and as I am more sure of his faith than any other's, I beg you will give my son into his care, for he can never hold his lands except through him.'[27]

A boy of nine and a man of eighty. Was it not in England's own interest that her throne go to Louis and Blanche? If the father had forfeited his right, he could not bequeath it to his son. Only the papal legate, the terrible Gualo, did not see it that way.

As for William Marshal, he was his suzerain's man come

what may, and if that suzerain happened to be a helpless child of nine, that was one more reason to be loyal to him.

An extraordinarily moving scene took place on Malmesbury Plain, where the last remaining barons faithful to John Lackland had assembled. 'There was Ralph of Saint-Samson, the young prince's governor, holding him in his arms. The child, who was well-tutored, greeted the Earl Marshal and said to him: "Sir, you are welcome. I yield myself into God's hands, and yours. May God do you the grace to keep me well." The Earl Marshal answered, saying: "Sire, on my soul, I will omit nothing to serve you in good faith so long as I have strength." All who were present wept, the Earl-Marshal as the others, and then set out for Gloucester.' Advised by the papal legate, the barons decided to have the child crowned King at once, and entrusted to William Marshal the duty of knighting him. 'None other of us measure up to him. It is William who must gird the sword upon the knight. Then shall he have knighted two kings.' In fact, long ago, William Marshal had knighted William, the eldest son of Henry II, whom they called the 'Young King'. 'The child was clad in royal vestments to his measure. He made a handsome little knight . . . Gualo, the Pope's legate, sang the Mass and crowned him, helped by the bishops who were assembled there.'[28]

Meanwhile, what of Queen Isabella the boy's mother, the former Isabella of Angoulême? None of the chronicles mentions her. Moreover, she was pregnant and would soon give birth to a girl. But another woman was watching from afar, a woman who felt for the boy-king the same dogged loyalty as William Marshal. It was Nicole de la Haie, said to be 'a crone most cunning, trouble-seeking and forceful'. The year before she had wished to give King John, who was visiting Lincoln, the keys to her castle. 'I am old,' she had said, 'and have suffered many hardships and woes, such that I cannot endure more.' John had refused, saying: 'My dear, it is my will that you hold this castle, as you have done until now.' It was probably the best decision John ever made, as shown by what followed.

Nicole was a strapping Norman woman, from La Haie-du-
Puits, near Coutances, of the same breed – as she would prove
– as the famous Arletta, mother of William the Conqueror, and
Matilda, his wife.

To Blanche's joy her husband had returned to France to spend
the Christmas season with her. During his last two weeks in
England Louis had taken two strongholds, Hertford and Ely.
Campaigning was difficult in winter, and he had judged the
conquest of England so nearly complete that he need no longer
hasten matters. He had agreed to a truce until Easter 1217.

Louis's and Blanche's only anxiety concerned the religious
question. They could not even begin to plan their coronation
in England while they were still under excommunication. But
Pope Innocent III had died on July 16, 1216, at the high point
of Louis's triumph in England, and his successor, Honorius III,
was a good-natured old man who they hoped might be expected
to show a bit of understanding.

It was a vain hope. 'John . . . placed into our hands and under
our protection his kingdom and his sons. We are not to be
compared to a hireling who deserts his flock and takes to his
heels because he spies the wolf.'[29] And Honorius had sent
legates to the King of France with urgent instructions: 'Beseech him, by the blood of Christ, that he should pardon our
English wards whatever offences their father John did commit
against him. Beg him that he will, with a pure heart, urge his
son Louis to return from England.'[30] Stephen Langton, Primate
of England, had been vexed by the coronation of young Henry
at Gloucester. As Archbishop of Canterbury, he should have
crowned the king. But Gualo of Beccaria had excommunicated
him too, and had given still further proof of his adroitness by
assembling a few churchmen and barons at Bristol, where the
boy-king had sworn to them to respect the Magna Carta.

When Louis took to the sea again, on April 22, 1217, it was
with the intention of winding up matters promptly. Although
his father Philip, not eager for quarrels with the Church, had

held aloof from the plans, Louis and Blanche had sufficient means to allow them to carry on the struggle.

The question was where to strike the decisive blow. Nicole de la Haie was still holding out in her castle at Lincoln, and she had let it be known that she would take in and help any of the rebellious English barons who did homage to young Henry. Her example stiffened their resolve and won some of them over. Louis sent the constable of Arras to Lincoln. He laid waste the countryside, but could not take the castle. Louis learned that William Marshal was assembling knights and crossbowmen, and he rushed in reinforcements: six hundred knights and a thousand foot soldiers, with orders to give battle. He himself was at Dover when the news of the outcome reached him. It was disaster for the French.

Louis's troops were twice as numerous as the English, and they had felt they could take the castle by storm. They had gone at the walls stoutly and were beginning to break in when a hail of arrows from the battlements had suddenly driven them back. William Marshal's crossbowmen, advised by Nicole de la Haie that the French were not guarding the northern approaches to the castle, had been able to slip through in haste and take up positions on the ramparts. Some of the French assailants got through none the less, and there was a furious mêlée at the town gates. William Marshal, with all his eighty years, was in the thick of it, fighting like a lion. He went straight for the banner of the Count of Le Perche, who was directing the French assault. After a few minutes of fierce fighting the Count was seen to topple from his horse, and his attendants raised him up, 'fresh dead'.

The engagement had a ludicrous ending. The French army was jammed against Wigford Gate, which was so low and narrow that two horses could not pass through it abreast. A stray cow had somehow got herself wedged into the opening and had to be killed and hauled away. While this was going on Nicole de la Haie's men were taking French prisoners to their heart's content. Four hundred were captured, as many as there were knights in the army still faithful to the young King Henry III. It was a fierce battle, but we must see it in the context of its time, for at the end of the day three dead men were removed from the field, one of them the Count of Le Perche.

It was May 19, 1217. The battle at Lincoln Castle had changed the tide of war. The boy-king Henry III reaped the fruits of the victory, and the unhoped-for triumph rallied many waverers to his side.

Louis quickly sent word of the reverse to his father, 'and to his wife, the Lady Blanche'. He was aware of the loss of prestige it meant for him. All around him the English barons were going over to the side of John Lackland's son. John had been universally loathed (the saying at the time was that hell itself, in receiving him, had been befouled). But the feeling that 'the iniquity of the father could not be imputed to the son,' as Matthew Paris put it, was gaining ground. 'I must tell you,' Louis wrote to his father and wife, 'that I shall be able neither to fight on, nor leave England, if you do not send me a strong warlike help.'

When the King of France learned of the defeat at Lincoln he asked: 'Does William Marshal yet live?' 'Yes,' they answered him. 'Then I fear not for my son.'[31] Such was his tribute to the old Earl Marshal, whom he knew to be as upright an enemy as he was a loyal vassal. Philip was accustomed to studying events in perspective, and he knew the game was lost.

Blanche was less easily reassured, also less easily discouraged. She now showed her mettle. The merry Ménestrel of Rheims, who wrote a number of fictionalized biographies, called '*vies romancées*', provides an eloquent anecdote on the subject. It tells us much about Blanche's character, even if it is not, perhaps, completely factual.

Sir Louis . . . sent to his father for help and money, in God's name. And the King answered, by the sword of St James, he would send nothing, and would not, for him, be excommunicated. When the Lady Blanche learned it, to the King she went and said: 'Would you let His Royal Highness, your son, die in a foreign land? Sire, 'fore God, he must reign after you. Send him his needs, be it only the rents of his lands.' 'Nay,' said the King, 'Blanche, I'll send naught.' 'No, Sire?' 'No, in truth,' said the King. 'In God's name,' said the Lady Blanche, 'I well know what I shall do.' 'What then?' said the King. 'By the blessed Mother of God, I have fair children of His Royal Highness. I shall give them as pledges and shall surely find one who would lend to me for them.' And she went from the King as if in high dudgeon. And when the King saw her leave thus, he thought she had spoken in earnest. He had her called back and did say: 'Blanche, to you of my treasure I shall give what you please, for you to do as you will, and as you think best, but know that in truth I myself will send nothing.' 'Sire,' said the Lady Blanche, 'you say well.' And so was great treasure delivered to the Lady Blanche, and she did send it to her lord.[32]

What actually happened was that Blanche herself rode through Louis's domains, alerting the barons and burghers of Artois and 'toiling and moiling', as the chronicles say, in order to send her husband efficacious help. 'The Lady Blanche, the wife of Louis, was at Calais, and there summoned all the knights and people she could to send them to England to succour her lord. Robert of Courtenay was come there to cross the sea, and Michael of Harnes, and other knights, but in all they were not a hundred.' William Marshal's own biographer paid the following tribute to her energy: 'Were all those that she did so bring together come in arms to London, they had conquered England.' The fleet assembled and reached Dover. 'On the morrow, as they thought to make for the mouth of the Thames, there did come a gale and high sea that drove them back to the Flanders coast in great alarm.'

With renewed confidence the followers of young Henry marched on London. The French came out and made ready to fight, whereupon, says the *Chronicle of the Dukes of Normandy*, the papal legate mounted a palfrey, 'but did not forget his spurs. He fled all the way to Windsor without pause.' Negotiations, however, were going on constantly. A Cistercian monk and papal penitentiary took it upon himself to make numerous peace proposals. Queen Isabella herself reappeared on the scene and held a peace 'parliament' with the Count of Nevers. William Marshal was worried about Blanche's activities in Calais. She had in fact managed to send off some eighty ships, 'both great and small', on August 24, 1217. It was not a very large force, but it was headed by Eustace the Monk. There were high hopes.

A battle took place at sea not far from the Isle of Thanet where Louis had originally landed. Eustace the Monk's ship was surrounded and attacked by three English ships. 'Hardily did the English have at them and lash them with stones and lime, with which they blinded them all. So hardily did they do battle that they took them all by their might.'[33] Eustace the Monk was downed. A sailor who had in times past served under him, one Stephen Trabe, cut off his head. That was the end of the expedition Blanche sent to England.

This time the negotiations were conducted by Louis, William Marshal, and Queen Isabella in person. They were held on the Thames near Staines. Louis's people were on one side of the water, Henry's on the other, and between them the Queen and the legate, 'all clothed in scarlet'. The affair was conducted as was usual in those days. Both sides swore to keep the peace. Louis was granted compensation. The following day tents were set up for a chapel and solemn pledges were sworn before the altar. The heir of France was then escorted by the legate and the barons of London to the coast, and England rang with cries of 'the King's peace'.

It was a bitter pill for Louis and Blanche, but it had to be swallowed. The boy-king's claims, upheld by two old men, one in Rome, the other the heroic and fearless Earl Marshal of England, had been duly sanctioned.

*

Louis sailed from Dover on September 28, 1217. His defeat had not been a shameful one. His compensation of 6000 marks (the details of the payment were in the hands of a burgher of Saint-Omer with the reassuring name of Florent the Rich) was enough to cover the expenses he had incurred in equipping his men.

But Louis's and Blanche's ambitions were to undergo further trials. Their eldest son Philip, he of whom they had said that Blanche had 'given a lord to the French and to the English', died the following year, 1218. He was only nine years old, and the cause of his death is not known.

In the same year, on the other side of the Channel, old William Marshal also died, whose loyalty had twice kept the Plantagenets on the throne of England. He could afford to die, his work done. Henry III had now rallied round him all the barons of his realm.

III

THE REALM OF THE FLEUR-DE-LIS

O happiness for us most meet
That gives us back our royal line!
Philip of France's first-born son,
His father's glory come to him,
And justly famous for his own,
So many painful labours past,
So many happy outcomes won,
This land of Gaul is rightly thine,
O thou to whom the newborn reign
Turns now to beg thy clemency,
Thou King whom God's own finger marked.
Come, Holy Ghost.
> *Verses in honour of Louis VIII's coronation,*
> *written in Peter De Medicis's antiphonary.*[1]

Not only a King, but a King with his Queen were crowned at Rheims on August 6, 1223, the feast of the Transfiguration. Louis and Blanche stood together before the altar as they had stood together twenty-three years before, on their wedding day.

King Philip had passed away on July 14 of that year, at the age of 58. His last words on his death-bed had been for his son: 'Fear God; glorify God's church; give justice to God's people; protect the poor and the humble against the encroachments of the overbearing.' Overcome with tenderness the dying King had added: 'My son, you did never cause me grief.'[2]

It was true. For all his ambition, his love of action, and even the ferocity that had won him the nickname 'Louis the Lion', the new King of France had been a devoted son who had always followed in his father's footsteps. In comparing the dynasties of England and France, the Welsh chronicler Giraldus Cambrensis had praised the good and pious kings, modest and chaste, of the 'realm of the fleur-de-lis'. In his imagination the chronicler set up the lily of France against the leopard of England. The scent of the lily, he said, had the power of putting wild beasts to flight.[3] One can well imagine the symbolism that Giraldus drew from this legend, for he detested the Plantagenets, who had always seemed a family in which each member was bent on destroying the others. Yet to call King Philip 'modest and chaste' was going a bit far. A devil had been gleefully carrying off Philip's soul to hell, according to contemporary legend, when in the nick of time he had been snatched to safety through the personal intervention of St Denis. Philip's sister-in-law, Sibyl of Beaujeu (the sister of Isabella of Hainault), spread the story eagerly, claiming to have had it from a cardinal in Rome, who had heard it straight from the lips of the monk who had seen it in a vision at the moment of Philip's death.[4]

Ten years earlier, in 1213, Philip had restored Queen Ingeborg to her rightful place in the French court. He had tried everything to prevent it: all the tricks of civil and canon law, threats, intimidation, appeals and delays. He had imprisoned her in the abbey of Cisoing, near Tournai, then in a tower at Étampes. The marriage had been declared invalid several times by obliging primates, only to be reinstated each time by the Pope's legate. Ingeborg had fought on for twenty years, defending her right so tenaciously that Philip, King though he was, had finally had to yield and Queen she remained until her own death in 1236. They called her the 'Queen of Orléans' during her last years, for as a widow she spent most of her time in Orléans and Corbeil. A stalwart woman, like most of the women of her day.

Philip seems to have been more or less faithful to Ingeborg during his last years. In his will he referred to her as *carissima uxor*, his 'dearest spouse'. As for Louis, all contemporary sources agree that he treated her 'not as a step-mother, but as his own mother'.

Louis had a natural gift for personal and family relationships. He was a dutiful and loving husband. In the first town-charter in which his name is mentioned, by which he had the burghers of Aire and Saint-Omer swear fidelity to him, he made a point of adding: 'Saving the right of our most dear Lady Blanche,' and the words were used in the oral vow that the townsfolk took at Louis's request.

As they stood side by side on their coronation day Blanche well knew that her husband's heart was hers alone, without rivals or secrets. They were a blameless couple as the Archbishop of Rheims, William of Joinville, anointed them with the holy chrism. Even Louis's worst enemies in England could find nothing to reproach him with in his personal life. Unlike his father, he was a man of one love only, and Blanche knew it. Others knew it too. When they wanted something from the King, they went to the Queen. Even the Pope, whose legates kept him well-informed, addressed himself to Blanche when he had some request to make of Louis.

Louis and Blanche were full of high hopes as they came to the throne. They were thirty-five, the age of sober and fruitful enterprises, the age of maturity. The power they held in their hands, which they could use to do great things, was more than any of their forebears had possessed. So much had been achieved since Philip's coronation forty years ago. The King of France was now at home in areas where formerly his wishes had been openly flouted. Vast domains once belonging to the King of England were now his fiefs: from Paris to Calais, through the lush farmlands of Artois and Flanders; from Orléans to Rouen, with all of rich Normandy in between; lands in Touraine, in Anjou, in Berry.

Everything augured a splendid reign for Louis. At court they took pleasure in pointing out that in Louis VIII the line of the great Charlemagne had returned to the throne. The poet Giles of Paris dedicated his *Carolinus* to Louis. He recalled that Louis was descended from the Emperor through his mother, Isabella of Hainault, and told how, according to legend, St

Valerian had appeared to Hugh the Great (father of Hugh Capet) to foretell that after seven generations the realm would return to the line of Charlemagne. Five sons of Blanche and Louis now surrounded them, giving every chance that the prophecy would be fulfilled. These were young Louis, who had become heir to the throne when his elder brother Philip died, Robert, John, Alphonse (whose Castilian-sounding name was a reminder of Blanche's family), and another Philip, born the year before, 1222, and to whom, oddly, the second name of Dagobert (that of the Merovingian Frankish kings of the 7th century) had been given.

Blanche could count her blessings. She was a happy wife and mother. When she and Louis had made the customary tour of the kingdom after their coronation, their subjects had come out to greet them gladly everywhere. They had received the oaths of loyalty spontaneously, without undue display of pomp or might. In September 1223 they were in Touraine, Anjou, and Normandy. In November it was Flanders, Picardy, Artois, the regions round Douai, Saint-Riquier, and Abbeville. 'None did revolt nor turn his arms against the Royal Majesty. Normandy raised not her head. Flanders did not refuse to bend her neck humbly to the yoke of such a master.'[5]

It was in Normandy and Flanders that rebellion could most easily have broken out on Philip's death. Since Bouvines in 1214, Count Ferdinand of Flanders had remained locked up in the fortress of the Louvre, and Normandy was a recent conquest, a heritage which William the Conqueror's descendant, Henry III of England, could be expected to claim.

But young Henry did not so far seem inclined to press any claims. A kind of holy truce had fallen on France and England upon the translation in 1220 of St Thomas Becket's body to the choir-loft in the 'Trinity Chapel' of Canterbury Cathedral. The Archbishop of Rheims had celebrated Mass and the ceremony had taken place in the presence of Queen Berengaria, widow of Richard Lionheart. The English barons had shown a punctilious courtesy on the occasion, which was a memorable one for all Christendom. They had gone out of their way to leave the best lodging-places in Canterbury to the visitors from overseas, among whom the French were particularly numerous. Only William Marshal the younger had remained in the town, where, thanks to his name, he pretty much conducted himself as lord and master.

Fortune seemed to smile as Louis and Blanche began their reign. Their main residence was at Saint-Germain-en-Laye. When they went into Paris they stayed in King Philip's beloved Cité, where Blanche could observe the progress being made on the cathedral of Notre Dame. The nave had been completed before their coronation. Now the façade had risen as high as the rose-window, on which work was beginning. It was a delicate operation, but one which the master-architects were no longer afraid to tackle. The great hollow circle was latticed with lacy stone mullions forming a star and supporting stained glass representations of cosmic and seasonal themes which the liturgy would use as points of departure in developing its symbolic meanings. The techniques developed by the builders now allowed them to use bold new designs – in particular the circle, the perfect geometric figure and the symbol of the earth itself – which their predecessors of the Romanesque period could have produced in wood but not in stone.

With other Parisians Blanche could now admire the carvings over the north and south portals, the central one being still unfinished. The south portal told the story of St Marcel, with the Blessed Virgin Mary enthroned in majesty above and attended by Bishop Maurice of Sully, who had urged that the cathedral be built and had laid its cornerstone, and also Barbedor, dean of Maurice's chapter. The north portal showed the Virgin being crowned by her Son. It was a subject that had already been used on the portal of Senlis, within the royal dominions, and which was to become very dear to the faithful from now on: the notion that she who had brought Christ into the world was queen of this world and the next.

Blanche fully shared the piety of her day, which specially

attracted her towards the Cistercian order. She felt an affinity between the personality, at once vehement and meek, of its most famous son, St Bernard of Clairvaux, and her own. The year before the coronation she had been associated, at her own request, with the prayers and good works of the Cistercians at the time of their general chapter assembly. The document to this effect contains the earliest mention of Blanche in the French National Archives. It attests to the religious predispositions which would later cause her to found two convents for cloistered Cistercian nuns.

The first book dedicated to Blanche dates from the same period: *The Mirror of the Soul*. 'Most noble and puissant Lady Blanche,' says the dedication, 'Queen of France by the grace of God, I send you this book, called *The Mirror of the Soul*, which I have caused to be written for you.' Later the notion would be taken up again and yield a whole literature of 'mirrors': a 'mirror of the world', a 'mirror of history', etc . . . This was the first time it was used, in French at any rate. The author explained:

As to why it is called the Mirror of the Soul, there is good reason. For just as a person will study himself in a corporal mirror, so as to remove what is unseemly, it is as fitting that the soul have a mirror whereby she may remove the vices and sins which come from the body and lead the soul to hell, and so that, looking into this mirror, she may adorn herself with those goodly virtues which lead soul and body to the bliss of heaven.

We do not have the original manuscript that was presented to Blanche, but the treatise[6] has reached us in the form of an unpretentious manuscript with the initial letter illuminated on a gilt background. It shows a seated queen being handed a mirror by a kneeling nun who wears the white mantle and black veil of the cloistered Cistercian. The text could well be the work of a woman. It addresses the Queen gently, almost intimately. Urging her to be generous in her alms-giving, it says: 'I mean not, Lady, that you do scant herein, but say this that you may be the more endued with nimbleness to't.' Probably the writer was a nun who had already benefited from the royal open-handedness. Her study of feelings is not without its subtlety, even poetry. 'Even such is the heart,' she writes, 'that will not suit itself, but must leap from one purpose to the next, changing its will, varying its counsels, doing what is new, undoing what was done, re-doing what's undone . . . It wants and wants not, as one which cannot stay himself . . . It is drawn hither and thither by all manner of things, seeking where it may rest . . .' She lists the heart's ups and downs: 'Vanity cozens it; curiosity buffets it; covetousness pulls it; delights lead it astray; lust besullies it; envy plagues it; anger saddens it and sadness angers it . . .' And she concludes: 'This bootless world is less substantial than a dream, a shadow, or a puff of wind, and little grace is in't . . .' But against this futility stands the happiness of heaven, to which the largest part of the work is devoted: 'You shall be a free-woman of that Holy City whose citizens are angels. God the Father is its Cloister, the Son its Light; the Holy Ghost its Clarity.' She lingers on that vision of God: 'Light of the enlightened, Rest of the over-wrought, Peace to supplicants and Life to the living, the victors' Crown.' The treatise ends with enthusiastic reflections of the joys of heaven: 'Dearest Lady, think on that fine City. It is a firm habitation, a country where are all joys for all, whose inhabitants dwell in peace and murmur not, suffering not, nor discomforted . . . Think, Lady, of the light those souls shall have, when the body's light shall be as is the sun . . .'

We cannot know what precise influence that little treatise may have had on the Queen to whom it was dedicated, but it helps to recreate a mood. Its delicacy, its emphasis on the 'happy' life ('happy through love's sweetness and contemplation's ease') betoken the cheerful optimism of its day. It is the true contemporary of the angels carved in the archivolts of Notre Dame and of those gracious Blessed Virgins being triumphantly crowned, in the tympanums of the cathedral, by their Son.

It would be pleasant to be able to say more about Blanche's personality, and also describe her outward appearance and her habits more fully, but texts are sadly lacking. None of her contemporaries provides us with a picture of her as she stood beside her husband on their coronation day. They are content to tell us in a general way that she was beautiful: 'Well endowed in body, in carriage, in beauty, rich with nature's noblest gifts,' all of which is emphatic enough, but scarcely detailed.

The picture that remains of her, on her seal, her personal hall-mark, confirms her beauty. She is shown standing, a noble and extremely elegant silhouette, draped in a cloak of royal fleur-de-lis, with her left hand at the fastening. The gesture reveals what must have been a handsome metal clasp at her throat. In her right hand she is holding a fleur-de-lis. A belt worn low seems to lengthen her waist and its hanging ends let one sense the moving body beneath the folds of her dress. Her crown, and the veil framing her face, add to the feeling of grace and firmness. Even Matthew Paris, an Englishman who suffered from no excess goodwill towards France and who spared Blanche none of his caustic comments, called her the 'magnificent' Queen. The word suited her well, particularly in its contemporary meaning, for it referred not only to personal appearance but also to a taste for the beautiful, and to generosity.

There is no doubt that Blanche was generous. The ledgers give a day-by-day record of her gifts and charities. Such things were customary at the time, but Blanche's charities clearly exceeded those of the other royal houses. She gave lavishly to the poor, to the monks and cloistered nuns, to lepers, to the hospitals, to the messengers reaching her from Spain and elsewhere, as well as to her own retainers: her private secretary; William her cook; her groom Girardin, to whom she gave ten *livres* upon his marriage; and the members of her own family, to whom she distributed furs and jewels. There were regular charities: ten *sous* each day to the poor, adding up to twenty-eight *livres* from Candlemas (February 2) to Ascension (forty days after Easter); and bread: a *livre*'s worth distributed each day. There were also occasional charities: a hundred *sous* to the poor folk of Corbeil upon her arrival in that town; 160 *livres* for white woollens and other cloths for the cloistered nuns of Pontoise; ten *livres* for the lepers of Dourdan: 20 *sous* to two old women of Montargis and the same to two others in Nemours; a hundred *sous* to the prioress of Oursan for the board of an indigent girl; eight *livres* to the messenger who brought the news of the successful confinement of the Queen of Navarre; and so on. Besides the gifts of money were gifts in kind, such as the breviary given to Hugh of Athies, which to judge by its cost (fourteen *livres*) must have been richly illuminated; the chess-set given to Louis; and another chess-set of ivory, whose recipient is unknown.

Unfortunately we cannot be sure of the details of Blanche's artistic tastes. A certain smock-frock which she bought for 20 *sous* is simply said to be 'painted' without further details. She had her chariot draped with blue, but we cannot infer from this that she had a particular fondness for that colour, since it was France's national colour. It was perhaps not by accident that both the croziers that she presented, one to the abbess of Maubuisson, the other to the abbess of Notre-Dame-la-Royale, were of crystal – an excellent rock-crystal, finely carved. The illuminated psalter that was very probably hers is one of the finest of its kind even in a century that cherished grace and beauty.

There are enough references in Blanche's ledgers to purchases of clothing for us to be sure of her feminine taste for finery. Contemporary sources tell us also of her care that the royal children should be 'nobly clad'. Here too the term 'magnificent' applies to her. We find that in 1234 she spent 150 *livres* on her dresses, and 25 *sous* on two rugs for her room; also a silver vase worth 108 *sous*. She bought a number of things at the Lendit fair. Thus in 1241 John of Ermenonville, most likely one of the Queen's valets, purchased cloth for her: fine dark-dyed woollens, also blue; camelshair (sometimes called 'triple' because it came from the town of Tripoli); and skins of hare and other animals – for a total of 75 *livres*, quite a tidy sum. Another purchase of furs during the same year came to 42 *livres*.

A knowledge of the cosmetic practices of the time enables us to round out the scant details in the ledgers. Blanche was undoubtedly expert in the beauty care of her day, since her contemporaries vouch for the fact that she remained lovely and attractive to the end of her life. There were, of course, all the perfumes of the East, mostly made with musk as a base. But simple home recipes were more frequently used. The whole secret of elegance consisted in not appearing sunburned at a time when everyone was outdoors most of the day, walking and riding on horseback. To whiten one's face one began with a steam-bath, after which came an application of white make-up, either fine flour or white lead, diluted in rose-water. Oil of peach kernels was used to heighten colour, or else, according to a book of recipes called *The Adorning of Ladies*, peas or chick-peas, ground to a dry powder, mixed with egg-white and made into a lotion with lukewarm water. Blemishes and skin ailments were treated with yellow arsenic, the juice of patience-dock and wormwood, or soapy water. Wrinkles were attacked with a decoction of mallow and violets boiled in wine. Teeth were made whiter with a mixture of barley flour, powdered alum, and a touch of salt, worked together with a tiny bit of melted honey. Hair was dressed with olive oil, honey, and alum in equal parts, to which a bit of quicksilver was added. An infusion of willow-leaves was thought to make hair grow more abundantly, and flaxseed in olive oil was used to prevent its falling.[7]

A few months after the coronation of Henry III, the English barons politely but firmly asked his mother, Isabella of Angoulême, to leave. She did not make an issue of it, for she realized how unpopular she was. She was often referred to punningly as 'Jezebel' rather than Isabel. She returned to the continent.

The Queen passed through Poitou and came to Angoulême, her native town, which was her heritage. She took the people's homage and remained thenceforth lady of Angoumois. She plighted her daughter's troth to the Duke of Lusignan, who was the son of Hugh Le Brun, Count of La Marche, so as to have his succour. But then did she dissolve that betrothal and did herself wed the Duke of Lusignan, which caused much talk thereon.[8]

One sees why. It was not only the off-hand way in which Isabella thrust aside her daughter in order to marry the man herself, but also her impromptu return, twenty years later, to the first love to whom she had been betrothed when she stunned everyone by deserting him to marry John Lackland. Isabella was in fact still young: only thirty when John died. Nevertheless, it was still a shock to see a man like Hugh of Lusignan swallow her earlier insult. The truth was that he was literally enthralled by her, so much so that the Poitou barons came to feel that they now were ruled by a queen.

Louis had scarcely been crowned six months when he found himself busily negotiating with Hugh of Lusignan. Isabella was vainly attempting to reclaim the lands in England that King John had previously assigned as her dowry. Louis, mindful of keeping such a powerful ally, quickly proposed instead an annuity and whatever lands he might conquer in Poitou. Louis even raised the possibility of giving him the town of Bordeaux as a present. The negotiations went so well that soon Hugh of Lusignan was doing liege-homage for his fief to the King of France.

Louis then undertook a sort of military excursion, going first to Tours, then Montreuil-Bellay, Niort, and Saint-Jean-d'Angély. The last two towns, each 35 miles from La Rochelle, surrendered without much of a fight. What about La Rochelle itself? It would be no small plum for the Capetian dynasty to acquire a sea-port, particularly La Rochelle, which supplied the entire north of France with wine and salt. But La Rochelle was defended by a skilful soldier, Savary of Mauléon, who had shown his mettle during the struggle with England and now put up a stout resistance. The difficulties of the siege caused grave concern in Paris. 'Savary of Mauléon and three hundred knights and other soldiers, who were therein, held the castle hardily against the King and his people. Forasmuch as the siege and war had already endured for eighteen days, the clergy and religious and the people of Paris took alarm and did go a solemn procession barefoot and shirted from the Church of Notre Dame to the abbey of Saint-Antoine, for that God might send the victory to the King of France. And in the same procession were three queens: the Lady Ingeborg, who erstwhile was the wife of King Philip; the Lady Blanche, wife of King Louis; and the Lady Berengaria, wife of King John of Jerusalem.'[9]

The procession was on June 2, 1224, On the following day La Rochelle surrendered to King Louis, after a tragicomic incident. Savary of Mauléon had opened a coffer sent him by King Henry III which he believed to be full of money. It turned out to be full of stones and bran. The story seems to sum up the penury in which the King of England, himself facing many difficulties, left his defenders at La Rochelle. In any case it discouraged Savary and he decided to capitulate.

For a time Louis dreamed of conquering Gascony as well as Poitou. Everywhere he went he found submission and loyalty. The burghers of Limoges had surrendered to him, also those of Pui-Saint-Front and Sarlat, in Périgord; Sarlat thereafter included a fleur-de-lis in its coat of arms. Aided by the Count of La Marche, Louis felt himself on the verge of taking Bordeaux. The people of that town, however, firmly repulsed all French overtures, declaring they would have neither peace nor truce with the enemies of King Henry. At this point Louis had to return to Paris to deal with a strange affair centring on Flanders. But he had acquired his sea-port, brought Poitou entirely under his control and gained the fiery Lusignans as his allies, not to mention Savary of Mauléon, whose sword was now at Louis's disposal – all in a few months. His nickname 'The Lion' suited him better than ever.

Ferdinand, Count of Flanders, had been a prisoner in France for almost ten years. In 1224 his wife Johanna was still ruling firmly over his lands. Some curious rumours now began to spread. Johanna's father, Count Baldwin, was said to have returned from the Holy Land after an absence of twenty years. Baldwin had left in 1204 with a number of other lords to lead the Fourth Crusade, whose story was told by the chronicler Villehardouin. He had been elected the first Latin Emperor of Constantinople. Two years later he had been captured in an ambush, and had disappeared.

In 1224 a mysterious hermit was living in the forest of Glançon between Tournai and Valenciennes, and was thought by some of the Flemish knights to resemble their long-lost count.

A man came into Flanders and did proclaim himself Count Baldwin of Flanders, once Emperor of Constantinople, saying he had escaped by a miracle from the captivity of the Greeks. Many Flemish folk, high and low, found him wondrous like unto Count Baldwin . . . and they received him for their Count and lord. And inasmuch as they did hate the Countess Johanna, Baldwin's daughter, they did reject her and take from her almost all the lands of Flanders, agreeing in all things the while with the false Count. And when Countess Johanna did find herself thus rejected from her lands, which were her own inheritance, she was most marvellously discomfited and did therefore come to King Louis of France, and besought him, 'fore God, that he should take pity upon her and do her justice, in that he could and might restore her lands and county.

In a well-known sculpture at the Cordeliers' church at Nancy we see a striking depiction of what a crusader's unexpected return, years after his disappearance, must have been like. The artist shows a knight in rags, held by his wife in a close embrace.* Some think it represents Count Hugh I of Vaudémont, in Lorraine, who had gone off to the Holy Land with King Louis VII of France around 1147 and who for a long time thereafter had been thought dead. His wife, Anne of Lorraine, refused to marry again and more than fifteen years later, in 1163, had the happiness of seeing her husband return. It was no surprising thing in those times for a knight to disappear during a battle and then, in a series of extraordinary adventures, survive a massacre, eke out a long captivity in some Saracen prison or in the service of some emir, only to reappear after everyone had thought him long dead.

The Flemish hermit must have closely resembled the former Emperor of Constantinople, and those who let themselves be taken in may well have acted in good faith. Some people, such as the abbots of Saint-Jean de Valenciennes and Saint-Vaast d'Arras, sincerely believed that it was their old lord back, though others said the real Baldwin had been a bigger man, and his former clerk (we would say secretary), Walter of Courtrai, confronted him without being recognized by the claimant. Nevertheless, there were those who meant to capitalize on the aura of curiosity, and then enthusiasm, which rapidly surrounded the mysterious hermit, in order to get the unpopular Countess Johanna into difficulties. Many of the wealthy burghers and petty country squires saw here a chance to assert their independence. The whole business finally reached the proportions of a *coup d'état*. The fake Baldwin was escorted in triumph from town to town, all over Flanders. He played his part admirably, pulling up his clothing to reveal scars, which he told the gaping onlookers were those he had received as Emperor of Constantinople. Finally, on Whitsunday, May 19, 1225, he solemnly assumed the coronet and started dubbing knights, granting fiefs, and generally conducting himself as the lord of the land. Countess Johanna, who had refused to

* The statue is in the Cordeliers' church in Nancy. A moulding may be seen in the Museum of French Monuments in Paris.

credit him, had no recourse but to take refuge in Paris and beg Louis's help against the impostor.

Louis of France was the nephew of Count Baldwin of Flanders through his mother Isabella of Hainault. Before taking action he wished to be very sure of the true state of affairs. He began by sending his aunt, Sibyl of Beaujeu, to Flanders to have a look at the man in question. Sibyl was Baldwin's and Isabella's sister, and immediately realized that the hermit was a remarkable and determined impostor. Quickly playing her own game, she advised the 'Count', as sister to brother, that his best course was to go and see the King of France, who, she promised, would certainly receive the true Emperor of Constantinople with all the honours due to his rank. The ball was then in Louis's court. He went to Péronne with Blanche, who was personally interested in the adventure, 'and bade him feigning to be Count Baldwin to appear before him.' The man accepted the challenge and came to the King, assuming 'a mighty and overweening manner'. The Bishop of Beauvais was there and asked the man: 'In what place were you wed?' When he did not answer, according to the chronicle, the King at once saw that he was a 'cozener'. He none the less continued to question him, asking him where he had done homage to King Philip for the county of Flanders, and where Philip had knighted him. The man evaded these questions, 'asking for that evening his supper and his bed and proclaiming he would answer on the morrow'.[10] Louis, angered at his 'madness and arrogance', 'ordered that he quit his lands and realm within three days and did give him safe-conduct that he might betake himself again whither he came.' 'Baldwin' did not make an issue of it. He cleared out while the King was returning to Valenciennes. Attempting to avoid the unpleasant homecoming he might expect in Flanders, he got as far as Burgundy in the opposite direction. There, however, a knight recognized him and handed him over to Countess Johanna. Early in October 1225 she had him summarily hanged in Lille.

One result of the incident was a rapprochement between

France and Flanders. Johanna started to negotiate for the release of her husband. What made Louis all the more ready to grant this was the knowledge that Johanna wished to have her marriage with Ferdinand annulled in order to marry Peter Mauclerc, Count of Brittany. It was agreed that Ferdinand should be freed at Christmas of the following year, 1226, in return for certain pledges and the payment of a ransom. This release took place, but in circumstances quite different from those that Louis had expected.

Blanche was again pregnant. In 1225 she had given birth to Isabella, the royal couple's first girl. Her last son, Charles, would be born in 1226.* That year, destined to be such a grievous one for Blanche, began with the news of a new crusade in southern France. The papal legate, Romano Frangipani, had for some months been going about the country trying to raise an army to send down to Languedoc to suppress the Albigensians.

Louis had already gone south twice, but his brief visits had been more like a suzerain's tours than the campaigns of a crusader. The second, however, had involved the frightful massacre at Marmande (between Bordeaux and Agen), described with a grim zest in the *Chanson de la Croisade Albigeoise*.[11]

The second part of the *Chanson* ends with Louis's preparations for the siege of Toulouse. It describes the archers posted on the Bazacle bridge being built over the Garonne, a splendid 'work of art', both a dam and a foundation on which mills were built. But Louis did not finish the siege, whether because he felt unable to, or simply because his forty days of pledged military service were up. At that time, 1219, Louis had evinced no greater interest in the Albigensian situation than his father had. His major concerns were elsewhere, in Flanders and

---

* It is not known for certain whether it was Charles who was born in March 1226, or Stephen, who did not live. In the latter case Charles would have been a posthumous child born in 1227.

Normandy, and in England, Blanche's heritage, where his bitter disappointment was still so recent.

Six or seven years later things had changed. Louis, as King, was obliged to concern himself with Languedoc, for he was suzerain there. The Count of Toulouse, Raymond VII, was Blanche's first cousin, since he was the son of Joan, a daughter of Eleanor of Aquitaine, and had received some of his upbringing in England. Whatever might be said of his father, Raymond VI ('a limb of Satan, son of perdition, enemy of the cross, attacker of the Church, protector of heretics', according to Peter of Vaux-de-Cernay),[12] the present Count could hardly be held responsible for his father's misdeeds. That had been Innocent III's decision, and a parliament held in Paris in 1224, in the presence of King Louis, had 'acknowledged and declared that Raymond VII, Count of Toulouse, lives a good Christian conformably with God's will and the faith.'[13] But now the almost permanent war in Languedoc had taken a ferocious turn, and it was time to intervene.

Early in 1226 the situation had become intolerable. After the sack of Béziers and the taking of Carcassonne in 1209, the crusaders had chosen as their leader Simon de Montfort, Earl of Leicester, who a few years before had refused to take part in the capture of Zara ('I am not come hither to destroy Christians'[14]), for which the Venetians had threatened to kill him. This man had subsequently exhibited such vast ambitions that they both ruined him and did real damage to the cause of the crusade, which had actually been compromised from the start. It had quickly degenerated into a personal rivalry between Simon and Raymond VI. The people of southern France had become more and more disgusted with their purely political wrangling. This was as true of the faithful as it was of the heretics, as witness Toulouse itself, where only the tradesmen's quarters were friendly to the Albigensians.

On September 12, 1213, at Muret, Simon won a great victory over the combined forces of Raymond VI and Pedro II, King of Aragon and Catalonia, who had come to Raymond's aid with an impressive army. This had enabled Simon to extend his authority to Toulouse itself and to both banks of the Garonne. But even with such triumphs the equivocal nature of the whole undertaking created chronic difficulties. Toulouse would not stay conquered; it had constantly to be besieged and captured anew. Simon was killed by a stone in the forehead in one such action outside its walls in 1218. His son Amaury was not the man to take over such a heavy responsibility. Raymond VI died in 1222, and his son, Raymond VII, not only recaptured Toulouse and the region round Agen, but went on to take Lavaur, Puylaurens, Montauban, Castelnaudary, Moissac and Carcassonne as well.

It was a hopelessly tangled situation, calling for the King of France, the natural suzerain of all the northern French barons, to settle it. In addition, Amaury had, in 1225, ceded to Louis all the rights he had inherited from his father. At a synod held in Paris on January 28, 1226, the Count of Toulouse was once more excommunicated, for his conduct had been causing grave concern to the papal legate.

Romano Frangipani, Cardinal of Sant-Angelo and papal legate, had a powerful personality and had immediately acquired an ascendancy over both Louis (to whom he was related) and Blanche. To hear him talk, it was imperative that the crusade against the Albigensians start up again at once. The heretics were on the march, he said. They were preaching their false doctrine all over the country, through the mouths of such men as Peter Garcias and Raymond Niort, the castellan of Sault. The Cathar 'bishop', Guilabert of Castres, was actually conducting services at Fanjeaux, and had presided over a veritable synod of heretics at Pieusse. This false preaching placed Christian souls in mortal danger. Something had to be done.

Louis was all the more willing to heed the legate's request for knowing that young Raymond VII was negotiating with the King of England. He decided to act promptly.

The marshalling of the crusaders was set for that spring (1226) at Bourges. The King of France was to have all the great lords of his realm at his side: his cousin Humbert of Beaujeu; his bastard half-brother Philip Hurepel; Archibald of Bourbon, Count of Saint-Pol; Enguerrand of Coucy; Robert of Courtenay; Theobald of Champagne; Peter Mauclerc, Count of Brittany; John of Nesle; and of course Amaury de Montfort, as well as some churchmen, among them Brother Guérin, who had been with King Philip at Bouvines. Even so, Louis was far from having the hundred thousand knights that one imaginative chronicler talks of, or even the fifty thousand mentioned by another.[15] But he had an impressive army, and a great many of the petty barons in southern France decided that the better part of valour was to claim Louis's protection immediately.

'We are eager to come under the shadow of your wings and within your wise authority,' Bernard Oton, lord of Laurac, wrote to Louis. The people of Béziers and Saint-Antonin did likewise, as did many more, such as Raymond of Roquefeuil and Pons of Thézan. Nuñez Sancho, Count of Roussillon, and Jaime I of Aragon, both traditional allies of the Count of Toulouse, also went over to the King of France. It seemed clear that a standard campaign of forty days should suffice to re-establish the King's authority over the formerly rebellious provinces. Louis wavered a little over what itinerary to follow, then opted for the valley of the Rhône, his previous route. It was the quickest and easiest of access.

The journey down passed without incident. At Montélimar the King received an embassy of the townspeople. Beaucaire and Avignon both sent out embassies to meet the King on the way. Avignon was a rich and powerful city, which had traditionally always made much of its alliance with the counts of Toulouse. Raymond VII, in a special gesture, had dispensed the burghers of Avignon from paying tolls while travelling over his lands.

Nevertheless Louis did not expect to meet with serious resistance in Avignon. He camped at Sorgues, eight miles upstream, on June 7, 1226, and received a deputation. Avignon agreed to let him have free passage through. But two days later the right of way was suddenly denied, and the King almost fell into an ambush. The crusaders started fighting with the townspeople and the Avignon authorities ordered a wooden bridge destroyed that had already been used by part of Louis's troops to cross the Rhône. It was the end of any agreement. The King immediately ordered the town to be besieged. It was the first obstacle, and an unexpected one, in a campaign that had got off to a flying start.

Avignon possessed two towers, Quiquenparle and Quiquengrogne, which made it a strongly defended place. The prosperous burghers had laid in abundant supplies and had even hired a band of Flemish and Brabant mercenaries, all of which made it look as if the break with Louis had not taken them entirely by surprise. Furthermore Raymond of Toulouse had used scorched-earth methods to hinder the advance of the French army, having gone as far as ploughing up the plains so as to deprive the horses of fodder. Contrary to the usual state of affairs in a siege, it was the besieged who had everything they needed and the besiegers who were starving. The summer was intensely hot that year. The French army soon began to suffer from the inevitable epidemics, among them dysentery. On August 8 an attempt to scale the walls turned against the crusaders. The wooden bridge they had thrown out collapsed under their weight and almost three thousand men were drowned. And a few days later, while the French were eating, the Avignon forces made a lightning sortie and killed a large number of the besiegers. The news reaching Blanche in the north must have been grim. The siege was as interminable as it had been unexpected. There was even talk among the King's counsellors of raising it.

Amid the general discouragement Louis once more gave proofs of his energy. He ordered hygienic measures, including throwing the corpses that littered the camp into the Rhône. He dug a huge moat between the town and his forces, in order to

forestall any more surprise sorties. He also let it be known that
the siege would go on as long as necessary. 'The Lion' was
rousing himself, and his determination was not lost on the
enemy. Towards August 15 the Avignon burghers opened
negotiations. Hostages were demanded, and when these had
been delivered the papal legate made his entry into the town on
September 9. The people of Avignon would be spared, but
their walls were to be razed.

The neighbouring peasants went at this work with a will, for
Avignon's power had been formidable and had been harshly
wielded throughout the countryside.

Louis left the town under the control of William of Orange,
whose father had been flayed alive in Avignon years before. He
decided to build a fortress at Villeneuve-lès-Avignon, across
the river and upstream, to deal with any possible future re-
bellions. It was called the castle of Saint-André.

Even during the worst moments of the siege Louis had continued to receive the homage of the southern barons. The
remainder of his crusade was one long triumphal march, via
Béziers, Carcassonne, Castelnaudary, Pamiers, and Puylaurens.
His power was universally acknowledged.

But the Avignon siege had done severe damage. There had
been great weariness, discontent, and murmuring. Many of
the barons had come within an ace of deserting their suzerain,
and there had been one serious defection: Theobald of Champagne. During the worst days of the siege, in the first part of
August, he had decamped, alleging that his forty days were
up. The King had threatened to go in person and devastate
Champagne if Theobald deserted; he had still done so. But he
only dared slink away after dark, and his knights were hooted
by the grooms and butchers and cobblers of the French army,
who 'clamoured at their falseness and folly'. Their departure
had a smell of treason about it. It was a scandal.

Along with this, untimely deaths were leaving gaps in the
King's entourage. William of Joinville, the Archbishop of
Rheims who had crowned Louis three years earlier, died of an

illness. So did Philip, Count of Namur, and Bouchard of Marly, both of them counsellors of the King. Louis himself seemed extremely fatigued when he started on the homeward journey in October, leaving his cousin Humbert of Beaujeu in charge of the whole region which, in general, could now be considered pacified.

Everyone was worried. The King, who had spared himself no effort during that long siege in sweltering heat, was clearly exhausted. He had started home on October 29, 1226, travelling by short stages. When he reached the castle of Montpensier, north of Clermont-Ferrand, he felt unable to continue.

On November 3 he gathered round him all his closest companions. There were his half-brother Philip Hurepel; Enguerrand of Coucy; Robert of Coucy and John Clément, marshals of France; the Counts of Blois and of Montfort; also a number of prelates, including Walter Cornut, Archbishop of Sens, and the Bishops of Beauvais, Noyon, and Chartres. Louis made them solemnly swear to recognize his eldest son Louis as the heir to the throne. A document was drawn up on the spot, to which were affixed the personal seals of all those present. The King had made his will the previous year before leaving on the expedition to the south. He had specified that if anything happened to him his wife Blanche was to be in charge of the government. He had distributed various lands among his children for their support; such provisions were called 'apanages' at the time. His second son, Robert, had received Artois, the land which had come to Louis from his mother Isabella of Hainault. The third son, John, had received Anjou, and the fourth, Alphonse, the counties of Poitiers and Auvergne. The others were to go into holy orders, as did many younger sons in those days.

The King died on the Sunday next after the octave day of All Saints. Jesus Christ have his soul, for he lived a good Christian, always in great holiness and purity of body so long as life he had. For none ever discovered him to have commerce with woman other than her whom he took in marriage. Many they be who say that in the King's death is fulfilled that prophecy of Merlin's wherein he said: '*In monte ventris morietur leo pacificus*', which is to say: 'In the mount of the belly shall the peaceable lion die.' Louis the King was of his lifetime proud as a lion towards the wicked, and wondrously peaceable towards the good. And it has not been discovered that another King of France but this one did die at Montpensier, which means the mount of the '*panse*' [an old French word for belly], *monte ventris*.[16]

The splendid army which had set out six months before now became a funeral procession, one not only afflicted by the death of a King, but full of grudges, slanders and rumours which boded no good at all for that autumn journey home.

It was whispered that the King had been poisoned, that his enemy, Theobald of Champagne, who had deserted him so shamefully, had given him bad wine to drink. The deaths of others close to the King seemed to confirm these legends – and yet they are only that, for there is no need of poisoned wine to explain the illnesses caused by the poor sanitation and the latent epidemics present in any army. And as Theobald had left the King at the siege of Avignon in the first half of August, it is difficult to incriminate him for an ailment that occurred late in October. But his defection, so like a betrayal, had made a vivid impression on everyone, and presently its after-effects would be felt even by Blanche.

Louis had been a hardy warrior, fighting like a lion whenever his honour, his claims or his rights were at stake. Unlike his father, whose amours had kept tongues wagging, he had died with an untarnished reputation. Later the story was even told that when the King was very ill his friend Archibald of Bourbon had slipped a naked wench into his bed, with the idea that, one way or another, the King might warm himself. It was simply a standard remedy of the times. Perhaps, if the story is true, Archibald merely wished to cheer up his suzerain, after all the worries which had been capped by Theobald's departure. But Louis would have none of it. Be it remedy or soldier's 'at ease', he had declared that he would do without whatever might besmirch his soul.

Early in November Blanche had had her 'chariot' prepared and had set out with her family to meet the King halfway. It was Brother Guérin, the chancellor, who, riding a bit ahead of the barons, first met the Queen's suite led by twelve-year-old Prince Louis. The chancellor had him turn his horse round and go back to his mother.

'Mad with grief' – most phrases seem inadequate to describe Blanche's despair, for the chroniclers affirm that she would indeed have killed herself on the spot if they had not stopped her. Hers was an impulsive, absolute nature. This loss, so unexpected, tore at her inmost being, her every fibre. Louis had been her all, her tender spouse, her children's father, her still-young lord and King. His death was hers as well. The violence of her grief overwhelmed her entourage. Brother Guérin, who had till that moment kept his composure, now, according to the chroniclers, broke into a 'raging dole'. And the court of France was in great disarray, for it meant a third king – a child – within three years.

Yet in the midst of this tremendous grief one thing was overwhelmingly clear: the child must be crowned.

Did Blanche in that moment remember the venerable Bishop Hugh of Lincoln, who had told her when she was the same age as young Prince Louis that she must dry her tears, for 'a queen doth not weep'? From our twentieth-century vantage point a remarkable fact emerges when one compares two dates: November 8, 1226, the day Louis VIII died at the castle of Montpensier in Auvergne, and the 29th of the same month, the day that Louis IX was crowned King at Rheims. For it was a mere twenty-one days between the two events. When we remember that at that time the best speed was some forty miles a day, and when we think of all the preparations that were necessary for a coronation, we may conclude that Blanche was able to master her grief very quickly and not allow the woman in her to overcome the queen.

There were so many lords of the realm to be summoned, so many couriers to be dispatched in all directions, with documents (some of which we still have) bearing the seals of all those who had attended the King at his death. In addition there were all the practical details of the ceremony itself, which was becoming standardized procedure: the lodgings of the royal family at Rheims, the coronation vestments, the crown which must be adjusted to the boy's head . . .

Louis had explicitly left the administration of the kingdom in Blanche's hands. This was nothing unusual at the time, since women could inherit fiefs on a par with men. Feudal law had none of the restrictions of Roman law in this respect. Blanche would thus reign alone as Queen precisely as her sister Berenguela had done for a time in the kingdom of Castile and León. When later historians wrote of Blanche's 'regency' they were in error. The documents of the period were signed now by Blanche, now by the young Louis, so haphazardly that it would be impossible to set up criteria by which to distinguish which were her decisions and which were his. In any case, Louis at his coronation was twelve years old. In the years that followed Blanche was the ruler of France.

'Maintain our Queen and save her brood.' This was the sentiment of the people, as expressed by one Robert, a priest of Sancerre, in a rhymed sermon he composed 'the same month that good King Louis died'.[17]

At the end of the same month, on Saint Andrew's Eve, (November 29), in a moving ceremony 'sans lay nor rhyme', another Louis was crowned. The child to be anointed was brought in a chariot to the city wall, and then mounted on a charger. He was a handsome child, having inherited from his grandmother Isabella the Hainault family beauty: blond, delicate, fragile-looking. The boy riding astride his great horse to the cathedral doors must surely have roused the feelings of the crowd. A chronicler reports that they felt 'both weal and woe' on that occasion. A day or so before, at Soissons, he had been knighted. He was young for it, as we have seen, especially since it implied skill in handling arms; but a king must be a knight.

Brother Guérin helped him to dismount. The monk at the prince's side represented the faithful service due from a good and loyal vassal, just as William Marshal had represented it by Henry III's side a few years earlier. Indeed, it is impossible not to note the similarities in the two occasions. In each case a woman, an old man, and a papal legate – here the Cardinal of Sant'Angelo – watched over the destiny of a boy. Despite all her cares throughout those three hectic weeks – the practical details, Louis's funeral at Saint-Denis on November 15, her own grief – Blanche must have been aware of those similarities. On October 28, 1216, it had been her uncle's son. Now, ten years later, almost to the day, it was her own.

A striking testimony of Blanche's personal anguish during those momentous days has come down to us. It is a very simple little piece of parchment conserved in the French National Archives, a document sealed with a dab of lead hanging on a bit of hempen twine. It looks like any other papal document of the time, the lead and hemp – the cheapest materials with which it was possible to make a seal – being a reminder of the poverty of the apostle Peter. It is in fact a bull of Pope Gregory IX, dated December 7, 1227, at the Lateran Palace, and its purpose was to release Queen Blanche from an ill-considered vow which she was unable to keep. What was it – that promise Blanche had made to God which had become impossible for her? When and why had she made it? We shall never know. The Pope's letter gives no details. It must have been orally, through the intermediary of a faithful servant sent to Rome for that purpose, that Blanche had begged the Pope, chief custodian of vows made to God, to release her. Yet it seems unthinkable that, whatever the vow was, it had no connection with the tragic happenings of November 1226. And though we shall never know the Queen's secret, what we do know shows us that there was some trait of character, some deep-lying source of strength on which she felt she could draw when she had to face the most trying period of her life. Whatever that strength was, which allowed Blanche to give unreservedly of herself in the cares of the realm, it was perhaps the same as that which would cause her son to become a saint.

'Rejoice, thou happy France.'

Traditionally, new sacred music was composed for a coronation. The motet, called the 'King's conduit', which was sung for the anointing of Louis IX has come down to us. It was called *Gaude, felix Francia* and was sung for the procession of the Holy Ampulla ('La Sainte Ampoule'). The tiny flask of sacred oil was carried by the abbot of Saint-Rémi under a canopy held aloft by four monks. The boy who was to be anointed and crowned was already on a platform built in front of the chancel, surrounded by the great lords of the realm. He declaimed the solemn oath required: to maintain the Church, do justice to his people, keep the peace. The slender figure knelt, then stretched itself prone before the altar, as the chorus took up the Litany of the Saints:

> May it please God, hung on the cross above,
> To keep you, Gentle King, and those you love;
> And grant you, Sire, all virtue and all might
> To guard your throne and manifest your right.

Then the cathedral was filled with the strains of the *Te Deum*. The regalia were spread out upon the altar itself: the crown; the sword, sheathed; the golden spurs; the golden sceptre topped with a fleur-de-lis; the purple hose embroidered with golden fleurs-de-lis; the tunic and surcoat (a kind of cloak) of the same colours and design.

The ceremony began. Louis removed his robe, taking care to leave his shirt open at the throat. Bartholomew de Roye, the

Lord Great Chamberlain, drew on his hose. The Duke of
Burgundy, a very young man, attached his spurs. Since William
of Joinville, the Archbishop of Rheims, had died while with
Louis VIII in Avignon, it was the Bishop of Soissons, James of
Bazoches, who handed him the sword, now unsheathed, and
who would shortly anoint him. The little prince, holding the
sword across both palms, solemnly knelt before the altar, then
gave the sword to his uncle Philip Hurepel to hold. Then he
was anointed, just as Saul, David and Solomon were said to
have been in the books of *Samuel* and *Kings*. The holy oil was
touched to his forehead, his shoulders, his arms, his hands, and
his breast. Then he was clothed in the tunic and surcoat. The
ring was placed on his finger and the sceptre in his right hand.
The Bishop took the crown and placed it on his head – and at
once all the lords present stretched out their hands and sym-
bolically held it in place. The crowned King was then led to
his throne, draped with silk embroidered with fleurs-de-lis,
where he received the Bishop's kiss, then those of his barons
and peers. 'All were weeping, even the Countess Johanna of
Flanders' – whose loyalty was in doubt and who was not known
to be very susceptible.

The Mass went on. At the offertory the King held out a
lump of silver and thirteen gold pieces, as for a wedding.
Blanche, watching it all, must have been thinking of the
dangers and uncertainties that lay ahead for her. She had only
to glance round the assembly and note the empty places. Some
of the barons had sent word that they would not come on
account of 'the dole for the father and discomfort of the realm'.
It was an excuse, but it might also be a threat. Should grieving
for the father prevent them from showing loyalty to the son?
Blanche could list those she could count on. After Philip
Hurepel and Hugh of Burgundy, there were the two scions of
Dreux, Robert and Henry of Braisne, the latter soon to become
Archbishop of Rheims. There were the lords of Coucy, Bar,
and Blois, faithful to the oath they had sworn to their dying
suzerain. Only one great notable was present: John of Brienne,

King of Jerusalem, who was just back from pilgrimage to St James of Compostela, following which he had married a niece of Blanche, called Berengaria after her mother. Johanna of Flanders was there, with her kinswoman, Blanche of Champagne.

Of course there was a whole group of noblemen whose loyalty was beyond doubt, those who had been at Bouvines or La Roche-aux-Moines, and, three years before, at the coronation of Louis VIII. Here they were now, grouped round Brother Guérin, wholly steadfast: Bartholomew de Roye, the Lord Great Chamberlain; Robert of Courtenay, the Great Butler; Matthew of Montmorency, the Constable; John Clément; John of Beaumont; William des Barres the younger; John of Nesle; and the swashbuckling Michael of Harnes, whose whole life was a saga linked to that of his suzerains, a sort of French William Marshal whose exploits, unfortunately for us, were never recorded as were the Englishman's. Above all, there stood at Blanche's side the papal legate, Romano Frangipani, Cardinal of Sant'Angelo, who had been a bulwark for her during this troubled time, an unhoped-for comforter.

But along with these devoted supporters there were many disturbing gaps in the ranks. Hugh of Lusignan, Count of La Marche, and his wife Isabella, had not answered the invitation. Neither had Peter, Count of Brittany, called Mauclerc – 'bad clerk'. Many others besides were missing, some of them having had the impudence to say that the Counts of Flanders and Boulogne, still in captivity after ten years, should be set free before any coronation.

There was another absentee: Theobald of Champagne. But in his case Blanche had no doubt about the reason. She had learned the day before that he had sent his sergeants-at-arms to prepare a lodging for him at Rheims, and she had had the mayor send them packing. Theobald's banners had been thrown into the street and his servants ejected. Blanche was not about to pardon him for his behaviour towards her husband.

'Rejoice, thou happy France.' They sang the 'King's conduit' again as Brother Guérin helped little Louis IX up on to his horse at the cathedral door. Then, sceptre in hand and a smaller crown on his head than that used at the ceremony itself, he rode out into the cheering crowds.

Rejoice, happy France! How had the clergy of Rheims happened to choose that antiphon? What cause was there for rejoicing when a kingdom drowning in tears found a child, a woman and a greybeard at its head? Rejoice? When on all sides there were rebellious barons who now had a clear field for their long-awaited revenge? What else could be expected from the Albigensians in the south, from Flanders, Champagne and English Poitou? Let alone England herself, whose King had taken good care not to come and pay a vassal's respects at his suzerain's coronation.

Rejoice, happy France – what an ill-chosen phrase! Or was it some strange second sight?

IV

CHECK TO THE QUEEN

A new role awaited Blanche. She must no longer collaborate, she must command. No longer simply oversee her castles, her lands, her children, and that whole universe of kinsfolk, allies, clerks, servants, and dignitaries of all degrees who swarmed in and around a royal family. Now she must answer also for the king, for the kingdom itself.[1]

All the eyes that had hitherto rested on the royal couple were now directed to her and she must fathom all their looks alone, must guess what they told and what they hid, when they meant sincerity, flattery, or suppressed greed; when a smile was sham, when a friendly greeting meant treachery, when real honour might be concealed beneath arrogance, when she must contain her pity, when she must be indulgent . . .

Being a woman, she would often be hurt, upset, and taken in. But her very woman's intuition would also more readily let her distinguish between those whose appeal she might welcome and those she must turn away. It would let her focus on what was essential, see more than what was directly in front of her. Also at times – and here was the secret compensation for her solitude – her own glance would cause anxiety where there was good reason, create respect where it was lacking, calm or quicken the feelings of others.

She was alone, yet the life she had shared with her husband had prepared her for these confrontations. Louis had kept none of the kingdom's affairs hidden from her. For that very reason she would now be able to manage those affairs.

She also had the moral support of some close friends. She could count on the expert opinions of the Cardinal of Sant'-Angelo, and on Brother Guérin's wisdom. She elicited feelings of deep, even tender friendship among many of those around her. And in her loneliness she had the affection of her children, above all that of young Louis, 'whom she did love more than aught else in life'. Deprived of the main thing in a married woman's life, she at least knew how to make use of what resources she had, and draw her strength from them. What was most to be dreaded had happened to her. In one stroke she had lost her husband and been saddled with a responsibility that she would never have chosen. She must take the kingdom's destiny into her own hands and carry it forward successfully. Yet little though she dreamed it, it was in just that unwelcome task that she was to find her true calling, and to write in large letters in the pages of history the name of Queen Blanche.

The French barons had long been held in check by King Philip and his son 'the Lion'. But their quiescence did not mean a lack of discontent. This was just below the surface, needing only a pretext to burst out, as the difficulties during the siege of Avignon had shown. With Louis's death, the discontent surfaced throughout the land. Here a castle was threatened, there a province. It was mutiny almost everywhere, and must be met blow for blow, the right counter-move found for each bold stroke from the other side.

The first thing Blanche did, once her young son was crowned, was to liberate Count Ferdinand of Flanders. This had been Louis's plan and the coronation of a king was customarily a time for amnesties. Yet when we look at Blanche's life as a whole, and note the outstanding episode of her declining years, this gesture takes on symbolic value. It is significant that it was the *first* act of her reign.

Ferdinand left the Louvre prison on January 6, 1227, Epiphany Day. Accompanied by his wife, Countess Johanna, he returned to his domains in Flanders. He had been reinstated in all his rights. Blanche had even reimbursed half his ransom, 25,000 *livres*, and allowed him the revenues of the three towns which had been pledged for it: Lille, Douai, and L'Écluse. She had kept only the castle of Douai as pledge, thus adding a further favour to what had been planned. She had, however, taken the precaution of sending two of her retainers, Aubrey Cornu and her 'panter' Hugh of Athies (in charge of the royal pantry), to the principal towns of Flanders to receive the burghers' oaths of allegiance to Louis IX of France and to Blanche herself, in case Ferdinand and his wife should again contemplate treachery. But would he? He was not liable to forget his twelve years of captivity, or the special generosity Blanche had just shown him.

The other prisoner, Reynold of Dammartin, Count of Boulogne, undoubtedly hoped for a like indulgence. He had been removed from the harsh prison of Péronne, where King Philip had placed him, to the castle of Le Goulet in Normandy, where his captivity was scarcely easier. Unlike Ferdinand, he had been guilty of deliberate treachery. Moreover, Blanche could not set him free without alienating her brother-in-law Philip Hurepel, who had been granted the county of Boulogne. Reynold soon realized that he had no hope. He committed suicide about Easter 1227, causing sinister legends to grow up around the castle of Le Goulet, for suicides were rare in those days and filled people with horror.

Blanche was on the *qui vive*. The empty places at the coronation had been those of the most turbulent barons. Hugh of Lusignan would not see, hear, nor do anything contrary to the wishes of his wife, Isabella of Angoulême, who could not forget that she had once been Queen of England. She now made all those round her dance to her tune. Hugh had just signed an alliance with two other powerful western barons, the Viscount of Thouars and the Sire of Parthenay. Those were two names well remembered by everyone who had taken part, even at a distance, in the episode of La Roche-aux-Moines. Geography notwithstanding, it was only a step from Poitou to England. Two years earlier Henry III's own brother, Richard of Cornwall, had taken that step. He had landed on the continent, brazenly calling himself the Count of Poitiers, claiming to hold the title from his uncle and namesake Richard Lionheart.

Furthermore there was someone else, right on the spot, who was ready to effect the link between the western barons and England. This was Peter, Count of Brittany, the 'Bad Clerk'.

He was a dangerous man, this Mauclerc. He was one of those younger sons whose appetite for land grew greater the more they got. The second of three brothers, he was none the less well endowed. Robert, the eldest, called Gâteblé ('Spoilwheat') had received the county of Dreux. The youngest, Henry of Braisne, had entered holy orders and had just been elected by the canons to the archbishopric of Rheims in succession to William of Joinville. Peter had received no inheritance but had been well provided for by his marriage. King Philip himself had arranged for him to wed Alix, the heiress of Brittany. She had died five years later, leaving him three children: John called 'Rufus', Arthur, and Yolanda. John was to inherit the duchy of Brittany, over which his father kept watch. Kept an extremely tight watch, in fact, for he would entrust it to no one else and conducted himself like a high-handed baron, indeed like a despot. The church at Nantes had learned this through bitter experience. Peter had taken to pulling down all the houses in a parish, or in several parishes, in order to build up the ramparts of his castles in that region, and had locked up any churchmen who complained. He had even told a priest who had refused church burial to a usurer that he would bury him alive with the body! Some think that he had studied a while at the University of Paris; others that his name 'Bad Clerk' meant that he had once been in holy orders. We cannot be sure. What is certain is that his brushes with the clergy had taken him all the way to the ecclesiastical courts in Rome. He had nevertheless been entirely loyal to his suzerain Louis VIII, and had fought valiantly with him in Flanders, Anjou, and England.

But his stay in England had evidently aroused his ambitions. The dukes of Brittany were also the earls of Richmond. Now came the sensational news that Peter had betrothed his daughter Yolanda to Henry III, the King of England himself. They were only waiting for a papal dispensation to celebrate the marriage, as they were within the prohibited degrees. At the same time a story was going about to which Peter Mauclerc could not help but turn an attentive ear. It was to the effect that Peter's ancestor Robert, first Count of Dreux, had been not the second but the eldest son of King Louis VI, 'the Fat', and hence should have been King of France. The story claimed that Robert had been kept from the throne because he was duller than his brother, who became King Louis VII. With France now in the hands of a woman and a child, it looked like the right moment to put in a claim. Peter Mauclerc was just the man to press a claim. He had spent his life pressing claims.

Blanche knew Peter well enough to be on her guard. She had kept informed of the network of new alliances being created in the old Plantagenet realm. Now it began to look like an actual conspiracy. Mauclerc had drawn Theobald of Champagne himself into his orbit. Blanche regretted having made him so angry at the coronation. His ally Henry of Bar had also gone over to Mauclerc. A little more and the whole kingdom of France would be caught between two powerful sets of enemies.

Blanche did not wait till spring. By the end of January 1227 she had summoned her vassals and got under way, accompanied by her son the King and their faithful barons. In the first ranks of these were Philip Hurepel and Robert Gâteblé, the elder brother of Peter Mauclerc. On February 20 Blanche and young Louis were in the cathedral of Tours. They went as pilgrims to the monastery of Saint-Martin, the famous native of Tours whom everyone in the region revered. Next day they were south-east of Tours in the former Plantagenet castle of Chinon, and from there they travelled about fifteen miles in the same direction to Loudun. The rebel army was concentrated at Thouars, another fifteen miles east and slightly south of Loudun. The royal army and the rebellious barons were keeping a close watch on each other. An extraordinary deployment of pawns began on the chess-board. The fifteen miles of terrain between Loudun and Thouars were criss-crossed with the comings and goings of messengers from both sides, their favourite meeting-place being at a charming spot on the river Dive near the village of Curçay, half way between the two towns. The conspirators decided to make Theobald of Champagne their chief negotiator because he was well-known at the French court. He and the Count of Bar were given safe-conducts signed by young Louis. They were soon deep in serious discussions with their opposite number on the King's side, none other than Blanche herself.

In a very few days the impression grew in the rebel camp that the negotiations were going almost too well. Theobald seemed constantly ready to cross the Dive for another round. Richard of Cornwall became worried and communicated his suspicions to Savary of Mauléon. Both had the same impression: the more Theobald saw of Blanche, his cousin and his 'Lady', the less eager he seemed to press their claims. Richard of Cornwall and the others became so convinced of it that one day, as they strolled back from that idyllic spot on the river, Theobald and Henry of Bar got wind of an ambush awaiting them. They turned round and went back to Loudun, coming not as negotiators this time, but as refugees requesting asylum. Needless to say they were warmly welcomed.

> Lady in whom wisdom and honour bide . . .
> If noble love for me thy heart betide,
> Command me not to dwell far from thy side.
> Loyalty and high courage spring in me
> From this my song which wings its way to thee,
> One day in May.

What should the next move be? Blanche offered to meet the conspirators in Loudun. They refused and suggested Chinon. She agreed, but when the day came the irate barons had not yet managed to soothe their injured pride; they failed to put in an appearance. Another rendezvous was arranged, this time in Tours, and the same thing happened. This time Blanche lost patience. She ordered them to appear at Vendôme; if not, the royal army would go into action. Peter Mauclerc gave in. He went to Vendôme with his ally Hugh of Lusignan and submitted.

It all ended on March 16, 1227, with a proper treaty in due form. As was usual in that day and age, the quarrel ended with a number of betrothals. Instead of Henry III of England, Peter Mauclerc's daughter Yolanda was now to wed a scion of France, Prince John, who was to inherit Maine and Anjou. His younger brother Alphonse would marry Isabella, daughter of Isabella of Angoulême and Count Hugh of Lusignan. Another Isabella, Blanche's only daughter, would marry another Hugh, the son of Count Hugh. Thus three royal children were betrothed to three of the rebel barons' children. The threat of an English marriage was averted and Poitou was safely back within the French orbit. Richard of Cornwall decided that the best thing for him was to sign a truce and return to England. Blanche, realizing that this was not the time for penny-pinching, distributed lands to Robert of Dreux, money to Philip Hurepel, and tax exemptions to the burghers of La Rochelle, who had remained loyal to France amid great temptations.

So the Queen had won the first round. She had dismantled a whole conspiracy without shedding a drop of blood. But those who knew Peter Mauclerc knew that he would seek revenge, for it was only Theobald's inconstancy that had foiled him. He would get even with Theobald some day. Meanwhile there was a better game to play. The great problem of the rebels had been their own disunity, each fearing that another would oust him should they succeed. But there were other ways of tackling young Louis IX than meeting him head on. Why not detach him from his mother, secure his person and rule in his name? The scheme was subtler than outright rebellion, and surely cleverer. If they could make the boy feel ashamed to be tied to his mother's apron strings they could probably get him to see things their way

It happened that Louis was touring his lands and was at

Orléans when this notion gained favour with the barons. The barons gave as their opinions 'that the Lady Blanche, his mother, ought not to rule so great a thing as the realm of France, for it was not meet that a woman do such things.' The King gave as his answer that he needed no other help in ruling than that 'of the good folk of his council'.

But he was on his guard. When he reached Arpajon, twenty miles south of Paris, and learned that a large army was concentrated at Corbeil, ten miles to the east, he decided with a prudence beyond his thirteen years that his small escort would not be able to protect him. The castle of Montlhéry was close by, with its powerful walls and towers. He had often heard stories of that castle and how it had been such a thorn in the side of his ancestor, Louis the Fat, by preventing him from travelling in security between Paris and Orléans. Now it would *provide* security for Louis the Fat's great-great-grandson. Young Louis hurried there, pulled up the drawbridge, manned the battlements, and sent two messengers to his mother in Paris.

As was her habit, Blanche sized up the situation rapidly. She had no time to summon her vassals, yet she did not wish to let the conspirators invest Montlhéry properly. She knew she was well-loved in Paris. She had spent most of her childhood and youth there, had been among those present to hail each stage in the progress of the great cathedral of Notre Dame (whose façade was now complete with a handsome gallery enclosed by slim, graceful columns), and had recently become a member of a charitable association of Parisian clergy and laymen called the *Confrérie Notre-Dame*. She decided to appeal direct to the people of Paris. She summoned the burghers and told them of the trap her son had almost fallen into. They agreed unanimously to go to his rescue, and they advised the Queen to summon also 'the free towns of France' – meaning those of the Ile-de-France.

Then did the Queen at once send letters throughout the neighbouring lands to ask that help be sent to those of Paris who meant to deliver her son from his enemies. Thus did knights and other good folk from all the country thereabout gather in Paris. When all were come they armed and sallied forth with banners unfurled and set out for Montlhéry. No sooner had they done so than the news of it reached the barons. The same were sorely vexed at seeing such folk come, saying amongst themselves that they lacked the forces wherewith to do them battle. So did they betake themselves away each to his own country, and those of Paris came to the castle of Montlhéry. There did they find the young King and brought him to Paris, all in close ranks about him and ready to fight should there be the need.[2]

Blanche had appealed to the people and they had not failed her. The would-be ambush had turned into a triumphal popular demonstration which made a great impression on all who witnessed it, first and foremost on young Louis himself. Much later, in his conversations with his chronicler, the Sire de Joinville, it became one of his favourite reminiscences. 'From Montlhéry all the way to Paris, the road was crowded with armed and unarmed folk, all crying out to Our Lord that he should give me a goodly life and long, and keep me and guard me from mine enemies.'[3]

Indeed, there could have been few sights more likely to strike the imagination of a boy of that age. When, later, Louis IX 'placed his life in peril for his people', which Joinville saw him do four times, as he states explicitly, he must have done so not only out of a sense of duty, but also, surely, in repayment of what he felt as a debt of gratitude.

The barons were beaten for a second time, and by an adversary whom they had not yet correctly sized up, but they were still not ready to admit defeat. They inveighed with redoubled fury against 'Dame Hersent' – the she-wolf in the popular story, the *Roman de Renart* (Reynard the Fox), which all the townsfolk were avidly reading. They added slander to name-calling. This foreign woman who was ruling France had

Blanche of Castile was born in 1187 to King Alfonso VIII and Eleanor of Castile. She had eleven children by her husband, Louis VIII. Among them was St. Louis, in whose name she ruled France until he came of age. Blanche died in 1252.

n lan de lincarnation. ay.
cc. ou mois de may fu la
pais refource entre le roy
plp: et le roy jehan dengle
terre. entre vernon et lisle dandeli. Si
est plainement contenu es istrumes

John and Philip Augu
exchange the kiss of p
after signing a treaty.

British Museum, London

Letter to Blanche and
Louis VIII from a Castilian
noble, Rodrigo Díaz, showing his silver seal.

Archives Nationales, Paris

cognoscant misericordiam ⁊ dei petat misericordiam.

ḊE EXAUDI orationem meam: et clamor meus ad te veniat. Non auertas faciem tuam a me in quacunq; die tribulor: inclina ad me aurem tuam. ❀ In quacunq; die inuocauer

Blanche at prayer. An illuminated capital from her psalter.

Blanche's seal.

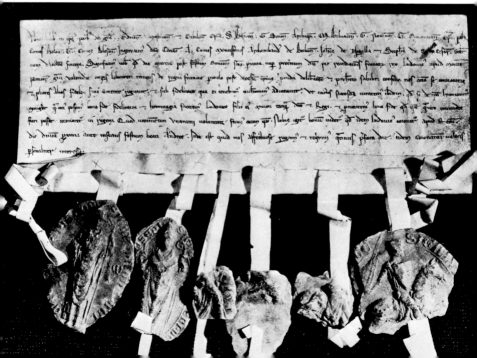

The witnesses of Louis VIII's death invite Blanche to assume the government on behalf of her son.

Archives Nationales, Paris

Summons to the coronation of Louis IX (St. Louis).

Archives Nationales, P

The birth of St. Louis *(top left frame)*.

Seal of Theobald of Champagne.

Archives Nationales, Paris

Reliquary purse with the arms of Theobald, now in the cathedral treasury of Troyes.

Archives Photographiques, Paris

Sir Edmond's cope, now in the church of St. Quiriace, Provins.
Blanche and Louis attended his canonization ceremonies.

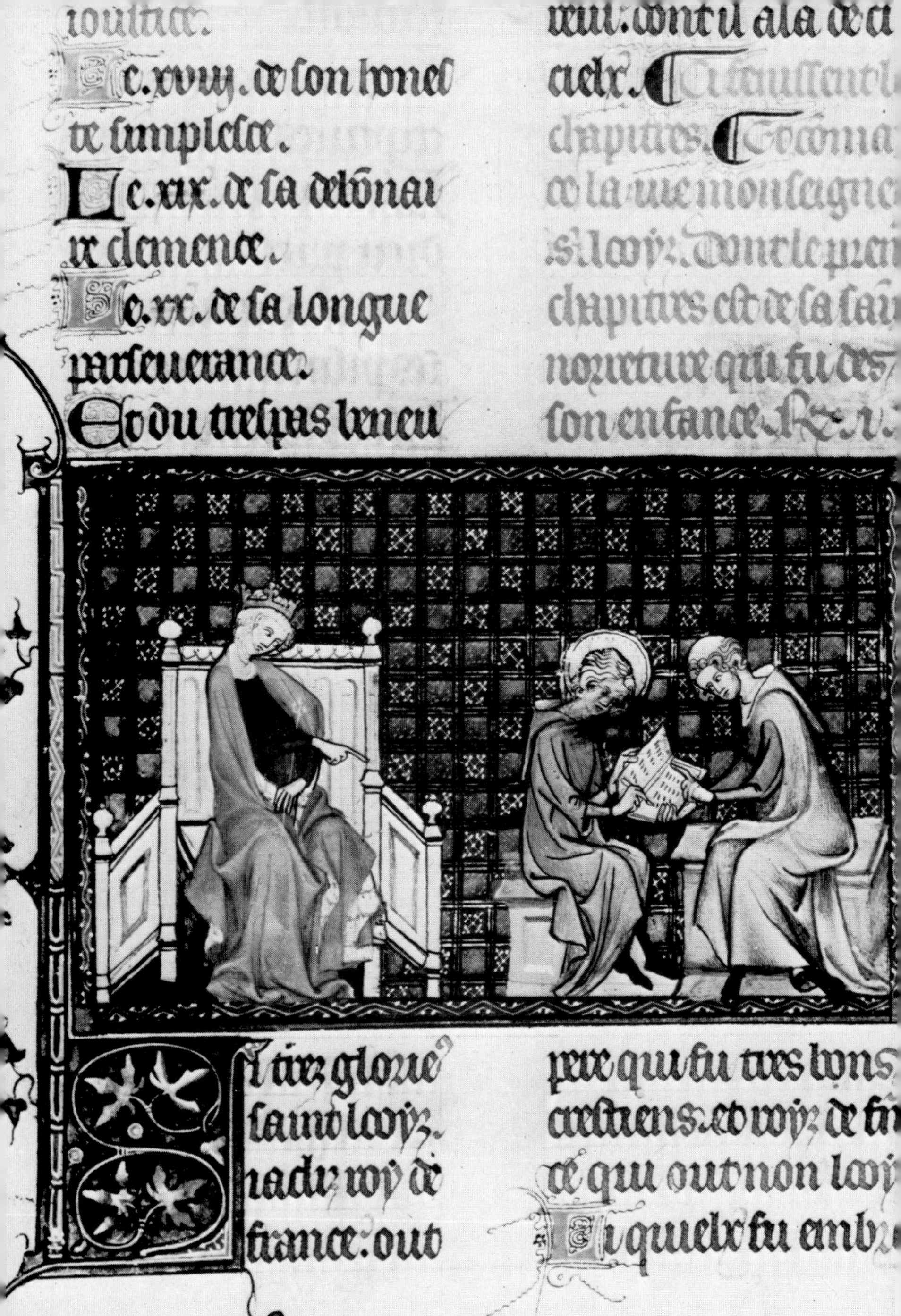

Bibliothèque Nationale, Pa

St. Louis.

allowed her affair with the Count of Champagne to become scandalously obvious. And who knew but that the two of them had plotted from the start to get rid of Blanche's husband, who had been so treacherously deserted by her paramour at Avignon? And look how she was squandering the wealth of France! She preached thrift to her son the King, but she herself scattered largess to the courts of Castile and Champagne.

> The truth touching my lady shall I tell,
> Of how she loves her babe so tenderly
> She doth not wish that he should much excel
> At opening of his house's treasury.
> Yet she herself doth lavish it right well
> And sendeth of her plenty much to Spain
> And much also to reinforce Champagne.[4]

Some unusual activity on the lands of the Count of Boulogne, Philip Hurepel, next attracted Blanche's attention. He was fortifying Boulogne; building ramparts and a castle at Calais; increasing the fortifications at Hardelot and other places. All that masonry boded no good. Since the suicide of Reynold of Dammartin, Hurepel had no fear of losing his county, and that very assurance made him cock an ear in the direction of Brittany, where Peter Mauclerc, despite the Vendôme agreements, had not really disarmed.

Why should not the realm, and the young King, be in the care of a baron like himself, Philip? Bastard though he was, he was of royal blood. Why should a woman and a foreigner be in charge? For that matter, since a king was needed, why not one of the barons? There were several who felt able to assume the responsibility, especially now that the dynasty seemed to have toppled over on to the distaff side. Peter Mauclerc's tireless scheming had brought him another ally: Enguerrand III of Coucy, a close kinsman of Peter and likewise a descendant of Louis VI through his mother, Alix of Dreux. Enguerrand was another baron who felt able to take the helm. What was needed this time was a really well-thought-out and thorough conspiracy, one that would use force and not let itself be out-witted by 'Dame Hersent'. There was no dearth of malcontents in France, and further afield there was someone else merely waiting for the end of the truce in order to renew hostilities. In 1228 the King of England had held his Christmas court at Oxford, where he had received delegations from Bordeaux, Guienne, Poitou and Normandy, all begging him to make a show of force by landing on the continent.

All these unusual alliances and activities were not lost on Blanche, who made her own counter-moves. She had learned that the free towns could provide much help and it was to them that she again turned. During the month of October 1228 all the royal bailiffs between the Seine and the Flanders borders were requested to see the mayors and aldermen of the principal free towns and obtain their oaths of allegiance to the Queen and her son. It was the first glimmer of an alliance between the King of France and the bourgeoisie which one day would come fully into its own. Two hundred and fifty years later Louis XI merely followed the example set by Blanche. Two hundred years after that Louis XIV chose every one of his ministers, without exception, from among the bourgeoisie. The circum-stances were of course quite different in the three cases, but they all had one vital feature in common: the monarchy's need to hold an increasingly restless, ungovernable, even mutinous nobility in check.

A number of small pieces of parchment still in the files of the French National Archives attest to that allegiance sworn by the burghers 750 years ago. Each bit of parchment bears the seal of a town: Amiens, Compiègne, Senlis, Arras, Montreuil-sur-Mer, Tournai – a total of 28 – for which a written instrument bears witness to their oath. All these towns had in times past – as long ago as the middle of the 11th century in the case of Saint-Quentin – either rejected the authority of their hereditary lord outright or bought their freedom. Now they were declar-ing themselves ready to stand by their little King and his mother.

Blanche felt much strengthened by their promised support

– promised unconditionally, too, which showed the confidence
that the burghers had in the Capetians.[5]

On their side the barons were organizing and agreeing carefully among themselves just how they would go about it to
prevent another fiasco. Peter Mauclerc himself would decide
when hostilities should begin. They knew that Blanche's
strategy would be to call up the 'seigneurial host', that military
assistance which she could rightfully request of her barons.
The rebels planned to respond to her call, but each would go
to court with exactly two knights. In that way they could not
be accused of breaking their oath to the King, but they would
have tricked 'Dame Hersent' for she would have no army or at
best a ridiculously insufficient one, and so would have to
dance to the barons' tune. Checkmate. In any case, wasn't it
about time that Hugh Capet's dynasty, which the barons themselves had elected to the throne, be replaced by a younger,
stronger one?

It was the end of the year 1228. Louis IX held his Christmas
court at Melun and summoned Peter Mauclerc for December
31. Peter did not answer. It meant war. Blanche waited for a
further signal. She knew that she could count on the townspeople of the entire region to the north and east of the royal
domain, so she decided to surprise Mauclerc by carrying the
war into his own lands. And surprised he was, for – contrary to
all the rebels' expectations – she arrived with an imposing army,
and as one might have guessed, there was Count Theobald of
Champagne in the midst of them. He had not brought two
knights with him, like the rebels, nor yet the three hundred
cited later by Joinville, who, being too young himself to take
part in the action, went by hearsay. There were eight hundred
knights with Theobald, a fact attested to by his own recruit-
ment list, which has been preserved.[6]

Beyond Chartres and Nogent-le-Rotrou, on the road to
Brittany, in the Perche country formerly entrusted by King
Philip to Peter Mauclerc, stood the castle of Bellême. Despite
his feudal oaths, Mauclerc had fortified it so powerfully that it

was considered impregnable. It was the objective of the first military campaign led by Louis IX in person. He was three months short of fifteen, but he knew that at the same age his grandfather Philip had led his first campaigns.

Louis's plan was bold. Apart from the castle's grim fortifications, it was mid-January of a harsh winter. Peter Mauclerc had begun marauding in the nearby royal lands, not expecting a counter-move until spring. The young King knew that the siege he planned could be a long one. He lodged his troops with care, following the advice of the Marshal of France – probably John Clément, a battlewise old veteran. Some were housed in the surrounding villages, but most were in tents. Bivouacs were set up, and all the necessary supplies for men and horses were brought in from the neighbouring hamlets: Saint-Martin-du-Vieux-Bellême, Saint-Jean-de-la-Forêt, Saint-Ouen-de-la-Cour, Sérigny, and several other places were called upon to help meet the expenses. Much later, when the King inquired into the losses and damages suffered during the campaign, the local peasants had some grim tales to tell. The parishioners of Saint-Sauveur and Saint-Pierre-de-Bellême complained that their houses had been burned by order of the Count of Brittany; whereas other villagers had had their grain and livestock requisitioned by the King's own quartermasters.

Finally the besieging forces were in position, but in no happy mood, for meanwhile the winter had set in in earnest. Everything was frozen stiff, including the besiegers. They had to break the ice in the watering-troughs so that the horses could drink.

Blanche came to oversee the situation personally. She was well aware that it was a critical one. She and her son and all those with them had become committed to a very dangerous operation, one that could not be allowed to fail. The kingdom depended upon it.

Any commander-in-chief would have said the same. But Blanche had a woman's reactions in addition to those of a strategist. These were her people and they were freezing. Somehow they must be kept warm. Her maternal instincts buttressed what ordinary common sense made plain.

It was so cold, the peril had been too great for man and horse had not Queen Blanche, who stood to siege before the castle, sent word throughout the army to all those who would fain win the day, that they go forth and hew down trees, walnut and apple, and all firewood they might find, to bring it to the army. No sooner said than the common varlets went and cut down what they did find and lugged it back by horse and wain. And those in the army made great bonfires without the tents and pavilions, so well that the cold could not harm man nor horse.[7]

The forest of Bellême was close by, and even the beams of old houses in Bellême and Sérigny were burned. The 'great bonfires' that sprang up everywhere put fresh heart into the men and horses, so much so that the castle of Bellême, that impregnable fortress, surrendered after two days of attack. Louis, whose first military success was thus due to Queen Blanche's maternal gesture, spared the garrison. And the villagers, well aware of what they owed to Blanche, later raised a cross in memory of the siege commanded by a woman. Centuries later they were still calling it La Croix-feue-Reine: 'The Queen's Fire Cross'.

The news spread quickly. Hugh Le Blond, castellan of La Perrière, to the west of Bellême, lost no time in surrendering his keys. Blanche, meanwhile, had sent her bailiff of Gisors, John des Vignes, against one of Mauclerc's allies, the Sire de La Haie-Paynel, who owned important lands in England. John des Vignes had merely to announce that he came in the Queen's name for La Haie-Paynel, thoroughly taken aback by the success of Blanche's dogged campaign in mid-winter, to surrender as well.

'You told me that this young King would get no help from his men,' the King of England wrote sourly to the Count of Brittany some time later; 'but I see that he has more people than you or I.'

The main source of Louis's strength was no secret. For Mauclerc and his friends, furious since their first set-back, the arch-enemy was now Theobald of Champagne, whom they meant to repay.

> Envious Theobald, full of felony,
> Thy fame comes not from feats of chivalry,
> But only from thy skill in physickry.

He had long been suspected of being a poisoner. 'Had thy master lived, thou wert disseized.'

So the rebel barons turned their forces against Champagne. It was just at a time when Theobald, no politician, had managed to quarrel with Count Hugh of Burgundy. And even worse, he had in a fit of unjustifiable anger seized the person of Robert of Auvergne, Archbishop of Lyons, whom he accused of plotting with the Burgundians against him. It was a veritable kidnapping. The Archbishop had been waylaid while passing through Champagne and taken by night, blindfolded, to a castle where he was held as hostage. He might have been there a long time but for an unexpected deliverer: the Count of Bar, who was indignant at such proceedings and insisted on his release. So Theobald had made himself three new enemies at one stroke: the Duke of Burgundy, the Archbishop, and the Count of Bar, who till then had been his ally. Theobald became the butt of jests and ballads which went the rounds of the castles and fairs, calling him 'old, vile, and a huge hill of flesh'. (Theobald's corpulence – he was not yet thirty at the time – was to be the subject of witticisms all his life.)

But it did not stop at words. The Duke of Burgundy and the Count of Nevers lost no time in invading Champagne. They sacked Saint-Florent, put the torch to the castle of Ervy, and besieged Chaource, south of Troyes. The minstrels began to sing a new ballad about Theobald, depicting him in rags, with only 'ribalds' for companions, and seeking whatever friends he could find to come to his rescue. The rhymester had ended it with a couplet full of sly implications.

Then to his ribald quoth the Count:
"'Tis plain as hair upon the head
That with one pennyworth of bread
I might well surfeit all my friends,
For I have none, my wit intends.
None may I trust in this mischance,
Unless it be the Queen of France.'
She did his loyal friend remain,
And proved she did not him disdain,
Through her his foes were brought to hand,
And repossessed was all his land . . .
And many tales thereon be told,
As on Sir Tristram, and Ysolde.

Clearly, if Blanche was at times ruled by her motherly impulses, there were other times when she knew how to be a woman – which must be understood within the context of the era of 'courtly love'. Be that as it may, Blanche and her son, with their army, set out at once for Champagne. In a few days they were in Troyes. Moreover Blanche had sent Ferdinand of Flanders, now her friend, to deal with Philip Hurepel, who had become a declared enemy of Theobald. Ferdinand took the offensive and marched on Calais, burning down the Castle of Marck and the farm at Oye on his way. Not long after, the Minstrel of Rheims gave an amusing account of Philip's beating about the bush.

The Queen's counsels would have her defend the lands of Champagne and Brie, as the Count of Champagne was her kinsman and true to the King. She did gather a great army at four leagues from Troyes, she and the King being there besides. She bade the Count of Boulogne and the barons that they be not so bold as to do aught ill in the King's fief, for she stood ready to do justice for the Count if they should say wherein they were aggrieved. And they did send word to her that they did not mean to plead, saying it was a woman's way to prefer him who had murdered her husband to another. Then answered the Count of Boulogne, having marked their treachery, and he said: 'By my troth, you say ill. None of you has made plain his grievance 'gainst the Count. We would, moreover, perjure ourselves before the King, if hereafter we did him wrong despite this prohibition. What's more, the King is my nephew, the son of my brother. He is my liege lord and I am his liege man. Wherefore I would have you know that I am no more of your alliance nor of your counsels, but shall be the King's true man with all my might.' When the barons heard the Count say thus, they did gaze upon each other and marvel and said to the Count, who was their chief: 'Sire, herein have you abused us, for you make peace with the Queen, but we shall lose our lands.' 'In God's name,' said the Count, ''twere better to renounce folly than to pursue it.' Whereupon he did cause to be written to the Queen and sent her word that he meant not to infringe her commandment, nor the King's, but stood all ready to perform it. The which, when the Queen did learn of it, made her well content. And the Count of Boulogne took leave of the barons and they went their ways, each to his own lands with heart uneasy. For they had not won their way but rather the Queen's harsh rancour, she who well knew how to show her good favour and ill towards those that did deserve them, and give to each according to his deeds.[8]

Philip had not in fact been a very staunch ally to the injudicious barons. He had learned a lesson from Ferdinand's exploits and he knew when enough was enough. Hugh of Burgundy, for his part, had no wish to encounter the royal army; he made peace. A whole new network of alliances sprang up; some were broken, others renewed. There were truce proposals and threats of war. If we are to believe the chroniclers of the day, some of the barons went as far as requesting Blanche's personal permission to settle their quarrels with the Count of Champagne by judicial combat. It was

probably at this time that the irascible poet called Hugh of La
Ferté wrote a new song depicting Blanche as so haughty that
she would not even deign to answer such requests, for by the
beginning of the 13th century judicial combat was quite
obsolete. To name champions and agree that he whose man
was defeated was in the wrong was to turn the clock back to
Merovingian days. Blanche's icy silence on the matter was
understandable. Some years later a brief decree issued by her
son the King would declare the outmoded practice illegal.

Mauclerc still did not admit himself beaten. In October 1229
he arrived in England with the intention of dispelling Henry
III's last doubts and having him mount an invasion. This time
it was outright treason. True, King Henry was in any case
making plans to recover what his father had formerly lost,
and the invasion would have taken place sooner or later. But
Henry had just had a frightful row with his chief justiciar,
Hubert de Burgh, who thirteen years before had so loyally
defended the fortress at Dover and enabled him to be crowned
and whom Henry now accused of preparing the expedition half-
heartedly. The ships Hubert had assembled in Portsmouth
harbour were far from sufficient to transport the required army,
he maintained. In his anger Henry went so far as to accuse the
old minister of taking a bribe from the Queen of France.

With Peter Mauclerc's arrival King Henry regained his
optimism. Together they planned the invasion for Easter of the
following year, 1230. Peter did homage to Henry for his
duchy of Brittany.

So Blanche and young Louis had to take up arms again and
if possible forestall the English landing. King Henry was
planning it with extreme care. He did not conceal his designs
on the French crown. In his luggage, along with his solid silver
table ware, he ordered his household to pack a royal mantle of
white silk, a sceptre, a baton of gilded silver, and parade sandals
and gauntlets. If Enguerrand of Coucy was nursing designs on
the French throne he clearly had a competitor.

Blanche and her son, however, were still to be dealt with.

In January 1230 Louis had already reached Saumur at the head of the royal troops; from there he went on to Angers. He was to handle the fighting, Blanche the bargaining. She managed to pry loose from Peter Mauclerc some of his closest allies, such as his brother-in-law Andrew of Vitré. Then the Count of La Marche himself, a former traitor, who might well have been expected to join the Plantagenet alliance, opted for the King of France. Two other Poitou lords, Raymond and Guy of Thouars, also came over to Louis's side and signed a treaty to that effect at Clisson, south-east of Nantes. Shortly after that young Louis took Ancenis, Oudon and Champtoceaux (all on the Loire up-river from Nantes) one after the other from the Count of Brittany. During all this King Henry, who had effected his landing, was taking his troops on a tour of western France which (whether through prudence or some other reason) did not seem to include an encounter with the army of King Louis. In July 1230 Henry besieged and captured the small fortress of Mirambeau, north of Bordeaux. He then stopped in Bordeaux itself for a while, after which he returned to Nantes, and shortly afterwards took ship again at Saint-Malo to regain his island realm on October 28, 1230. The much-trumpeted invasion had fizzled out. The mountain had given birth to a mouse.

Philip Hurepel had parted company with his fellow-conspirators in the autumn of 1230, after the royal armies had parried new attacks on Count Theobald's domains and on Troyes. His defection undoubtedly had something to do with the discreet departure of the King of England. In any case it left Philip's former allies disappointed, furious and very uneasy. 'The Queen of France has sworn she will disinherit me,' Reynold of Pons wrote to the King of England. As for Enguerrand of Coucy, he withdrew to his ancestral acres, comforting himself with the proud personal motto which more or less confirmed the demise of his old ambitions:

> No king I be,
> Nor prince, nor duke, nor high county;
> I am the Sire of Coucy.

And he set himself to build the splendid keep, at Coucy-le-Château, north of Soissons, which was to remain the largest and finest in Europe right down to the 20th century.*

Peter Mauclerc, however, seething with rage, still would not give up. They had begun to sing ballads about *him* now. One of them, in the form of a dialogue in alternating stanzas, well conveys the people's impressions of those rebel barons' interminable, vacillating struggles, never able to finish the job they set themselves.

'Walter, you come from France and have been with those barons. Pray tell me what they mean to do. Will their quarrels last forever? Will they never come to terms? Will they never even come to blows?'

'Peter, according to our Count Hurepel, and the Breton, and the valiant Lord of Bar, and the Burgundian chief, we shall, before Rogationtide, see the braggart Basques so well repulsed and brought to heel that no king lives who could defend them.'

'Walter, these worthless threats go on and on. One would not think these men seek real revenge. Yet, by my faith, they do. Each day I see them gather from afar, in numerous companies. They lose their lands, their honour, and their gold, for they can neither speak well nor keep their peace.'

'Peter, too much confusion often spells misfortune. They wittingly would mock the Cardinal, and the King, who now, on Dame Hersent's advice, has dealt them grievous blows. Their plans are thus in ruins, and each thinks only of himself.'

'Walter, there's no trusting them. They are too slow in getting under way. They have let the fair weather slip by, and now come rain and snow. When they seem most angry, even when they quit the court, they always leave two or three of their own men to parley and prolong the truce.'[9]

---

* It was blown up in March 1917 by the retreating Germans, who considered it to be an observation post endangering their movements.

In the midst of all this Blanche had accomplished what was perhaps the most important act of her reign, the one which, in perspective, surely had the most lasting effect on the destiny of the kingdom of France. In any case it was, in her own time, the act most typical of her own policies, and one that deliberately broke with the policies that had preceded her. She made peace with Raymond of Toulouse.

Clearly Blanche was not the only one who wanted peace. The war against the Albigensians had been the Pope's decision, undertaken for the purpose of fighting the heretics. But it had dragged on for twenty years now, and no one could any longer distinguish religious from political motives, high-minded ambitions from covetousness, or even the role of nobles from that of prelates. Church councils had attempted to settle the Languedoc question several times. The Counts of Toulouse were now excommunicated, now absolved. The only thing certain was that everyone was thoroughly sick of the poorly started, poorly managed, never-ending business. Who could tell by now what the fighting in southern France was all about? Even those who had been against the heretics had now lost patience with the good Christians. The constant warfare had accomplished nothing except the death of the King of France. Some different way must be found.

Blanche found it and was greatly helped in it by the Cardinal of Sant'Angelo. He had been ordered by Pope Honorius III to bring the Albigensian war to a successful conclusion, and he finally succeeded in doing so.

To begin with, the Cardinal energetically collected the subsidies due from the clergy. Since it was a religious war, it was only right that the clerics pay their share. The Cardinal fully understood the Queen's difficulties and how all her own resources were required to maintain the royal army needed to hold the arrogant barons in check. When Blanche saw how whole cathedral chapters of her kingdom kept on indefinitely finding excuses for putting off payment of the tax levied for the crusade, she became furious and complained to the legate. He told her that in order to collect the tithe (one-tenth of the cathedral's revenues) he would if necessary even sell the canons' cloaks. This upset the canons and they complained directly to the Pope. After many irksome misunderstandings, complaints, appeals and protests, the recalcitrant chapters, those of Rheims, Tours, and Rouen, finally paid over five thousand *livres tournois*.* It cost Blanche a few whispered charges of anti-clericalism, but at least she had the funds needed to deal with the Languedoc situation as she intended.

At the death of Louis VIII the Constable of France, Humbert of Beaujeu, had been left in the south of France with five hundred knights. He had undertaken a few tentative operations which had resulted in his being defeated at Castel-Sarrasin, north-west of Toulouse, by Count Raymond. The Count had been apprised of his movements and had prepared an ambush.

When the French were come to that place where he lay in ambush against them, he rushed upon them with his army. The French were taken unawares. It was a bitter fight. More than five hundred knights of France were captured, and many killed. Some two thousand sergeants-at-arms were taken prisoner. They were stripped naked, and the Count caused some to have their eyes torn out and their noses and ears cut off. With others he had their hands and feet hacked away, and sent them back thus shamefully mangled to their own people, so that the horrid sight of them should strike dismay into the hearts of the French.[10]

The English chronicler probably exaggerated the incident, but the fact remains that the French were undoubtedly badly beaten.

A little later, however, a victory helped to make up for this. The imposing fortress at Termes, south of Carcassonne, which had given the crusaders in southern France so much trouble, and which is constantly mentioned in the *Chanson de la Croisade*,

* *Tournois* meant money minted at Tours and came to have the same meaning in France as *sterling* in England.

had been yielded to the King of France. The lords Oliver and
Bernard were allowed to keep it in return for doing homage to
the King. It is not clear whether their act was outright defection, or whether they were simply weary of war. Shortly before Christmas, 1228, Count Raymond of Toulouse had sent
Hélie Guérin, the abbot of the monastery of Grandselve, to
tell his cousin Blanche that he meant to swear allegiance to the
King. Thereupon, while the Cardinal of Sant'Angelo held two
councils to thrash out the matter with the churchmen, Theobald of Champagne undertook the practical negotiations. In
due course the Count of Toulouse arrived at Meaux, in
Theobald's lands, most eager to settle the matter. He wished to
be reconciled with the Church and he accepted the clauses of
the treaty drawn up by his envoys. After a few days of discussion, Blanche received this powerful vassal in Paris. The
wording of the letters that Raymond wrote to her subsequently
left no doubt that so much sympathy, even affection, had developed between them that Blanche would be reproached for
it.

The major concern was lifting the excommunication.
Raymond was obliged to undergo a ceremony of expiation.
As his father had done in former times before the gate of
Saint-Gilles-du-Gard, he appeared on Holy Thursday, April
12, 1229, before the gate of Notre Dame de Paris, barefoot and
clad in his shirt and hose. With the Cardinal as witness, he
solemnly swore obedience to the Church. The Cardinal pro-
nounced the remission of all condemnations that had been laid
upon him, and led him by the hand to the altar. Next day
Raymond gave further confirmation of his resolution: he
would take the cross. He promised to spend five years in the
defence of the Holy Land.

The chapter of history begun twenty years earlier with the
murder of the papal legate was ended. Possibly Blanche had
had the benefit of a fortunate combination of circumstances,
although the whole affair had taken place at a time when the
throne was still in the midst of its struggles with the barons,

and when an attack by the King of England seemed imminent. But the fact remains that, in this most painful conflict that had involved almost all the political powers of Western Europe, her role had been the most fruitful. Where her husband, by force of arms, had achieved only distressing results, as at Avignon, or horrible ones as at Marmande, she had brought peace.

As was customary, the treaty called for a marriage. One of the King's brothers was betrothed to Joan, daughter of the Count of Toulouse. She was Raymond's only child and his sole heir. The Count himself could now resume the peaceful enjoyment of almost the whole of his domain. He still had the county of Toulouse, the northern half of the county of Albi, parts of Quercy and Agenais, and Rouergue, all lying for the most part between the Aveyron and Aude rivers in southern France. Raymond had yielded to the Pope his rights over the marquisate of Provence, which was a dependency of the Holy Roman Empire. Joan's dowry comprised the duchy of Narbonne, the southern half of the county of Albi, and the two domains of Castres and Mirepoix. Finally, the King of France was to retain Carcassonne and Beaucaire in his personal realm. Various clauses of the treaty specifically guaranteed the agreement. The citadel of Toulouse in particular, called the Château-Narbonnais, was to be garrisoned for ten years by the King's troops, and twenty burghers from the town were to remain within it as hostages until the walls had been razed. Yet amid all these precautions the most precious pledge of peace was clearly Joan of Toulouse, then only nine years old. In accordance with custom, she was to be brought up at the court of France, in the company of her fiancé.

Blanche must have witnessed the arrival of the little girl at court without undue illusions. The proposed marriages in Brittany had fizzled out almost as soon as they had been contracted. Would the Toulouse marriage plans fare any better?

The Count of Toulouse remained at the Louvre until his daughter arrived. He would be coming back to the court of

France more than once, and each time the presents showered on him would prove the warmth of his welcome there.

The mission of Romano Cardinal Frangipani was at an end. He had had the satisfaction of seeing it fulfilled in every way. 'We, Romano, by divine mercy Cardinal of Sant'Angelo, considering the humility and piety of the Lord Raymond, son of Raymond, erstwhile Count of Toulouse . . . have been mindful to grant him the benefit of absolution according to the ritual of the Church . . .'[11] It was also the Cardinal, without a doubt, who had taken the greatest part in the drawing up of the treaty. It has in fact been pointed out in recent times that the treaty of Meaux-Paris[12] was the first to be written according to a logical scheme, at a time when the matters dealt with in treaties were usually broached haphazardly, the wording jumbled, and with no great attention to logical order. Here each clause is as clear as a treatise. Two of the clauses were more important than anyone realized at the time. One of them required the Count of Toulouse to use his power to repress heresy. The other stipulated that he should furnish the sum of four thousand marks to the masters of the University of Toulouse – which did not yet exist, but which was to be founded for the very purpose of combating heresy.

It so happened that just as he was preparing for the foundation of a university at Toulouse, the Cardinal, and Blanche too for that matter, were to experience an all-out confrontation with the student world.

It began trivially enough, according to the English chronicler Matthew Paris, on Shrove Monday of that year, February 26, 1229.

Some few clerks of the University of Paris did betake themselves to Saint-Marcel so as to take the air and sport about as was their wont. Once there, and having frolicked some little time, they did chance to discover within a tavern a most excellent wine, delicious to drink. A quarrel as to the

price of this wine broke out between the same clerks and
the taverners. They did begin to seize one another by the
hair, and to deal out many blows, until the townsfolk
running up did deliver the taverners from the hands of the
clerks. But they did wound them, the same not wishing to
leave go their hold, and did compel them to run away,
being well and mightily thrashed. The same clerks, returning
to the town in tatters, did incite their companions to avenge
them. Returning on the morrow with swords and cudgels
to Saint-Marcel, they did violently break into the house of
the taverner, stove in all his wine-casks and let out the wine
on to the paving. Then they went about the streets and
squares of the town, pursuing all those whom they did
chance to meet, both men and women, and leaving them
half stunned.[13]

The dean of the chapter of Saint-Marcel, then a town in the
suburbs of Paris, at once took up the defence of his townsfolk
against the students. He complained to the papal legate, the
Cardinal of Sant'Angelo, and to the Bishop of Paris, William
of Auvergne, who both listened sympathetically.

The Bishop of Paris had not been in that office for three
months when he had had a brush with the students of Saint-
Thomas-du-Louvre College: a small group of overstimulated
lads had forced their way into a nunnery one night. As for
the Cardinal, his contacts with the Paris students had been
disastrous. Four years earlier they had come and asked him to
pronounce an official confirmation of their privileges, which
had only been in existence for about fifteen years. The Cardinal,
full of the authority that the Pope's mandate conferred on
him, had summoned the masters and had before their very
eyes, and without even listening to them, broken the seal of the
University. The seal! Those present were at first flabbergasted,
then furious at an act that amounted to denying the University's autonomy, its very right to exist. But that autonomy
had been recognized by the King, the Pope, and by the pre-

ceding papal legate, Robert of Courçon. The news of the outrage spread immediately throughout the student world. Masters and scholars had taken up arms on the spot and actually besieged the episcopal residence, to which the Cardinal had withdrawn after his exploit. Luckily for him, the King, Louis VIII, was in Paris at the time and, having received word of the riot at the palace, had speedily sent knights and soldiers to restore order – not before two men of the Cardinal's retinue had been killed. The Cardinal himself had discreetly left town the next morning, and had lost no time in excommunicating his assailants. Yet in less than a month the eighty excommunicated masters had been absolved. Needless to say the University and the legate were now at daggers drawn. And the business at Saint-Marcel seemed to afford the Cardinal an excellent opportunity for getting back at these perpetually rampageous University people.

So the Bishop and the legate, greatly agitated, went to see the Queen. She also seemed ready to listen sympathetically, for she clearly had no great love for the students. Perhaps she remembered the nights of rioting that had upset her as a child. Here is how Matthew Paris tells it:

The Queen, being by nature hot-headed, did with womanish impetuosity send all in haste to the city provost and some of his men to go at once without the walls and punish the instigators and relent not. Those people, ever ready for cruel deeds, came in arms without the gates and did find behind the ramparts some students at their sport, the same having had no part whatsoever in the crimes committed. For indeed those which had provoked the tumult and combat did come from far-off regions in Flanders and were called in the vulgar tongue, Picards. Notwithstanding, the armed men rushed upon such of them as they chanced to find, the same being innocent and unarmed, and did kill some, wound others, and thrash still others without mercy. Some took to flight, seeking refuge where they might find it . . . Among those wounded were two clerks of high repute and most esteemed, which died, the one a Fleming, the other a Norman.

This monstrous transgression coming to the ears of the masters of the University, all did assemble in the presence of the Queen and the legate, having beforehand suspended their lessons and disputations. They did earnestly beg that justice be done them for such an outrage, for in truth it did appear shameful to them that for so slight a cause the fault of some few blameful students should redound to the prejudice of the whole University . . . But forasmuch as all manner of justice was denied them, by the King as much as by the legate and the Bishop, all the masters and students did with one mind disperse themselves, breaking off the doctors' studies and the scholars' discipline, so much so that not one was left, and the city was deprived of those very students of whom she was wont to glorify herself.

It was no laughing matter. Paris had lost her students, the courses were suspended, and the 'disputations' that habitually echoed throughout the dwellings of the clerks were heard no more. Recalling that in accordance with the privilege granted to the clerks by King Philip the royal sergeants-at-arms were forbidden to lay hands on the students, the spokesman for the University did not hesitate to deliver an ultimatum to the Queen: if by Easter (April 15, 1229) masters and students had not received reparation, a general strike of six years' duration would be called. In the 13th century they did not go in for half-measures.

Blanche felt that she was supported by the legate and also by the Bishop of Paris, who had formerly had jurisdiction over the city's schools. She decided to confront the clerks as squarely as she had the mutinous barons. She lived to regret it. The general strike was called. The students left Paris, some going to Rheims, others to Orléans, many to Angers in the territory of Peter Mauclerc, Duke of Brittany. The masters of the newly-created University of Toulouse quickly turned the situation to their own advantage. They sent circulars to the Paris clerks offering them hospitality in Languedoc. Still another person tried to profit from the situation: King Henry III of England. On July 16, 1229, he promised the masters and students of Paris that the way would be made smooth for them if they came to settle in England. On top of all this, slanders and satires in ribald Latin (of the genre called 'Goliardic', written most often by defrocked priests and monks) were being bandied about, suggesting, as might be expected, that there was more to the alliance of the Queen and the Italian legate than met the eye.

Whereat there was spread abroad a tale so shameful that one should forbear to repeat it. It was said that Master Legate did bear himself toward Dame Blanche in no fitting manner. But 'twould be impiety to give it credence, such talk having been put about by the enemies of the Queen. In the like uncertainty the well-meaning spirit must rather believe for the best.

These lines are from Matthew Paris, who himself was anything but well-meaning. He goes on to claim the reason some of the barons had refused to be present at the coronation was the too-intimate relationship the legate was accused of having with the Queen. The accusation was certainly false, but it died hard. Even in Latin, it is impossible to quote the ballads of the 'Goliards', who in later times would have been hanged or imprisoned for *lèse-majesté*. Long after, at the end of Louis IX's reign, the facetious Minstrel of Rheims adapted this gossip in a scene narrated with his own inimitable zest:

The good Queen and wise took counsel with herself, for she yet minded the wicked things . . . they had told against her. Wherefore did she strip away her raiment down to a simple shift and threw thereon a mantle, and thus apparelled left her chamber. She betook herself to the hall where sat the lords and prelates, and had her ushers cry peace. When the clamour was abated she mounted upon a wall-table of two legs, and said . . . 'My lords! Do you all look upon me. There are those who will have it that I am with child.' And anon she let fall her mantle upon the table and did turn about this way and that until all had seen her and it well appeared that she had no child in her belly. When the barons saw their lady thus naked, they did leap in front of her and drape her in her mantle again, and they led her to her chamber and bade her clothe herself. Then did they return again to the hall, where much was said of this and that.[14]

Needless to say the episode is entirely apocryphal.

One might have expected that the Pope, when apprised of the matter, would lay the blame on the trouble-making students, but the opposite happened. On November 24, 1229, Pope Gregory IX sent a severe letter to the King of France and his mother, and he wrote similarly to the Bishop of Paris. He disavowed King and Bishop alike and came down firmly on the side of the students and their masters.

By the time Blanche received this letter she had already, of her own accord, done what could be done to resolve the dispute. In August 1229 young Louis had reaffirmed the privileges granted by King Philip to the University. The provost of Paris had even taken his oath to respect the University's immunity. The strike went on nevertheless. It was to last two years.

Finally a letter from the Pope dated April 14, 1231, indicated that a friendly settlement might be reached, though he continued to side with the University. The King must again reaffirm the privileges, although this had been done in August 1229. He must set the maximum rents that could be charged for lodgings let to students in Paris and the suburbs, which meant the Mont Saint-Geneviève and the 'Latin Quarter' generally. Finally, he must pay appropriate damages. Studies at last resumed on a normal basis during the year 1231.

It was dawn. Everyone was still asleep in the palace of the Cité except Blanche, who sat listening to what a Black friar was reading to her. He was one of those who had followed Brother Dominic and had just set up a monastery in Paris, on the highroad of the pilgrimage to St James of Compostela. It was the Queen's habit to make use of the morning calm for prayer and meditation; once the day was started she had scarcely the time. Suddenly the monk, who was on his knees near the window, beckoned to her. Blanche came over and looked out to where he was pointing in the courtyard of the palace. It was always open to one and all, and the poor people of the town, beggars and vagabonds, came each morning to ask alms. It was too early to expect anyone in the royal residence to be stirring, yet down in the courtyard was a young boy, dressed as a simple squire. He must have slipped out by some side door. He was moving about among the wretched people there, giving a few coins to each. Blanche, startled at first, took some time to recognize the lad by his well-combed blond hair, worn halfway down to his shoulders. It was her son Louis. It was the King.

As the lad was returning to his room, the Black friar met him in the corridor and led him to the Queen. 'Sire,' said the friar, 'I witnessed your audacity.' Louis was taken aback and blushed a little, but he said: 'Friar, those people are the true soldiers of the realm. They fight for us against our enemies. They are the ones who keep France in safety and peace. If truth were told, we have not paid them all the wages they deserve.'[15]

Blanche knew her son better than anyone, and she knew that such gestures were already habitual with him. She marvelled to see how he surpassed her fondest hopes. Naturally she was bringing all her watchfulness and love to bear on his training, on preparing him carefully for the great role that awaited him. She obtained the best tutors, supervising his studies herself, taking care that his upbringing was confided only to clerics as pious and upright as they were erudite. The King and his brothers received the normal training for their time. This meant that prayers and religious offices were part of their daily routine. They went to mass each day and attended the singing of vespers. For the royal family, however, these things were not merely formalities, routine and social ritual; not for Blanche, and above all not for Louis. They *believed* these things, they had received and accepted them in the innermost fibres of their being: the daily prayers; the liturgical year measuring out the rhythm of life in the up-beats and down-beats of worship, of penances and rejoicings, fast-days and feast-days. It was from the secret, intimate logic of faith that young Louis drew the strength on which he built his life. There was no need to make him go to church and sing psalms. He was naturally inclined toward the life of worship. Later on his intimates would declare that in the worst moments of his career 'he was constantly praying'. The proof was there in his youthful preoccupation with poor and humble people. He looked upon those poor, whom he called 'the soldiers of the realm and his protectors', as an incarnation of Christ himself. Such a feeling could come only from the heart of the gospels.

Yet these predispositions would probably not have come into their own without the tender and watchful eye that Blanche gave to her sons, especially to the one 'whom she loved before all the others'. It is a remarkable fact that the two sisters, Blanche and Berenguela, each had a saint among her children. They were not saints themselves, but they must have been the right kind of mothers.

The only thing that Joinville, Louis IX's chronicler, tells us in this respect is that Blanche said 'that she had rather see her son dead than guilty of deadly sin'. It shows her high ideals, but seems a little insensitive. According to Geoffrey of Beaulieu, the Black friar who was the saintly King's confessor and who must have understood the inner life of worship better than Joinville, the fellow-soldier, there was more to the story. It seems (according to Geoffrey) that Louis himself told how, before his marriage, a monk had been informed by perfidious witnesses that Louis had some concubines with whom he occasionally sinned. The witnesses claimed that Blanche knew all about it and concealed her son's carryings-on. The scandalized monk had gone to Blanche and voiced his dismay. 'Most humbly did the Queen disclaim such falseness and did add this, saying, for which she may well be praised, that were her son the King, whom she loved above all mortal creatures, sick to death, and she be told that he could be made well by lying with a woman other than his wedded wife, she would rather he die than he offend his Creator even once through mortal sin.'[16]

Thus the true meaning of the anecdote is seen from the context. It reminds us of the similar story told of the King's father, Louis VIII, on his death-bed. And it agrees with the general feeling of the times that the death of the body is preferable to the death of the soul. It simply expressed in the rough imagery of that century what we read in the gospel of Matthew, x: 28: 'And fear not them which kill the body, but are not able to kill the soul: but rather fear him which is able to destroy both soul and body in hell.' Or again (v: 29): 'And if thy right eye offend thee, pluck it out, and cast it from thee: for it is profitable for thee that one of thy members should perish, and not that thy whole body should be cast into hell.' St Louis was to take up the same thought in another way when he put a much-quoted question to his seneschal Joinville: 'Which is better: to commit mortal sin or to be a leper?'

Thus, to return to Blanche, her irritation is easily imagined when a simple-minded monk came to her with such stories. Other evidence has survived which shows more clearly what kind of upbringing she was giving her children. First and foremost, Louis's psalter. Its illumination is still Romanesque in style and it bears the moving inscription: 'The Lord St Louis, the same who was the King of France; his psalter, wherein he did learn to read as a child.' One's psalter was one's primer. The large illuminated 'B' on the first page stands for 'Beatus': 'Blessed is the man that walketh not in the counsel of the ungodly . . .' (Psalm 1: 1). It is the beginning of a book familiar to Christians through the centuries, but it was also, in Louis's day, the beginning of schoolwork. Like every other pupil at his age, the young King had to start by finding in the manuscript the words he heard sung in the holy offices day after day. All studies began with the Bible, that treasury of prayer, poetry, and wisdom that was the bedrock of learning in all Christendom at the time. When someone said that he 'knew his psalms' he meant that he knew how to read. All Blanche's children knew their 'letters'; in other words they had learned Latin. (Louis's sister became so erudite that she was able to correct her chaplains when they made mistakes in their Latin.) They had also studied music. Louis's psalter shows five instruments: a hurdy-gurdy (or 'vielle', on which the four strings are rubbed by a cranked wheel – not the barrel-organ of more recent times); a cithern; a harp; and two kinds of viols played with bows. It was a period when great strides were being made in music. The arts of musical notation and calligraphy had both been perfected. St Louis loved books all his life. It was his collection that became the nucleus of what is today France's Bibliothèque Nationale, after having been the Bibliothèque Royale for some centuries. This love of books undoubtedly came to Louis from his mother. The *Psalter of Blanche of Castile* is one of the finest manuscripts of the period, rivalled only by the splendid *Psalter of St Louis*.

We do not have complete information on how the royal children spent their time, but we do know that a part of it was devoted to recreation and excursions. Later, Louis's first biographer noted how, at his mother's bidding, the King 'did at times agree to go out to play by wood and stream',[17] and how the Queen was always at pains 'that he should betake himself thither with a noble bearing and in fine array, as befitted so great a King.' In no other period of our history has a genuine love of poverty been so well reconciled with a taste for display.

On October 24, 1227, Blanche and Louis were at Longpont, near Soissons. They had come at the request of the abbot to be present at the consecration of the new abbey church, which took the place of the one built some hundred years before by Jocelyn of Vierzy, Bishop of Soissons, when the abbey was founded. It was a splendid edifice, 105 metres long, vaulted with those ogival arches that were becoming more and more familiar. It had a triple nave, transept, and an ambulatory from which radiated seven chapels. Despite its size, it had been built in only twenty-seven years.

Cistercian monks from Clairvaux had founded the abbey at Longpont in 1132 and had thereafter added the names of a number of saintly personages to the annals of their order. One of these was John of Montmirail, who was held in particularly high esteem at the court of France. He had been the Constable of France until he entered the order at Longpont at the age of forty-four. He had died ten years earlier in 1217, in the odour of sanctity, and his memory was very much alive beneath those new arches he had watched being built.

As was customary, a great banquet was given after the liturgical ceremonies. The King's cup-bearer, Ralph, Count of Soissons, had the honour of carving the roasts for his royal master. He used a knife with a handle of engraved gold, which had been given to the abbot of Longpont two years before by the abbot of Westminster, Richard of Barking, then on a diplomatic mission in France.

Today only ruins remain of what was once the largest and probably the most handsome abbey church in the region of Soissons. It was savagely vandalized during the French Revolution, and more particularly during the period following it, when the destruction was specially cruel and systematic because it was the work of merchants who resold the stones for profit. Oddly, however, Count Ralph's carving-knife still exists. It was found at the end of the 19th century in a grocer's shop at Villers-Cotterêts, not far from Soissons. The gold handle was gone, but the steel blade still bore traces of its original gilding, as well as the inscription which leaves no doubt as to its origin. It is the only remaining relic of what was a landmark in the history of church architecture. Shortly afterwards, in 1228, the King, then fourteen, was at his castle at Asnières-sur-Oise, where the royal family often stayed. He was there for the purchase of a property called Cuimont, on which in accordance with his father's wishes he intended to found an abbey. Louis VIII had stipulated that the pearls and precious stones of the King's crown be sold in order to build a monastery. Thus Royaumont – the Royal Mount – came into existence. Blanche, who is known to have been specially fond of the Cistercian order, undoubtedly had a hand in the founding of Royaumont and in the decision that it became a Cistercian monastery. Louis VIII's will had stipulated that the monks of Saint-Victor be in charge of the new abbey. But the change had been made without difficulty, since the abbot of Saint-Victor, John le Teutonique, and the Cistercian, Walter of Chartres, were among the executors of Louis VIII's will, and both agreed to the arrangement.

In founding Royaumont young Louis had fulfilled both the will of his father and the fondest wishes of his mother. As the foundation stones were laid Blanche's emotions must have been similar to those she had felt on discovering that the young squire distributing alms in the palace courtyard was none other than her son, the King. The work was carried forward so briskly that a few monks were able to settle there the following year, 1229. From an early age Louis had manifested that interest in building which was to characterize his reign as markedly as his interest in books. He often went to Royaumont to observe the progress being made. He would oversee the work, take part in the architects' planning, and even at need lend a hand with the common labourers. Many of the scenes of Louis's youth, which biographers later were so fond of relating, took place at Royaumont.

The King then staying in his manor of Asnières close by the same abbey, did often come to hear Mass and other offices and to visit the place. Whenas according to the custom of their order of Cîteaux, the monks came out after Terce to work at carrying the stones and mortar wherewith the walls were built, the King would take the barrow full of stones and carry it at the front, the same being carried at the rear by a monk, And thus did he several times. And the King did likewise cause his brothers, the Lords Alphonse, Robert, and Charles, to carry the barrow, there being with each of them a monk at the nether end. And the same did he have other knights of his company perform. And whereas his brothers would rather at times converse and sport, the King would address them thus: 'The monks now keep silence and so ought we.' And when the King's brothers did lade their barrow too heavily and sought to stop on the way to rest them, he would say: 'The monks take no rest, neither ought you.' And thus did the devout King incite his people to do good.'[18]

William of Saint-Pathus, from whom we have the preceding account, said of Blanche: 'She desired that each should do well in all things, and rejoiced when all was well, herself readily doing as well as lay within her power.' Clearly her own son more than once gave her the opportunity to rejoice.

In 1230 Louis held his Christmas court at Melun. During four years on the throne he had had his share of difficulties, and more than once his reign had seemed about to collapse. Nevertheless, most of the great lords of the realm were to be found gathered about the sixteen-year-old suzerain on that Christmas day. They included the loyal and the not-so-loyal. There were Philip Hurepel, now definitely rallied to his young nephew; the Count of La Marche, who four years earlier had not attended the coronation; Theobald of Champagne, who would have been only too glad to have attended. Amaury of Montfort was there, having ceded to the King all the lands he had acquired in Languedoc. There were the Duke of Burgundy; the Count of Vienne and Mâcon; John of Braisne (one of Mauclerc's brothers); Enguerrand of Coucy; and many more. All of them affixed their personal seals round the royal seal on the ordinance proclaimed on that occasion. That ordinance, which has been much discussed in our own time, forbade usury, that is, lending money at interest. It applied to everyone, but in particular to the Jews, who were accused at the time of being much inclined to such transactions. All such debts were to be repaid without interest. Each Jew was placed under the tutelage of the lord of his place of residence. They were allowed to continue living where they were on condition that they abstained from all usurious lending.

For Blanche the ordinance of Melun was important for other reasons besides the juridical ones. Seven hundred and forty-odd years later we can still see, on the simple rectangle of parchment, the eighteen almost intact seals of the lords who endorsed it. Surrounding the royal seal, showing the King on his throne, crowned and sceptre in hand, parade a dazzling cavalry of noblemen's seals of the equestrian type, each man shown on his charger, armed and caparisoned.[19] Blanche must have been delighted to watch the procedure. Each of the lords present had in turn produced the metal die of his personal seal, had gone up to the document on the table, and had pressed his die into the hot wax prepared for him. Among those eighteen, many had been among the 'blacks' on the chessboard not long before, enemies to be met only with sword drawn. Now most of them were with the 'whites', who previously had counted so few names; Amaury of Montfort, who had just become Constable of France; Robert of Courtenay; and – it goes without saying – Theobald of Champagne.

Which was not to say that all struggles were at an end. But Louis now had the advantage; it was the young King who would take the offensive, going into battle with all those warriors riding at his side, just as they have ridden with him down the centuries on the ordinance of Melun. So much so that the very next year he was able to obtain a cessation of hostilities by a mere show of force, without a blow being struck. Though not a final settlement, the agreement signed at Saint-Aubin-du-Cormier on July 4, 1231, was a three-year truce, which meant that until Midsummer's Day (June 24) of 1234 all hostilities pitting France against England and Brittany were to be suspended.

Nevertheless Blanche remained watchful, and she continued to gain so many new alliances for her son that Mauclerc began to feel like a rat in a trap. One by one the castles near the boundaries of Brittany paid homage to the King of France. Ralph, lord of Fougères, came into the fold. Henry of Avaugour, head of the house of Penthièvre, in exchange for becoming the King's liege man, received a castle whose name was to go down in history: Guesclin (then called Guarplic), near Cancale, east of Saint-Malo. When Amaury de Montfort became Constable of France (the commander-in-chief of the army, in the absence of the King) Blanche took care to have him forfeit all claim to the county of Leicester, to which he relinquished his rights in favour of his younger brother Simon, named after their famous father. Too many problems had arisen from the fact that the lords of Normandy, Brittany, and Poitou also possessed fiefs in England. The younger Simon de Montfort, who appeared to be as ambitious as his father had been, lost no time in crossing the Channel to make good his claims in Leicester. King Henry III received him with open arms, thinking to make him his ally against the Queen of France and little knowing what a viper he thus pressed to his own bosom.

Blanche began to face the future with confidence. Like it or not, the malcontents among the French barons were one by one accepting the situation. And that prince of poets, Theobald the Troubadour, continued to address his most fervent appeals to her:

> Sublimest goddess, Love, who deigned to stoop
> To find a humble lodging in my heart . . .

Blanche had become used to his passionate avowals, even his reproaches:

So fair thy name, yet bringest so much woe . . .

She did not mind being cast in the role of great Lady, playing opposite the lord of the court of Troyes (where another poet, Chrétien, had once sung), a new Queen Guinevere to his Launcelot. In fact, ten years earlier an unknown author had started to make a prose version of Chrétien of Troyes, linking the adventures of Launcelot with the quest of the Holy Grail, that mysterious chalice long sought after by the knights of King Arthur. The origin of this theme, which has never failed to stir men's imaginations, goes back to the mists of age-old Celtic legends. It now became the basis for three superb new works: *Launcelot*; *The Queen of the Holy Grail*; and *King Arthur*, whose rich structure has been compared to that of the many cathedrals being built in the same century. These stories undoubtedly delighted the courts of both France and Champagne. In them the traditional knightly hero is transformed into an almost sublime being. While Launcelot, because of his lapses, is denied access to the Holy Grail, Galahad, his blameless son, is granted that supreme vision of God's mystical gift to men. Galahad, the faultless knight, becomes the very embodiment of the ideals of chivalry.

Suddenly the court of France was rudely jolted back to reality from these lands of fiction by the news that Theobald, Count of Champagne, who had been widowed for the second time the year before, wished to marry again, and had chosen as his prospective bride Yolanda, the daughter of the archenemy Mauclerc himself.

This new misconduct on the part of her troubadour cut Blanche to the quick. Yolanda had formerly been betrothed to a brother of the King, at the time of that first treaty with the Count of Brittany, which he had so treacherously broken. To choose the daughter of a former enemy, who is still the chief adversary of your closest friend and ally, argues a lack of political common sense. Perhaps Theobald thought that the marriage would be the means of ending all the long-standing

disagreements at one stroke. Blanche, however, did not see it
that way. She knew better than anyone else how pliable
Theobald was. With him on good terms with the court of
Brittany, all her careful plans for isolating Mauclerc would go
up in smoke.

Mauclerc had just sent his daughter to a nunnery of the
order of Prémontré, near Château-Thierry, in a place appro-
priately called Valsecret ('secret valley'). Theobald, all engrossed
in his personal plans, had left Château-Thierry to go and see
the girl there. Suddenly he was accosted by a friend of King
Louis, Geoffrey of La Chapelle, who said: 'My lord of Champagne, the King even now learns that you have agreed with
the Count of Brittany to wed his daughter. The King bids
you renounce the plan lest you lose all you possess in the realm
of France. For you do know that the Count of Brittany has
worked more ill upon the King of France than any man alive.'

Theobald was flabbergasted. His private plans were known
and he had been intercepted in the very act of accomplishing
them. After a moment of hesitation and a brief parley with his
retinue, he turned back crest-fallen towards Château-Thierry.

Theobald, who no longer even dared face the Queen, asked
his friend Philip of Nanteuil to be his intercessor with her. He
was badly in need of one. He was able to judge later what a
pitfall he might have landed in, but for Blanche's opposition.
For he learned that Peter Mauclerc, indefatigably offering his
daughter's hand to whomever seemed the best bargain, had
been negotiating with King Henry III of England at the same
time as he was making arrangements with Theobald . . . The
stout troubadour comforted himself by accepting the hand of
Margaret, daughter of Archibald of Bourbon, who was one of
the most loyal vassals of the King of France.

Theobald was as big a blunderer as he was a fine poet, and
he seemed destined to spend his life alternately outraging
Blanche and receiving her pardon. Four years later (having
meanwhile been crowned King of Navarre, at Pamplona – a
heritage from his mother, and having also declared his inten-

tion of going oversea as a crusader) he was again deep in matrimonial projects, this time for his daughter. As usual his unerring bad judgement led him to the worst possible choice: the son of Peter Mauclerc! As a transaction it was excellent, for the lad, John Rufus, was heir to the duchy of Brittany. But as might be expected the match did not suit Blanche. King Louis took up arms and arrived with his brothers Robert and Alphonse to lay siege to Theobald's castle at Montereau, southeast of Melun. Theobald did not even dare give battle. His recourse was to beg the Pope to intervene, since as a sworn crusader his property was inviolable. The Pope took up the matter with Louis, and it was again Blanche who arranged a settlement. Peace was restored, but Theobald had to hand over Montereau and Bray-sur-Seine to the King, and also come to the palace and renew his oath of fealty in the presence of Louis and Blanche.

The incident ended on a farcical note. Theobald came to the palace, but just as he was about to enter the King's audience chamber he was doused from head to foot by a basinful of curdled milk, purposely flung on him from the stairs. It was done by the valet of the King's brother Robert, Count of Artois, 'who had loved him never'!

In the opinion of a chronicler of the time, Philip Mouskès, 'It never yet was said that King or Earl had been so dealt with,' which put it mildly. The sight of the fat man all decked out in his court clothes, and dripping with curdled milk, was a jest in rather poor taste. Blanche, 'most ill-pleased', ordered the culprits apprehended and even talked of locking them up in the Châtelet prison, whereupon Robert of Artois, none too conscience-stricken, came forward. He said he had felt that Count Theobald deserved a lesson. The lad, then fifteen years old, may also have been annoyed by the constant attentions pressed upon his mother by the noble troubadour. At any rate Theobald sang no more ardent songs to Blanche after his dousing. Here is how the *Great Chronicles of France* relate the Queen's pardon and the poet's love:

The Count did gaze upon the Queen, so wise and fair her beauty dazzled him. He answered her: 'By my troth, Lady, my heart and arm and all my land are yours to rule. There is naught I would not attempt if it but gladden you. Never, please God, shall I go 'gainst you or yours.' Then all pensive he went his ways, and often in memory he saw again the Queen's soft look and her fair countenance. And then would steal into his heart sweet images of love. But when he bethought him how great a Lady she was, of so good a life, and pure, that she could never be a party to his pleasure, then would his soft thoughts of love turn to great sadness. And forasmuch as such deep thoughts engender melancholy, it was counselled him by certain sage men that he study the art of the vielle's pleasant notes and of sweet singing. He and Gace Brulé did make the finest songs, the most delectable and tunable that ever were heard. And he caused them to be written down in his hall at Provins, and in that of Troyes, and they are called the songs of the King of Navarre.[20]

After all this Theobald actually did take the cross and go oversea, doing great deeds and winning glory in the Holy Land. But he was never able to forget Blanche.

> O Lady who dost weave such love in me,
> I send thee greeting o'er the salty sea;
> It is of thee I think at dawn, at eve,
> And have none other joy, do thou believe.

V

THE TWO QUEENS

Louis, who King of France was made,
In everything truly obeyed
His mother's wishes, Blanche the Queen;
'Twixt him and her came none between,
Him did she love as never mother
Loved a son, or loved a brother.
He ordered that his barons bring
A noble maid to wed their King,
If her the Queen but did commend.
And Blanche would have it that they send
The daughter of Provence's Count,
Who was of birth so paramount
That never nobler woman dressed
Between the seas to east and west
(Thus do her own familiars tell)
Nor ever gentler damozel.[1]

The marriage of the eldest son is an important business, for the humblest as for the mightiest lord. The eldest son embodies the family's hopes, for he will receive the principal estates and the main part of the inheritance. When this son happens also to be the King of France the affair is more momentous still.

Blanche knew better than anyone how closely the fortunes of the throne were linked to the selection of the woman who would one day be Queen. Louis would be twenty in 1234, which meant that he had reached a very marriageable age. Blanche had thought long and carefully about the best choice for him. In 1233 Raymond VII of Toulouse had asked the King of France to arbitrate between him and the Church. Though restored to the faith, Raymond was constantly bickering with the local clergy. Blanche had appealed to the Pope several times on his behalf, in particular to help him regain the marquisate of Provence, which the Holy See had been keeping in pawn since the signing of the treaty four years earlier. Raymond was clearly in no hurry to keep his part of the bargain: the ten thousand crowns he had undertaken to pay the clergy, and the crusader's oath which he was doing nothing to fulfil. Nevertheless a French knight, Giles of Flagy, had been appointed to be the King's representative in arbitrating and if possible ending the quarrels between Raymond and the bishop and other prelates of Toulouse. Just as Giles of Flagy was leaving Paris Blanche sent for him. As a result of their conference Giles changed his planned itinerary. He left for Toulouse by the route down the Rhône valley.

Raymond-Bérenger, the Count of Toulouse, and his wife, Beatrice of Savoy, were a happy couple. The Count had many ties with the local nobility through his mother, Gersende of Sabran; on his father's side he was related to all the principal ruling families in Europe, Castile and Aragon among them. Beatrice came from the powerful house of Savoy, which formed part, as did Provence itself, of the Holy Roman Empire. Raymond-Bérenger and Beatrice had only one cloud over their happiness: they had no son to carry on the line. They had, however, four daughters, all beautiful, and according to one story the Count's trusted adviser, Romeo of Villeneuve, who worked wonders in restoring order in the Count's periodically depleted finances, had promised his master to make each of them a queen.

Giles of Flagy spent some time with Raymond-Bérenger, probably at the Count's castle at Les Baux, south of Avignon, then at the height of its splendour. After this he followed the Regordane Way via Nîmes, Béziers and the Aude valley to Toulouse, where he performed his functions as arbiter, and finally returned to the court of France. Here he again was closeted at length with Blanche. Then, according to the *Great Chronicles of France*:

The King bade the Count of Provence send him his daughter Margaret, for he meant to take her for his wedded wife. These tidings the Count received most joyfully and did much feast and reward the messengers thereof. He gave into their hands his daughter, who had been well taught and tutored from her earliest years. The messengers took the maid in charge, bade the Count farewell, and did ride till they came to the King again and delivered to him the maid. The King received her with much joy and caused her to be crowned Queen of France by the hand of the Archbishop of Sens.[2]

Margaret of Provence, thirteen years old, preceded by six heralds sounding their trumpets, and by a minstrel from her father's court, made her entry into Sens, 60 miles south-east of Paris, on May 26, 1234. William, Bishop of Valence, the representative of her father, led the escort of the young princess.

Blanche had sent the Archbishop of Sens, Walter Cornut, one of those most loyal to the French dynasty, to meet them, as well as a Parisian knight, John of Nesle. The King was waiting for his fiancée at Sens. He had left Paris in the middle of May and ridden out by way of Fontainebleau, Pont-sur-Yonne, and the abbey of Saint-Colombe, near Sens. His young bride had ridden up the valleys of the Rhône and Saône, stopping at the abbey of Tournus, south of Chalon, on May 19.

The town of Sens, dominated by its fine cathedral only some seventy years old, had been the scene of much activity. All the roads and streams leading into the old town had been thronged with carriages, wagons, horsemen and boats, and the bustle at Sens had radiated to some extent throughout France. Royal messengers were riding on all the roads of the kingdom, in all directions. One squire was sent to inform the Count and Countess of La Marche, the Archbishop of Tours, and the chapter of Poitiers. Another, Simon of Poissy, went off towards Soissons. Another, William of Coqueville, towards Angers. A squire called Lobert was sent to invite the Duke and Duchess of Burgundy, also Count Archibald of Bourbon, while another, Robert of Chamilly, was sent to the Count and Countess of Nevers. Naturally Blanche's own family in Castile were not forgotten. A scholar, Garcias, was dispatched to Spain with 32 *livres* (entered in the ledgers) for the trip and for the present Blanche gave her family on this occasion.

Two emissaries, Bigot and Peter of Crespières, had been sent on ahead to Sens to prepare the lodgings of the King and the royal family. The account-books do not specify where they were, but it is quite possible that the Archbishop of Sens lent his palace for the occasion. Mention is made of the special wagon that was needed to bring the royal vestments, jewels, and other coronation paraphernalia, to Sens. Special carts were provided to transport the money, which was usually carried in casks or sacks, naturally with a sufficient escort. The chief barons of France were also attending to their lodgings for the occasion. The royal accounts show that Blanche undertook to lodge the Countess of Flanders at Sens at her own expense. She also had temporary accommodations set up, many of them simply pavilions and tents designed to shelter either the horses or the men-at-arms, valets and grooms.

Between all such preparations, however, and the ordinary existence of the royal court, there was only a difference of scale, for life was a perpetual removal. The King spent all his time travelling over his domains. The chief barons, taking their cue from him, did the same on their own lands. In Blanche's day the King of France literally had no fixed abode. True, King Philip had shown great partiality for Paris, and his predecessors had enjoyed Orléans. But even the Parisian palace that Louis IX partly rebuilt and enlarged was only one among many residences. It was an everyday affair for the entire royal household to pack up their furniture; beds, coffers, benches, trestles and all the hangings and appurtenances that were once lumped together as the 'chamber', and carry them off a few leagues, to Saint-Germain-en-Laye, which had been Louis VIII's and Blanche's favourite residence; or to Senlis, north-east of Paris;

to Compiègne, further in the same direction; Pontoise to the north-west; Étampes on the road to Orléans, or others. All these castles were simply empty shells until the harbingers arrived and hastily unloaded their gear from the pack-horses, mules and wagons, hung up the tapestries, set up the beds, unrolled the mattresses and blankets, and, when the dinner hour was at hand, 'laid' the table upon its trestles.

Little Princess Isabella had an adventure on one of these occasions that was told long afterwards in the royal family. She used to say her morning prayers in bed, snuggled into her blankets. Once at dawn a valet, only half awake, came to take away her bedding and, not noticing the slim little body deep in the blankets, rolled up the whole thing, princess and all. He was dumbfounded when his bundle started to wriggle and cry out, and his blunder caused much amusement.

The ledgers that we still have for that year, however, indicate an unusual amount of moving about. Two extra draught horses had to be purchased, one for the kitchen gear, the other for the furniture and hangings. A 'sumpter' (the strongest kind of work-horse, worth fourteen to sixteen *livres* – more than a palfrey, which was a show-horse) brought the Queen's 'chamber' and another carried the fruit to be laid out on the banquet tables. The officers in charge of the pantry and the kitchen-garden supplies each had a pack-horse and a palfrey at his disposal. The Queen's cook, one William, supervised the efforts of two pack-horses, one carrying pots and pans, the other loaded with the money that would be necessary. Still other sumpters carried the young Queen's 'chamber' and the royal bed.

Blanche had had a new mattress made and covered with a quilt of embroidered silk for Queen Margaret; also other quilts. There were scarlet-draped coffers containing linen sheets, furs for the beds, and a whole assortment of nightshirts and body linen. She had also had the coronation jewels made ready, some of them bought from the Count of Flanders's goldsmith, and had had the Queen's crown made over new, since the coronation of Margaret, who like the King must be crowned, was to take place at the same time as the wedding.

The necessary table linen was also taken along: all that would be needed to spread white cloths on the banquet tables, both those of the court guests and those prepared for the commoners who would also have their share in the feast. There were 86 tablecloths, 240 pieces of unfinished bolt linen, and 100 napkins. There was a laundress called Rosette attached to the royal household; she was seconded by a girl called Laurence. Rosette probably hired locally the little platoon of washerwomen, armed with their battledores, needed to keep the Queen's linen immaculate.

Before leaving for Sens, Blanche had herself bled by her physician, Geoffrey Miniaz, probably a Spaniard. This may have been a routine precaution prior to the fatigue of the long ride, or it may have been intended to ward off the ill effects of the 'rising blood' which women felt threatened their complexion in the spring-time. She did not take her entire retinue with her. One of her ladies-in-waiting, Eudeline, was to come to Sens later by boat. Two others probably accompanied her: the one referred to as the Lady of Amboise, and Mincia the Spaniard, who is so often mentioned in the ledgers. Immediately after the royal wedding Mincia was to leave for Spain, and was given two pack-horses for her journey, along with money and some carriages that escorted her as far as La Rochelle. Several of the high officers of the court of France rode with her, among them the steward Bartholomew de Roye, called the 'fat knight'; the chamberlain John of Beaumont; Ferry Pâté, who later became Marshal of France; Countess Johanna of Flanders; and Count Raymond of Toulouse, who had prolonged his stay at court in order to be present at the wedding. The escort numbered 24 crossbowmen and 20 men-at-arms, who received their wages every fortnight and had their horses' maintenance paid for by the King. A blacksmith and his mobile forge travelled with the crossbowmen, in order to repair their lances and bolts, as well as the horseshoes.

The soldiers were rotated from time to time, a detachment of crossbowmen being sent off to accompany a particular baron who was to be specially honoured. Five of them accompanied Andrew of Vitré, for example, when he rode home after the coronation ceremonies.

The accounts of that eventful year, 1234, have been preserved. It is almost a blessing that they have reached us in a state of considerable disorder, for we look in on the details of the outfitting and moving about in catch-as-catch-can fashion, as they happened. Robin of Poissy bought three 'amitures' – probably in this case horse-cloths. Blacksmiths' vices and hearths were set up at a bivouac in the forest. Wolves had to be chased away at Pont-sur-Yonne and in the forest of Othe. There were the wages of the King's personal servants: six valets, nine squires on duty and seven in reserve. There were all the petty artisans and specialists whose services were constantly required: Simon du Louvre and a man called Stephen who made the spare parts for the crossbows; the two lackeys who tended the King's dogs; Simon of Moret, who looked after his falcons; all the huntsmen and their lads. Alms were distributed to religious orders along the way, such as those of the enclosed nuns of Pré and of Cour-Notre-Dame. In addition the King's almoner gave out small sums throughout the journey, as for instance the sixty *sous* he distributed between Paris and Fontainebleau. At the halts this almsgiving became more important. At Fontainebleau itself one hundred poor persons each received a *sou* on May 24. At Sens a man whose horse had been killed was compensated. There were similar instances every time the court travelled, some of them quite touching. A young girl about to be married had stationed herself on the Grand-Pont in Paris, in order to appeal to the King's generosity as he rode by. She was given forty *livres* via a squire called Hugh. Blanche often dowered girls whom she met on her journeys, such as the daughter of a poor lady of Anet, near Dreux, who received a hundred Parisian *sous*; a girl of the castellany of Nogent, to whom she gave fifteen *livres*.

There were also the lepers. Louis had given them twenty
livres and thirteen *sous* at the time of the ceremonies at Sens.
His largesse became increasingly generous. During Lent of
1234 he had 45,000 herrings distributed to the poor. There was
also, of course, the daily bread-line in the palace courtyard. It
cost a Parisian *livre* per day, which must have provided a good
many loaves.

Great care had been taken with the preparations at Sens, in
order to welcome the young Queen with all due honour. The
approaches to the cathedral had been put in trim. It had even
been necessary to knock down a wall, perhaps to build scaffold-
ings and platforms, or to make room for the banquet tables.
The cathedral of St Stephen had been all decked out inside
with tapestries and hangings as was customary on solemn
occasions, and outside an arbour enclosing silk-covered seats
had been built, to shade the King and Queen with leafy branches
during the jousting and tumblers' performances.

The town thronged with the invited guests, each accompanied by his own retinue and horses. On such occasions the
degree of pomp displayed could be accurately gauged by the
presents the King gave to the members of his entourage. Nineteen saddles were presented to the young men who had just
been knighted, plus those that the King had had made for his
brothers and for the son of Blanche's sister Urraca, called
'Alphonse the Nephew'. He had been brought up at the court
of France, where the two Alphonses were distinguished by
referring to them as 'the Son' and 'the Nephew'. Louis himself
had been presented with a sumptuous knight's outfit by his
mother: five saddles; six haquetons (stuffed jerkins worn under
the mail) for himself and his brother Robert; spurs; caparisons;
blankets of sendal; bridles with matching gold fittings on
reins, bits, stirrups, and spurs. For the King's young bride
there were two saddles, tunics, bridles, blankets, and ornaments.

Above all, 'robes' were given. Gifts of clothes were the most
usual, kings and lords giving them to their followers at
Christmas, Easter, and on their birthdays. The King's wedding

and the coronation of the Queen was also the occasion for such gifts.

Although the ledgers of the time were very terse by modern standards, they provide us with a glimpse of that same profusion of colours that one sees in the exquisite miniatures of the period. Members of the court, such as Ferry Pâté, John of Beaumont, and Henry the Falconer, received purple robes, as did the two Alphonses. The Queen's ladies of honour wore gowns of perse (a sea-green or bluish-grey) and scarlet, lined with vermilion. The Count of Toulouse was nobly arrayed in violet burnet (a kind of dyed wool cloth), on top of which were two more robes, green ones, all tokens of the King's munificence. Raymond was the object of special marks of esteem during his sojourn with the court and was given a palfrey and a pack-horse. His falconer's wages were assumed by the royal exchequer as were the various small gifts to his servants.

The King's brother Robert, later known as Robert of Artois, appeared in burnet robes of black, green, violet, and a red scarlet mantle ('scarlet' at that time still referred to a kind of rich cloth, not a colour), lined with ermine and with sleek and bushy vair. The youngest of the royal children, Isabelle, aged nine, and Charles, seven, had remained in Paris, where Blanche had explicitly given them into the burghers' care. To make it up to them for missing the wedding-day they were given handsome new clothes of rose and black burnet, to wear when they greeted their big brother and their new sister-in-law on their return. Blanche had had two recent bereavements, one after the other. Her sons John and Philip Dagobert had both died in 1232, but there is no record of the cause of their death.

The ledgers tell us that the King's robe on the coronation day was composed of perse-coloured cloth, of black burnet, red scarlet and violet scarlet. The Queen wore a mantle and a camail (short cloak) lined with sleek and bushy vair, with ermine and with sable.

A huge multi-coloured crowd swarmed through the streets

of Sens, in and out of the cathedral, and on to the fairgrounds. Blanche's haberdashers, Ivo the glover and John Godriche the hatter, had had their work cut out. All the young noblemen were wearing felt hats trimmed with peacock feathers, gold fastenings and silken ornaments. The jewellers had also received large orders: two gold bands for the King; gold belts and gold clasps for Robert and Alphonse the Son, and for Alphonse in addition a basin-case. Above all, however, they had worked on the jewels to be given to the young Queen. Blanche had spared no expense to see that she should be sumptuously welcomed. The gold crown that the King was to give her must have been magnificent, for it cost no less than 58 *livres*. He also gave her a gold diadem, two gold spoons, and rich ermines and sables. A gold cup was also made for the King and Queen, from which they would both drink during the banquet. According to custom, it was later given as a present to the King's chief butler. Cups, like clothes, were traditional gifts. That same year of 1234 Blanche gave her son a hanap (tankard) of heart-of-oak mounted on a silver base. A similar one, given by Blanche to the abbey of Maubuisson, can be seen in the Musée Lambinet in Versailles.

We can still get an excellent idea of what the dress of the time was like, for some remarkable specimens of it have survived. They can be seen in a museum unlike any other, that of the monastery of Las Huelgas at Burgos in Spain, which was to the Spanish royal family what Saint-Denis was to the French royal family. In it are the tombs of Blanche's parents and their successors on the throne, stone vaults which, thanks to the exceptionally clear, dry air, kept the fabrics almost intact. The burial clothes of certain princes were found in them, such as those of Don Ferdinand de la Cerda.

We can still marvel today at the magnificent robes in which he was buried, which were undoubtedly his ceremonial costume: a damasked cloth with a green pattern on a light background, lined with silk of amaranth purple; an embroidered baldric (cross-belt) with gold buckles; gold spurs; and for his head a kind of skull-cap embroidered with pearls among which are medallions showing alternately the lion and the castle, the heraldic symbols of Castile and León. Along with these still intact items are more fragments of cloth, some of embroidered silk, others of fine wool knitted with incredible skill, which constitute impressive evidence of the richness and variety of medieval textiles. The silken cloths must have been of eastern manufacture, as silk was not yet being woven in Europe. Some of the brocades show old Cufic Arabic characters, used ornamentally. But they display no greater skill than the knitted woollens which are undoubtedly of European manufacture. These must have required many needles and different colours of yarn. They show a multitude of designs, sometimes very subtle ones, blending greens, reds, and cream colours, and picturing here a swan, there a gryphon, or else flowerets, stylized foliage and the like, all on a lozengy background of alternating lights and darks.

Ordinarily only tiny fragments of cloth have survived from the burial vaults of the 13th century, but the Burgos museum, which has no peer in Europe, lets us really see what those sendal and scarlet cloths, those blankets and quilts listed in the account-books, must have been like. We can picture young King Louis in a long, iridescent robe like that of Ferdinand de la Cerda. We can picture the seat draped in brilliant silken damask where he sat with his bride watching the shows during those three days of rejoicing.

Louis's younger brother Robert, eighteen at the time, was closest to the King, though they were quite different in temperament. Robert had arranged the entertainment with the minstrels. Since he was inclined to do things lavishly he paid out 112 *livres* and 32 *deniers* (a *denier* being roughly equivalent to an English penny), as well as a gift of ten *livres* to a minstrel sent up from Provence by the bride's father. Unfortunately we have no details of the entertainments watched by the young couple from under their leafy arbour. No chronicler gives a description of them. There are, in general, only a few brief references to the minstrels and their 'Vanity Fairs'. Aubrey of Trois-Fontaines, writing of a similar occasion, describes a man, 'astride a rope, who did ride in the air, and those others, riding scarlet-draped beeves, who did sound their trumpets at each new dish served up at table.'[3]

Minstrelsy included everything pertaining to music, ballads and merriment. Part of the entertainment consisted of poetry, which was then always sung; part of it was tumbling and juggling, of the kind seen at a circus or an old country fair. By the same token, whenever there was a feast there was dancing, and there is no reason to suppose that Louis and his young bride did not take part as gaily as everyone else. The first biographies of Louis were written by persons eager to stress his saintly qualities. They make much of the three nights he spent in prayer before his marriage, and of the fact that he induced Margaret to join him in those prayers. Yet the ledgers are there to show that this saintliness and the reputation of his court for thrift did not prevent him from making merry when the occasion warranted.

The accounts show 118 *livres* spent for bread during those three days of merrymaking; 307 for wine; 667 for the main dishes and other kitchen expenses; 50 for lamps and torches. When one adds up everything, including the clothes worn by the royal family for the occasion, and given by them; the wages of the servants and grooms; the horses' oats; the costs of lodging retainers, and miscellaneous expenses, it comes to 2526 *livres*, 15 *sous* and 7 *deniers*. It is tempting to try to convert this figure into modern currency, but such attempts are invariably disappointing. However, in the 19th century the Parisian *livre* was evaluated at 22.474 francs, which means that the total expenses for Louis's wedding amounted to 5700 *francs or* (francs of 1928, convertible to gold).*[4]

* According to the conjecture mentioned in the Note on p. 33 which estimates the value of the *livre* in 1200 at about one gram of pure gold at modern rates, the approximately 2.526 kg of pure gold in question would have been worth about £3630 sterling in 1974.

From the moment they first met Louis and Margaret were deeply in love, and that love never once faltered. Margaret was only thirteen. All those who were present agree that she was very lovely and also 'well-wrought', which indicated that she had been perfectly prepared for her role of queen and was also well versed in letters, no detail of her education having been neglected. We still have some personal letters written by her in elegant Latin and French. It is even possible that Margaret, whose name means 'daisy', was the inspiration of that famous poem about a more exalted flower, the *Roman de la Rose*. It was written in the years immediately following Margaret's arrival at the court of France, by a scholar named William who hailed from that very town of Lorris, east of Orléans, where the young royal couple so often stayed.[5]

It is intriguing to wonder in what language the lovers first talked to each other. Margaret's native tongue was of course Provençal, but it is doubtful if Louis spoke it. It is more likely that Margaret had learned to speak the dialect of the Ile-de-France, for during that first half of the 13th century it was just beginning to form part of the required social equipment of a well-bred person. A didactic poem of the time, a sort of compendium of the current *savoir-vivre*, advises:

> Be debonair and strive to please,
> And learn to speak in French with ease;
> For 'tis a tongue well-loved these days,
> And gentlemen give it much praise.[6]

In the poem, of course, such advice was meant for the well-born, but the time was not far off when the study of French would form part of the standard education even of non-literary persons (those who had no Latin). Brunetto Latini, who was Italian by birth (we meet him in the 15th canto of Dante's *Inferno*), wrote his *Treasure* in French, which he called 'the most delectable tongue' and also the most widespread among the populace at large.

The functions of spoken language at that time were less

restricted than they are today; in a predominantly oral civilization the rich resources of speech were used by people who were still far removed from our essentially paper-and-ink civilization. As one leafs through contemporary documents, one gets a strong impression that everyone in the 13th, as in the 12th century, was bilingual if not trilingual. Even the rudest peasant was able to mumble a few words of Latin. Groups of people of vastly different origins, speaking innumerable dialects, were able to communicate with extraordinary ease. James of Vitry, for example, a priest from Champagne, landed in Italy and preached with such fire to the crowds in the churches that even women declared themselves crusaders. But in what language did he pour out this eloquence – French or Italian? Just as striking are the many poems of the period which alternate between French and Provençal, with no indication that the hearers were in the least disturbed.

Whatever the language they first spoke in, there is no doubt that Louis and Margaret remained very close all their lives. Their marriage, though not without incident, was never in real difficulties – between themselves, that is to say, for it cannot be denied that Margaret's advent created difficulties for Blanche.

She had wanted this marriage. She had worked for it and had rejoiced when it became a reality, even though she had not been able to gauge, as we can from our vantage point, the great importance for the French royal dynasty of this union with Provence. In the south of France the Rhône marked the dividing-line between the Holy Roman Empire and the area of Capetian suzerainty. France had just acquired the two seneschalsies of Beaucaire and Carcassonne, on the right bank of the river. Now Margaret further enriched the kingdom with lands on the 'Empire' side, which came under the direct control of her husband. Although a mere girl of thirteen, there was no doubt of her importance at the court of France. She was the 'Young Queen', and this plain fact, which had come about so quickly, was like a secret wound in the Queen's heart.

Blanche was then forty-six. Like every woman nearing fifty she was plagued by the worries, the half-conscious regrets and doubts that go with a difficult time of life. To these secret anxieties was added in her case an increased awareness of all that the holding of power entails. She had not asked to be given the reins of government, which had come as an added burden at the time of her widowhood, but she had become accustomed to responsibility; she may even have grown to enjoy it. At any rate she fully accepted her own responsibilities, and she intended that everyone else at court should accept his. No half-heartedness, procrastination, personal pleasures, or excuses, were to be tolerated in fulfilling this first duty.

The castle of Pontoise no longer exists. If it did, it might by now have become a place of pilgrimage for all the lovers in the world. For it contained a spiral staircase, with Louis's bedchamber above and Margaret's below, and these two 'had so ordered their affair that they were wont to hold their converse on a winding stair that did go down from the one chamber to the other; and their affair was so well ordered that when the ushers did spy the Queen Blanche coming towards her son's chamber they would knock at the door thereof with their staffs, and the King, hearing it from the stair, would run up hastily into his chamber so that his mother might find him there; and in like manner did the ushers before Queen Margaret's door when the Queen Blanche did betake herself thither, so that she might find the Queen Margaret within.'

Pontoise became the young couple's favourite residence.

Although Blanche was a peerless wife and mother, she appears to have been a trying mother-in-law. In our time, with psychoanalysis promptly offering an explanation of every human motive, it is tempting to say that Blanche was jealous. But such reasoning is completely brushed aside by a single remark of Joinville, who had a genius for putting simple truths in simple terms: 'The Queen Blanche would not suffer more than she could help that her son bear his wife company, except

it be at night when he did go to bed with her.' Blanche bore
Margaret no grudge for being Louis's wife. She begrudged her
the time that Louis filched from his King's duties to spend with
a mere child of thirteen, who had no role in government. But
for us it is reassuring to see this King, now called 'Saint', be-
having like any other lover, using stratagems such as lovers
have always used to show his affections.

Joinville tells another anecdote, which is more severe on
Blanche. 'Once was the King by his wife's side, she being
wounded from a child she had borne, and in great peril. The
Queen Blanche came thither and took her son by the hand
saying to him at the same time: "Come away. You have naught
to do here." And when the Queen Margaret did see that his
mother meant to lead the King away, she cried, "Alack, you
will not suffer me living or dead to see my lord." And thereupon she swooned and was thought to be dead. And the King
believing her to be dying, did return and they were at great
pains to revive her.' Yet even here, harsh as Blanche's attitude
may appear, her intention was only that the King should place
the duties of state before his personal feelings.

Even if Blanche were determined to see to it that her son
fulfil his 'austere duties', there was nothing austere about the
life of the court itself. It was an atmosphere in which a young
girl could blossom untrammelled into full, happy womanhood.
The time of mourning was past; the season of gaiety was at
hand. There were frequent banquets, and in the ledgers mention is often made of the minstrels. Some of them have amusing
nicknames: 'Mismatched', 'Peelings', and the one they called
'Four Eggs', who was the Sire of Courtenay's minstrel.

Three years after his own wedding, Louis celebrated his
brother Robert's knighthood with almost identical splendour.
The festivities took place at Compiègne at Whitsuntide, June
1237. One hundred and forty young lords received their
knights' spurs at the same time as Robert. All were given silken
robes for the occasion, and many other presents were given
to the principal guests. The ladies, such as the Duchess of

Châtillon and the wife of Enguerrand of Coucy, received emeralds. There were silver tankards for some of the men. There was a gold belt for the king and another for Robert. The young knight must have been magnificent in his robe of silk and of violet scarlet and his mantle of vermilion scarlet lined with fine vair and ermine, held at his shoulder by a gold clasp, all topped with golden headgear. The King wore a mantle of vermilion samite (a rich silk cloth) over his violet scarlet robe. The Queen was dressed in estanfort lined with ermine and sable, with a pelisse of fine vair. Possibly the King that day was mounted on his new dapple-grey palfrey. He had bought it only a short time earlier, paying all of 21 *livres*, the price of a charger. We have no details concerning Robert's mount. It was undoubtedly a splendid one, for he was known as an expert in horse-flesh. (At the festivities for Louis's marriage, Bishop Walter of Chartres had been able to think of no finer present for Robert than a horse.) Blanche's two younger children, at twelve and not quite eleven years, Isabelle and Charles, were now being treated more as young adults than as children. Isabelle and her future sister-in-law Joan, daughter of the Count of Toulouse, wore red *estanfort* robes. 'Master Charles' was dressed in a fine robe of striped scarlet, similar to that given on this occasion to Count Raymond VII of Toulouse, who had been invited to the ceremony.

Louis little dreamed that in knighting his brother he was dubbing the first member of the royal family who really embodied the failings of knighthood. The institution was then in its finest flower, but the signs of its deterioration could be seen in Robert of Artois. He had a kind of madcap bravery and recklessness that were to bring him to a premature death, and the King's army to catastrophe. He was also wildly prodigal. At the Compiègne festivities he distributed 220 *livres* to the minstrels, plus 100 *sous* to the trumpet-players and a like sum to the performer on the 'stive', a kind of bagpipe which Robert evidently fancied. But he had the warmest feelings for his own people, in particular Louis and their mother Blanche.

His letters to his mother, when he was off crusading, are full of affectionate touches.

Not only Robert's knighthood was fêted at Compiègne, but also his marriage, for he then wedded Maud, daughter of the Duke of Brabant. The time had come for the King of France to hand over to his younger brother the inheritance bequeathed him by their father. At the same time that Robert entered into possession of his personal domains a whole redistribution of fiefs took place, according to a family agreement that Blanche had presided over. She herself, thirty-seven years before, had received as wedding-dowry from her husband the castellanies of Hesdin, Bapaume, and Lens. Later she had acquired another property, Vilaines, in the same region. At the time of their marriage that group of fiefs had had the advantage of being close to her husband's personal domains. But this was no longer a factor. Robert had taken possession of Artois and Blanche herself preferred to live in the Ile-de-France, closer to the King and the crown lands. It was now agreed that a series of gradual exchanges were to be made, by which Blanche would receive various castellanies to compensate for the transfer of her wedding-gift lands to Robert. Over the next few years she thus acquired Meulan, Pontoise, Étampes, Dourdan, Corbeil, and Melun. The King added to these the domains of Crépy-en-Valois, La Ferté-Milon, and Pierrefonds, and Blanche gave up the dowry that had come to her from her uncle John Lackland: Issoudun and Graçay.

Blanche had always taken an active part in the administration of her personal lands. She had ordered the building of the covered market at Issoudun, and indemnified the owners of houses which had had to be knocked down in the process; she had journeyed from place to place to receive the homage of her local vassals. Her new possessions were closer to the theatre of her major concerns, and this would let her manage them more easily. A queen's dowry in those days was an important source of private revenues, which she would have been ill-advised to neglect. Even little Margaret received, at her marriage, a dowry consisting of the town of Le Mans with its dependencies, as well as the towns of Mortagne and Mauves-sur-Huisnes.

During the years following Louis's marriage Blanche pursued with imperturbable energy her strategy of encouraging some alliances and hindering others. Those that seemed to her to bring about reconciliations and stable consolidations of fiefs, she favoured; those that seemed dangerous to the royal dynasty, she opposed. Her son Robert had first been betrothed to Mary, daughter and heiress of Johanna of Flanders, but the girl had died. The heritage that would have brought about a union of Flanders and Artois had gone to her younger sister Margaret, whom the Flemings were later to call the 'Black Lady'. In marrying Maud (or Matilda), elder daughter of the Duke of Brabant, Robert was at least assured, failing the Flemish inheritance, of having a vital interest in the areas adjoining his own possessions.

Three other matrimonial projects were to cause concern during those years 1237-40: that of Johanna of Flanders herself, Ferdinand's widow, and those of the two Alphonses, the Son and the Nephew.

Flanders had given so much trouble in the past that Blanche had no choice but to keep a vigilant watch in that direction. As widow of Ferdinand of Flanders, who was also a son of the King of Portugal, Johanna was the object of a number of scarcely disinterested overtures. Among them, Blanche learned to her exasperation, were those of Simon de Montfort, of whom there was good reason to be wary. Amaury de Montfort's younger brother had inherited both his father's name and his ambition. He had been warmly welcomed in England by Henry III, who had confirmed his hereditary claims to the earldom of Leicester. Now he was back on the continent, obviously looking for a handsome alliance and not troubled by the fact that Johanna was considerably his senior. Blanche moved quickly. She journeyed to Péronne, east of Amiens, where she required Johanna to sign an undertaking whereby she relinquished any and all plans of marrying the Earl of Leicester. Such a threat would have been intolerable for the kingdom of France. It would have set up in Flanders a close vassal of the King of England, who seemed perpetually one jump away from waging war, and who would have acquired through this marriage the ideal base for his perennial invasion plans.

To make assurance doubly sure, Blanche followed this up with a matrimonial suggestion of her own: Johanna should marry Count Thomas of Savoy, the uncle of young Margaret of Provence, now Queen of France. Johanna, yielding to what her suzerain so firmly wished, accepted. The House of Savoy was just beginning to enter the pages of history, and doing so rather stormily, especially on the Italian side of the Alps in confrontations with the Holy See. For the time being, what mattered to Blanche was to create an alliance that would consolidate the French presence to the east of the Rhône. Once he was Count of Flanders, Thomas issued a pressing invitation to his sister Beatrice of Provence to visit the court of France, and great festivities ensued.

Beatrice went on from there to England, where her second daughter, Eleanor, had just become the bride of Henry III; her third, Sanchia, was about to become the wife of Henry's brother, Richard of Cornwall. All this added to the complicated network of alliances already in existence. But just such a network was the warp and woof of feudal life.

Simon de Montfort was vexed but not disheartened. He now set his sights on another lady of mature years, likewise an heiress with a considerable dowry: Maud of Boulogne, the widow of Philip Hurepel. Again Blanche snapped into action in order to forestall the matrimony-minded Earl of Leicester. Maud was promptly betrothed to Alphonse the Nephew, son of the King of Portugal and boyhood companion of Louis's younger brother, Alphonse of Poitiers. The disparity in ages was considerable, but Alphonse had the tact not to object. He had spent virtually his entire childhood at the court of France, and was only destined to leave it when an unexpected sequence of events caused him to become King Alfonso III of Portugal. When that occurred, in 1245, Maud's holdings were no longer of any great interest to him, nor was she herself, and he repudiated her.

Meanwhile the furious Simon de Montfort had gone back across the Channel. Perhaps to console him for two such disappointments one after the other, King Henry offered him the hand of his own sister Eleanor, then sixteen and the widow of William Marshal the younger, second Earl of Pembroke, whom she had wed at the age of nine.

Another wedding was now in order, that of Alphonse the Son and Joan of Toulouse. Theirs was destined to be another model marriage, like that of Louis and Margaret. Alphonse, Blanche's third surviving son, had a more fragile constitution than his brothers. He was the exact opposite of Robert. Where the older knight thought of nothing but deeds of derring-do and sumptuous festivities, Alphonse was a precise, conscientious, even finical administrator. His ledgers are models of perfection. Forward-looking as well as thrifty, he was the first nobleman to use paper instead of parchment for his ledgers. The less expensive writing material must have seemed in those days rather as plastic does today; it was used only for day-to-day notes and accounts. The novelty is seen in the fact that whereas John Sarrasin, at the court of France, noted his daily expenses on wax tablets, Alphonse, in Poitiers, was using paper for the same purpose.

Alphonse the Son was married in 1238; Alphonse the Nephew in 1239. During those years the court of France must have resounded with almost continuous merry-making. It was full of carefree youngsters. The young King and princes, their wives, the barons and their ladies, the minstrels and jongleurs – all helped to make it a lively, colourful court, perhaps the most brilliant in Europe.

Besides the civil festivities there were the religious observances, equally colourful. One of these was a red-letter day in

Louis's reign: the arrival in France in 1239 of the holy Crown of Thorns. Blanche made a point of going with her son to be present at the solemn reception, near Villeneuve-l'Archevêque, of this most precious Christian relic. Two Dominicans, Brothers James and Andrew, had brought the chest there with great precautions. When the King ordered it to be opened, it was found to contain a silver box, to which were affixed the seals of the Doge of Venice and of the principal barons of the Byzantine Empire. These were compared to the ones attached to the letters patent previously sent to attest to the genuineness of the relic that had been given into the custody of the two friars. When the seals were broken the silver box was found to contain a gold box. In this rested the Crown of Thorns, or, more exactly, a flimsy diadem of straw, to which were clinging a few fragments of what had from time immemorial been venerated at Constantinople as the Crown of Thorns worn by Christ at his Passion.

The moment, fraught with emotion, in which this relic was unpacked in France, had been preceded by a whole series of negotiations between Louis and young Baldwin II, who was presiding over the increasingly problematic destinies of the Latin Empire in the East, set up by the crusaders at the beginning of the 13th century. At his wits' end for lack of funds, Baldwin had been obliged to pawn the relic to a Venetian merchant, one Nicolò Quirino. A year later, while travelling through France on a trip he made to Europe in order to beg for help, he had admitted this to Louis. Louis had at once paid the pledge and advanced the most urgent of the funds that Baldwin needed. The relic was then brought from Venice to France, where it arrived on August 11, 1239.

When the procession reached the small town of Villeneuve-l'Archevêque the reliquary was placed on a litter carried by two men in their shirts and barefoot, like penitents. At the rear came Robert, Count of Artois; in front walked the King of France. From there all the way to Paris the precious burden was escorted by crowds on foot lining the roads. On Thursday,

August 18, three days after Assumption, it reached Paris. A platform had been set up outside the walls, at a place called La Guette, near the abbey of Saint-Antoine. There, in their turn, the people of Paris came to see and venerate the Crown of Thorns. It was said that the biggest crowds ever seen flocked out of Paris for the occasion. Then the reliquary was put back on its litter and, with the King and Robert at their places, it was escorted into the city amid singing of hymns. Going on ahead were a multitude of clerks, monks, prelates, and knights, who led the way to the cathedral of Notre Dame. There Mass was sung, after which the procession formed up once more to go over to the palace of the Cité, where the holy relic was placed in the chapel of St Nicholas.

Similar ceremonies and processions followed, for Louis eagerly added to his collection of relics whenever he could. The following year, 1240, he acquired a piece of the True Cross from the Knights Templar. It had been pawned to them, again by Baldwin, who was clearly determined to raise money by fair means or foul.

Paris turned out to watch these new solemn processions, which were headed by three queens: Blanche, young Margaret, and Ingeborg, the Danish 'Queen of Orleans'. A poet of the time, clearly a better chronicler than rhymester, gives us a glimpse of them. First comes 'Madame the Queen' – Margaret – who is 'dainty and true'. Then Blanche, 'prudent and frank'. Finally, 'she of Dannemark', who was 'courteous and wise'. We seem to see three legendary queens leading a pageant from some saga of chivalry, or from the *Quest of the Holy Grail*.

We get an insight into Blanche's own feelings about relics from an incident that had occurred a few years before. It shows that she could be reserved, if not suspicious. The abbey of Saint-Denis had been thrown into turmoil by the shattering news of the loss of the Holy Nail, a much-venerated relic of the Cross. It had occurred during one of those occasions when the abbey, like many other churches and places of pilgrimage, was overrun by swarms of the faithful. The sanctuaries were never big enough to hold the crowds that came to them, just as the roads were never broad enough to enable the pilgrims to travel in comfort. This was an unvarying aspect of the life of the time. When Abbot Suger began the building of the new abbey in 1137, he penned some striking descriptions of the mobs that used to push inside. Sometimes the crush was so great that the monks holding up the relics for veneration were overrun and thrown to the ground. People were trampled underfoot, writes the Abbot, shrieking like women in labour, and sometimes the only way to empty the place was to hand the precious relics out through the windows.

It was on such an occasion that the Holy Nail was lost underfoot in the mob. The news galvanized public attention. The chancellor of the Paris chapter, Philip of Grève, wrote a detailed account of the incident, as did the monks of Saint-Denis, all agreeing that everyone in Paris was in tears over the affair, the King and his mother not excepted. According to the accounts, Louis, then nineteen, said that he would have preferred to see the finest town in his kingdom swallowed up by the elements. He immediately promised a reward of a hundred *livres* to whomever should find it. Shortly thereafter it was found. The overjoyed abbot sent Blanche the good news, but she wrote him back advising caution. Was he quite sure that the nail that had been 'found' was the Nail that had been lost? And when the monks of Saint-Denis organized a ceremony to celebrate the finding of the Nail, Blanche politely excused herself and her son for not attending. A few days later Louis went alone without fanfare to the abbey to venerate the relic.

Blanche, however, did not show the same suspicion regarding the relics of the Passion that came from Constantinople. Louis had taken all possible precautions to ensure that he should not be defrauded. The circlet of thorns and the piece of wood deposited in the chapel of the palace were unquestionably the same that had had places of honour in the palace of the emperors of Byzantium. Though it is true that their authenticity prior to that was not investigated, no one had the slightest doubt about it. The relics' physical authenticity was vouched for by an unbroken tradition that went back to the beginning of the 4th century, when the Church was set free, back to the days of the Emperor Constantine and of his mother, St Helena, who had, according to writers of the same period, travelled to the Holy Land when she was over seventy years of age, founded basilicas on the Mount of Olives and at Bethlehem, and discovered the Cross on which Jesus had been crucified three hundred years earlier.

There is no doubt that in her personal attitude towards the relics, Blanche shared the prevalent devotion of her time. Doubts about that devotion did not start to crop up until much later. To us the veneration of relics can seem to divert true religious feeling towards idolatry, or even magic. But we cannot simply dismiss a trait so strongly rooted in basic human feelings, especially in an age ,when every human transaction, every decision, was symbolized by its appropriate concrete gesture, such as the handing over of a staff or of a clod of earth to seal the purchase of a piece of land. True, a relic, a fragment of bone that is taken to stand for the 'glorified body' of a saint, can all too easily lead the naïve into superstitious practices. But, overdone or not, the veneration of Blanche's contemporaries for such relics was in the temper of the time, a temper which, more than the need for scientific precision, felt a need for incarnate realities, for truths that could be 'touched and seen'.

The transfer to France of the Crown of Thorns and a fragment of the True Cross led to some noble results in terms of art and architecture. Shortly after the ceremonies attendant on their arrival, Louis decided to build a shrine worthy of them within the palace itself. This was the Sainte-Chapelle, conceived as a bejewelled reliquary in which stone was to take the place of metal and stained glass that of enamels and gems. It has triumphantly survived the ravages of seven centuries, which hurt it only in part, to come down to us as an incomparable testimony of the spirit of its times. In it sturdiness contrives to be elegant, the walls of shining coloured light eclipse the vaults and columns, and fragile grace enhances weight. We know that its architectural conception suited Louis's personal tastes, for he had it pictured on the bedside psalter that he later ordered for himself. We know that it amazed and delighted his contemporaries, and after them succeeding generations, for it was imitated not only in northern France, in the Sainte-Chapelle of Vincennes, and southern France, in the Sainte-Chapelle of Riom, but also in countries as far away as Bohemia and Norway.

The five years 1243–8 were a period of intense architectural creativity. Paris was one vast building-yard. Besides the Sainte-Chapelle, work was progressing on Notre Dame, where the south tower, like a great pointing finger, with the double blind arcades elegantly lightening the massiveness, was ready to receive its bells and become the voice of the Cité. Saint-Germain-des-Prés was also being partially rebuilt. Convents were going up, among them those of the Jacobins and the Cordeliers, also numerous hospitals and almshouses, similar to the well-known 'Quinze-Vingts' home which Louis was to build later, in 1260. The art historians of our own day discern in this architectural effervescence the distinct influence of the royal court, which they call 'court style' and which can be seen spreading and blossoming in all the creations of that century so in love with the stonemason's art.

Blanche presided over those court influences, which radiated outwards from the Ile-de-France. But she was no mere figurehead. Joinville the chronicler put his finger on the secret that enabled so much to be accomplished, whether in building or in the many military expeditions undertaken by the King, without increasing the taxes. He noted with astonishment that they had not risen during Louis's reign, although they had risen in England at that time, and they were rising in France during the reign of Philip the Fair, when Joinville wrote his *History of Saint Louis*, but 'the King,' he says, 'never imposed taxes such that they were complained of, neither on his barons, nor his knights, nor his yeomen, nor his bailiffs. And there was nothing marvellous in this, for he did all things by the advice of his good mother, by whose counsels he was always guided.' Blanche's good management was the secret behind the King's munificence. There was a 'thrifty housewife' side to her. She knew when to spend liberally, but she also knew how to make the court live within its means, on a simple scale and with careful book-keeping. A tally bearing her name has come down to us, one of those notched rods used when bailiffs and treasurers came to court to submit the accounts of their management. It is a fitting symbol of the woman who was both a magnificent queen and a good housekeeper.

'The King held a great court at Saumur in Anjou, and I was there and do bear witness that it was the most splendid that I ever saw,' writes Joinville – a lad of only seventeen at the time – of the festivities at Saumur which must have made a similar impression on everyone else who attended. They were for the knighting of the King's brother, Alphonse of Poitiers, a memorable ceremony held on June 24, 1241, so dazzling that it became known as the 'Peerless'. All the great lords of the realm were there. Joinville says that behind the three principal barons, Humbert of Beaujeu, Enguerrand of Coucy, and Archibald of Bourbon, there were a good thirty knights all clad in silken tunics. Alphonse had dressed his sergeants-at-arms in sendal tunics bearing the coat-of-arms of Poitiers, the county of which he had just taken possession. He himself wore a Spanish purple robe lined with sendal which his mother had given him for the occasion. Gifts of apparel were lavished on the knights dubbed along with Alphonse: robes of samite, cloth of gold, fur-pieces of vair, sable, civet and squirrel. Queen Margaret wore a short robe of Spanish purple and was given ermine furs. The King gave the new Count of Poitiers a magnificent charger and two palfreys. Among the newly-dubbed knights were two from the south of France: Pons of Olargues and Sicard of Villemur.

The wines from Le Blanc (east of Poitiers), Saint-Pourçain (above Vichy), and Saumur flowed abundantly during the banquet that followed. It was held under the great covered market built by Henry Plantagenet some seventy years before. Joinville's description lets us picture the arrangement of the tables aligned along the wall, while the young squires (of whom Joinville himself was one) busily carved meat for their lords from the roasts and joints laid out on sideboards. Joinville could not keep his eyes off Theobald of Champagne, now King of Navarre, who sat enthroned at the head of one of the tables, wearing a satin mantle with a gold clasp, and a hood of cloth of gold. The King presided over another table, and the young chronicler-to-be, who already had the gift of accurate observation, noticed an odd detail in his attire. Though Louis was sumptuously clad in blue samite with a mantle of vermilion samite lined with ermine, he wore on his head a plain cotton cap. It was the sign of that taste for poverty which was growing on the young King more and more despite all the splendour around him.

Blanche was of course at the banquet. She had sent her cook, Adam, to the Lendit fair to buy extra tableware for the occasion. She had appointed four roast-cooks from her own kitchen, and supervised the preparations of the whole affair – a banquet so huge, says Joinville, 'that there did dine a swarm of knights greater than I could count.' Blanche's table faced the King's and was served by three young lords: Alphonse the Nephew; the Count of Saint-Pol; and a young German baron whose mother, Elizabeth of Hungary, was rumoured to have performed miracles and had been canonized only four years after her death in 1231. Joinville tells how Blanche used to 'kiss this lad on the forehead, out of piety, reflecting how often his sainted mother must also have kissed him so.'

Three times as much was spent on the Saumur festivities as

had been spent to celebrate the King's own wedding. It amounted to 8700 *livres*, enough to satisfy the most sybaritic tastes. This 'Peerless' ceremony which so dazzled Joinville, and which was so unlike the usual court style of a Queen-Mother whom everyone knew to be thrifty, was so sumptuous that several of the guests suspected an ulterior motive for such opulence. Most of those present could only dimly guess the reason, but they were right in surmising that something unusual was afoot.

Perhaps only Blanche herself understood fully why the King, the two Queens, the new Count of Poitiers, and their entourage, had thrown the most lavish party ever seen beyond the Loire. Within the tangled skein of conflicting interests, bickerings, and ephemeral alliances, only she knew which were the master-threads. She knew on June 24, 1241, that mighty events were in the making. She could not guess their outcome, but she was aware of all that led up to them, down to the minutest details. And, as usual, she was girding herself for battle.

To size it all up we must, like Blanche during those festive days at Saumur, review the preceding events and the list of adversaries she had to face.

'Hereby learn, my Lady, that the town of Carcassonne has been besieged by him who calls himself the Viscount, and by his fellows, since Monday after the Octave of the Nativity of Our Lady.' Thus began a letter to Blanche in October 1240 from the seneschal of the King of France in Carcassonne, William of Ormes.[7] But what exactly was happening at Carcassonne, and who were 'the Viscount' and his 'fellows'?

Raymond Trencavel was the Viscount of Béziers. Both the man and the town summoned up disturbing memories for Blanche, from a time years before King Louis was born. That was probably why the seneschal sent his report directly to Blanche rather than to the King, feeling that she would more quickly grasp what was involved.

It all went back to the year 1209. The crusade against the Albigenses, which Pope Innocent III had finally reluctantly called for, had begun. Somewhat to their surprise, the crusaders had been promptly joined by the Count of Toulouse, Raymond VI, who had hastily made his peace with the Church by a spectacular act of penance performed before the portals of the church of Saint-Gilles-du-Gard, near Nîmes. He had then urged that the first blow be struck at Béziers, whose Viscount, Raymond-Roger, happened to be Raymond VI's hereditary enemy. A frightful massacre at Béziers had ensued, which did Raymond VI no good in the long run, for his own domains were appropriated by the redoubtable Simon de Montfort, who had himself designated Viscount of Carcassonne *and* Béziers as soon as he became the leader of the crusade.

All this was past history when William of Ormes wrote to Blanche. The protagonists in those grim events were all dead. Their successors had signed in 1229, under Blanche's auspices, the first peace treaty in twenty years of war in Albigensian lands.

But Raymond-Roger's son Trencavel had never laid down his arms. He was two years old when his father died while a prisoner of Simon de Montfort. He had been in the care of the Count of Foix for some time, then had found refuge in the court of Aragon. He had never subscribed to the peace sworn by Raymond VII in 1229 and for that reason he was considered a proscript, an outlaw of the kind called *faidit* (from a medieval Latin word for 'hatred'), the term applied to conquered Albigensians who had refused to submit and had been banished. From his point of view this had at least the moral advantage of leaving him complete freedom of action. Having sworn nothing, he could perjure himself in nothing. He could with an easy conscience set about reconquering his ancestral lands. He had suddenly made his appearance in the summer of 1240, sweeping in with a small band of Aragonese and Catalan knights to rekindle here and there the fires of rebellion. Small towns like Montolieu and Saissac, and larger ones like Limoux and Montréal, all in the vicinity of Carcassonne, began to heed his call and shake off the authority of the King's seneschal, sending their men to join up with the forces of Trencavel. Suddenly, on September 7, 1240, he appeared with strong support outside the walls of Carcassonne.

The seneschal had entrenched himself within the city. The Archbishop of Narbonne, the Bishop of Toulouse, and a number of other clerics and nobles of the region were with him, feeling safer inside the city-walls than in their towns or the open country. What followed showed that they were not mistaken. On September 8 some of the inhabitants of the town of Carcassonne (which lay outside the ramparts) came to the church of Sainte-Marie to take their oath of loyalty to the King of France on the altar of the Blessed Virgin. The very next day Trencavel burst into the town and massacred thirty or so priests and religious who had sought sanctuary in that same church.

There was a specific reason for this vehement anticlericalism. It was not that the majority of the people in that part of southern France, who had loaned their men to Trencavel, had suddenly become heretics. True, the crusade against the Albigenses had been horrible. The looting, the massacres, and all the other grim consequences of the fateful decision to extirpate the heresy by the force of arms, had left a residue of grudges and rancour which it is easy to understand. It was like dry tinder awaiting the spark. That spark had come, a few years before, in the form of a new and almost unbearable torment: the Inquisition.

The fight against heresy had taken a new turn, admittedly less violent than the crusade, but hateful to the people because of its cumbersome legality and the pervasive suspicions and vindictiveness that went with it. A special tribunal ordered by Pope Gregory IX in 1231,[8] was permanently in session, with the sole task of detecting and punishing heretics. It had begun functioning in 1233, when the Pope confided to the Dominicans the task of uprooting heresy in the kingdom of France. The main burden of investigation was removed from the shoulders of the archbishops and bishops, who now had simply to lend assistance to the Dominicans specially appointed to do this work. Numerous Inquisition courts had been set up, in Avignon, in Montpellier, in Toulouse, and elsewhere. In 1237 one was started in Carcassonne. The Dominican in charge of it, a Catalan called Brother Ferrier, performed his redoubtable functions with outstanding zeal and came to be known as the 'Hammer of Heretics'.

The south of France had no monopoly of these unwelcome tribunals. There was one at La Charité-sur-Loire, downstream from Nevers, whose jurisdiction the Pope had confided to a friar named Robert Le Petit. He was nicknamed 'Robert the Bougre', a term which then meant specifically an Albigensian heretic. Which was precisely what 'Robert the Bougre' had been, having converted from Catharism back to Catholicism. He had then thrown himself so enthusiastically into his job of repression that in February 1234, less than a year after he had gone to work, the Pope removed him. But only eighteen months after that he had been turned loose again, and in just one tour of the north of France – Châlons-sur-Marne, Péronne, Cambrai, Douai, Lille – the terrifying inquisitor condemned fifty people to be burned at the stake. The Pope was showered with complaints and protests, but it was not until 1239, after he had doomed the frightful number of 183 victims in the town of Provins alone, that 'Robert the Bougre' was definitely retired from active duty.

In the south, however, the Inquisition continued to engender fierce resentment, to which the occurrences at Carcassonne bore eloquent witness. 'Thus learn, my Lady,' wrote William of Ormes, 'that since they first laid siege to us they have not left off their assaults. For all that,' he added, 'we have such a number of good ballists and people well-resolved to defend themselves, that the rebels have lost many of their own in these attacks.' And his letter ended on a reassuring note: Trencavel's forces, having learned that reinforcements were on their way to the seneschal, had slipped away during the night of October 11-12, 1240, after burning the town of Carcassonne, a convent of Franciscan Friars Minor, and the Sainte-Marie monastery. So the siege had been raised the day before the seneschal wrote to Blanche, and the business ended on the whole not too badly for those loyal to the king. 'Of our own people,' wrote William of Ormes, 'not one, by God's grace, has been killed or even mortally wounded.' Nevertheless, his last sentence struck a disquieting note: 'As touching the other matters going forward in these lands, my Lady, we shall give you a true account of them in your own presence.'

Trencavel's adventure had ended shortly after the unsuccessful siege of Carcassonne. Blanche had quickly sent military reinforcements commanded by the chamberlain, John of Beaumont. She had also been prompt in expressing her gratitude to the people of Béziers, who had remained true to the King. 'We give you thanks,' she wrote them in that same month of October 1240, 'for this loyalty and beg you will so persevere in your constancy to our son the King that you should thereby deserve all aid and comfort from his hands, as from ours.'9 Trencavel had attempted to fortify himself in Montréal, but soon capitulated. He was let off with his life and went back to Aragon.

Blanche understood the state of affairs in the south of France too well to suppose that everything would now return to normal. The foremost question was: How would the Count of Toulouse react to all this? He had been at Penautier, three miles north-west of Carcassonne, during the siege. The seneschal had sent him an urgent request for help, but Raymond had replied evasively. He would first have to go back to Toulouse, he said, and take counsel. True, he had put in an appearance at the court held by the King at Montargis a few months before the festivities at Saumur, and had acted as one would expect a loyal vassal to. But Blanche knew her cousin too well to be deceived by his outward manner. She was fond of him personally (her contemporaries had even upbraided her for it), but this only enabled her to know him the better.

Raymond had caused her much worry in recent years. He had got it into his head that the way to solace himself for past disappointments was to seize the county of Provence; he was negotiating with the Holy Roman Emperor Frederick II; he had persuaded the people of Marseilles to give him the title of Viscount of their town. Raymond-Bérenger, lawful Count of Provence and father of Queen Margaret of France, had appealed to Blanche and Louis to arbitrate between himself and the Count of Toulouse. Raymond VII had accepted, but despite this he had laid siege to Arles and ravaged the Camargue region, between Arles and the sea. Pope Gregory IX himself had finally intervened. 'Whereas,' he wrote, 'we have, at the petition of the King of France and our most dear daughter in Jesus Christ, Blanche, Queen of France, consented to grant you a delay before you set to sea . . . we have not done so that you might go about wrongfully seizing the lands of faithful Christians and attacking them against all justice . . .' For Raymond of Toulouse, in returning to the bosom of the Church, had pledged himself to take the cross, but had repeatedly found pretexts for delaying his departure.[10]

Above all, and far more threatening than the danger from Toulouse, was the danger from Poitou. On that score Blanche nursed neither illusions nor personal affection. She distrusted the Count of La Marche, Hugh of Lusignan, and she particularly distrusted his wife Isabella, the former Queen of England, whose manœuvres she had observed for forty years. She distrusted them so much that she had planted an agent in their midst, a proper spy, her 'man in Poitou'. His name has not come down to us, but he was a burgher of La Rochelle, on familiar terms with the Count and Countess of La Marche, and someone in whom Blanche had complete confidence. His job was to see everything that was going on in Poitou, hear everything – and report everything to Blanche. At least one of his reports has come down to us. It is a little slip of folded parchment, only two inches long and thus easy to conceal. It is covered with fine handwriting, containing numerous abbreviations, and consists of a highly detailed account of all the doings of the Count and Countess of La Marche during the months following the festivities at Saumur.[11]

It was at Saumur that Louis's brother Alphonse had been solemnly invested with the title of Count of Poitiers and had taken possession of Poitou and Auvergne. The title could not be thought of as uncontested. It had been held only fifty years earlier by Richard Lionheart, King of England, and more recently – though admittedly in a theoretical sense – by another Richard, Earl of Cornwall and 'King of the Romans', the younger brother of the reigning King of England, Henry III. This is enough to show why Blanche and Louis brought every ounce of vigilance to bear on Poitou and the surrounding regions. They had been rebuilding and fortifying the castle of Angers during recent years, at great expense.[12] In the final analysis, the lavish festivities at Saumur had been part of the same enterprise: to impress all concerned by a royal display of power and wealth, so that any potential enemy would think twice before waging war on France.

The strategy had seemed effective. The Count of La Marche, who had earlier shown signs of reticence, had finally come in July 1241 to do liege homage to Alphonse in the presence of King Louis, after which he had invited them both to his castle of Lusignan. The King had subsequently bidden the two Counts farewell and returned via Orléans and Pontoise to Paris, while Alphonse had gone to Poitiers to settle in his ducal palace.

None of this was to Isabella's liking. Alphonse and the King had scarcely left the castle of Lusignan when she arrived in a rage and threw out all the furniture and household objects which they had used during their stay. Blankets, hangings, chests, stools, cauldrons and ladles in the kitchen, even the altar-cloths and ornaments and the statue of the Blessed Virgin in the chapel where they had attended Mass – everything that had touched or served them was thrown out by the furious Countess as her astounded and embarrassed spouse looked on and ventured to remark that if it was to furnish the castle of Angoulême that she had stripped that of Lusignan, she might have spared herself the pains. He would have gladly bought her as much, and more, to let her fix up her father's castle to her taste. This mild suggestion infuriated her, and she shrieked at him to get out of her sight, claiming that he was a base knave, a disgrace to his people, to have honoured the very ones who had disseized him.

She flounced out and ordered the wagon to get under way, leaving her bewildered husband rooted to the spot. When she reached Angoulême she locked herself into the castle.

It took Hugh two days to recover from this, and then he followed her to Angoulême. His wife would have none of him. He spent three despairing days locked out of the castle, sleeping at the Knights Templars' hostel. He kept sending messages and gifts to his wife, beseeching her to let him in. Finally she did so, but the interview was not a pleasant one for Hugh.

As soon as she saw him, Isabella burst into tears. From the reproaches she hurled at him Hugh gleaned that three days of rest and solitude had in no way softened her anger. We are able to read the details today in the complete, if anonymous, report from Blanche's 'man in Poitou'.

'Wretch! Did you not see, at Poitiers, how they kept me waiting for three days, to the delight of the King and Queen! How, when I was at last received by them, in the chamber where the King sat, he did not call me to his side, did not bid me sit next to him? It was done by spite, to disgrace me before our own people! There I was, kept standing like a kitchen-wench! They rose for me neither when I came nor when I departed! Did you not see their scorn? I forbear to say more – the shame and despair are stifling me, even more than their forwardness in stealing my lands! I shall die of it – of rage! – if God does not make them suffer for it! They shall lose their lands, or else I shall lose all I have and die of it to boot!'

Hugh was distracted, and could only murmur: 'Command me, Lady! I will do all in my power. You know it well.'

'If you do not you will never lie by my side again! I will not suffer you in my sight!'

He swore to obey, to do all exactly as she wished, and little by little peace was restored between man and wife.

When Blanche read this tragi-comic scene in her confidential report she knew that Hugh would betray his oath of fealty to the King and that Isabella would not rest until she had recovered those Poitou lands over which she had been suzerain when she was Queen of England. To please her, Hugh would become a conspirator and a traitor.

Secret conclaves were soon held, one of which at Parthenay, brought together a number of Poitevin barons. For more security Isabella had them come to Angoulême. ('She did them great honour, more than was her wont, for she loved them not,' wrote the spy.) When they renewed their former pact, made at the instigation of Hugh of La Marche, by which they swore mutually to revolt against the King of France at the first opportunity, the spy was in their midst. On another occasion, when they met at Pons, east of the port of Royan, he was not there, but he had sent one of his own men. By that time the plot was taking shape. Specific plans were discussed among them to besiege La Rochelle and close the road from Niort to prevent grain and other supplies from reaching the town. Blanche's spy warned her and advised how to outwit them.

It would be well, Lady, to order . . . the mayor of La Rochelle and of the other towns to guard the gates well, and let no one come in who is not known. I do know, in the utmost secrecy, that certain men mean to set fire to the town, and have been paid to do it . . . I beg you have the mayor and provosts drive away certain idle youths who openly keep a bawdy house in La Rochelle. In it many brawls have been hatched to trouble our city, and two men killed. I myself should have told the mayor this, except I fear he might thereby guess that I do write to you, or have said aught touching the Count of La Marche . . .

Blanche knew from other sources that a representative of the King of England, the seneschal of Gascony, had been among the plotters at Pons. The conspiracy was therefore being engineered with Henry's full knowledge, despite the truces he had already signed with the King of France. Thus, from the Channel to the Pyrenees, a vast powder-keg stood ready, waiting only for the spark.

Alphonse of Poitiers held his first court at Christmas, 1241. Hugh and Isabella put in an appearance, but, far from doing homage, they expressed outright defiance. Isabella violently announced that she was withdrawing her allegiance and that she considered Alphonse to be a usurper. Then she and her husband hastily left town, after setting fire to the house in which they had lodged.

At least both sides knew where they stood. War was inevitable. Louis summoned his barons the following Easter. Hugh of Lusignan went to England. 'He set to sea and crossed over and did put into King Henry's head that the King of France meant to disseize him and take his lands unjustly and without cause.'[13] Henry assembled his barons at London on January 28, 1242, and decided with them to take advantage of this golden opportunity to recover the lost provinces of Normandy, Poitou, and Anjou, and rebuild the former Plantagenet realm from the mouth of the Seine to the Pyrenees.

This time he made thorough preparations. Although Hugh of La Marche had assured him that once on French soil he would have all the help he needed (the people of Poitou, he declared, asking nothing better than to come under English rule again), Henry hired a number of German, Danish, and Norwegian mercenaries. He summoned his barons and, having a fair wind for France, landed at Royan, in the English territory of Guienne, on May 20, 1242. His mother, Isabella of Angoulême, was awaiting him on the shore. 'Fair son,' said she, kissing him most courteously, 'you have a great heart, who come to send succour to your mother, whom the sons of Spanish Blanche would vilely trample beneath their feet. But now, please God, it shall not be as they intend!' There was no doubt about it: Isabella's grievances as a vassal were inseparable from her woman's spite. It was with 'Spanish Blanche' she meant to do battle.

Meanwhile Louis had not been idle. He had summoned his barons to Chinon on April 28. The organization of his army showed his fondness for engineering. He was keenly interested in whatever was mechanical, or 'technical'. It is not certain whether his artillery master Jocelyn of Cournault was already in his service, but those around the King noted that his preparations consisted chiefly in constructing 'engines wherewith to fling stones', and having carpenters build siege-towers 'to shoot the nearer upon those who might be within the places besieged'. His engineer's curiosity matched his architectural interests, much commented on by his contemporaries. The two were closely related, for an architect was basically an engineer concerned with problems of weight and support, tensile strength and lifting apparatus. By the time Henry landed in May, Louis had already seized a number of small castles on the road to Royan, including Montreuil-Bonnin and the tower of Béruges, both just west of Poitiers. Early in June he took Fontenay-le-Comte, north-east of La Rochelle, and the castle of Vouvant near by.

About that time a strange episode occurred. Two men were found prowling about the royal camp-kitchens. Their behaviour had seemed suspicious to the cooks and valets and, according to the chroniclers, they were apprehended in the very act of 'throwing venom into the King's meats', this 'venom' having been given them by Isabella of Angoulême in person, who had hired them to get it into the King's dish or cup. They were hanged without further ado. One of the chroniclers relates that Isabella was sick with rage over their failure. 'The tidings came to the Countess that the two knaves had been seized in their wicked act and hanged. She was so wroth that she took up a knife and would have struck herself, but that her people took it from her. And when she saw that she could not have her will she rent her wimple and her hair and was so downcast that she took to her bed and remained long uncomforted.'[14]

Isabella's behaviour did not slow down the march of events or the customary procedure. Ambassadors and challenges were exchanged. Meanwhile Louis consolidated his conquests in Poitou. He had a dependable ally in the province of Saintonge, along the east bank of the Gironde, in the person of Geoffrey of Rançon, lord of Taillebourg, who detested the Count of La Marche 'for a great outrage the Count had done to him, so it was said; and he had sworn on the relics of the saints that he would never have his hair cropped after the fashion of knights, but would part it and wear a head-band, as do women, till his vengeance be taken on the Count of La Marche, whether by his own hand or another's.'[15]

As for the barons of Poitou, still unsure of where their loyalties lay, Louis did not leave them the time to make up their minds. One after the other he took the castles of Frontenay (later called 'Frontenay the Demolished'), Villiers, Prahecq, Saint-Gelais, Tonnay-Boutonne, Matha, and Thors, all lying between Poitiers and Royan. At Thors the garrison surrendered without even putting up a fight. The armies of the King of France reached the Charente without having to engage in anything that could be called combat. Geoffrey of Rançon, thirsting for his revenge, had managed to keep King Henry immobilized by endless, futile palaverings, until that day, July 20, 1242, when Geoffrey knew the French were at the gates of Taillebourg.

The King of England, almost backed up against the sea, was obliged to stand and fight, but the rapidity of the French advance had deprived him of part of the forces he was counting on. 'Being advised that the King of France was drawing near to Taillebourg, we did the same from our side. But having been unable to take a stand earlier, because few of our English were with us, and because the French clearly had the greater numbers, we sounded retreat and withdrew to Saintes,' Henry later wrote of the engagement to the Emperor Frederick II. At the moment of confrontation Henry had sent his brother, Richard of Cornwall, on embassy to the King of France. Richard was well-chosen for the role. He had recently returned from the crusades, where he had himself ransomed a number of French knights who had suffered a disastrous defeat at the hands of the Saracens. Louis received him courteously, but allowed him only a few hours' truce. When Richard returned to Henry he said privately: 'We must decamp quickly, or we shall be taken.' They dined in haste, 'for the French were crossing the bridge', and followed helter-skelter by their army, they rode without stopping until they came to Saintes. The English forces were in danger of being taken from both sides, for in addition to using the stone bridge at Taillebourg, Louis had had a wooden bridge thrown across the stream, over which it was said more than five hundred foot-soldiers and bowmen had already crossed.

Next day, July 22, Louis himself crossed the Charente and turned towards Saintes. Hugh of La Marche, in Taillebourg, came out and gave battle. The first clash was received on the French side by troops commanded by Alphonse the Nephew, but the fighting quickly became general. The English arrived. The two kings were now face to face in a long awaited encounter. Their armies shouted their battle cries: 'Royaux! Royaux!' from the English; 'Montjoie! Montjoie!' from the French. Before long Louis had forced his adversary to flee. Henry fell back on Saintes again. He was so hotly pursued that one of the French knights, John des Barres, who had pushed through the gates of Saintes with a few men, almost on top of the English rear-guard, found himself a prisoner when the gates were closed. These Frenchmen later described the 'great discord' and recriminations which they witnessed between Henry III and Hugh of La Marche over this fiasco.

'Well, what of your promise? Were you not to bring us as many soldiers as we could wish for, all eager to face the King of France?' 'I never said that.' 'I have your writing to that effect, here with my chamberlain.' 'I neither wrote nor signed it.' 'What's this? Did you not send me messengers and letters till I was weary of them, all beseeching me to return hither, and chiding me for my delay? Where are these men you promised?' 'It was not I. God's body! Do you blame your mother, my wife! She it was contrived all that, myself privy to none of it!'[16]

The day after the battle Henry retreated towards Pons to the south. Then, not feeling safe, he fell back on Barbezieux, to the east; then again to Blaye, at the head of the Gironde estuary. He was well-advised in this, for Reynold, the lord of Pons, went to tender his submission to Louis, who was then at Colombiers, just below Saintes. At the same time Hugh of La Marche sent his eldest son as hostage to Louis. On July 26, he came himself, with his other children and Isabella.

They cried him mercy with many sighs and tears and began to say: 'Most gentle King, and debonair, do you forgive us and have pity on us! Through wickedness and arrogancy did we turn against you! Sire, of your franchise, and out of your great mercy, forgive us our fault!' The King, seeing the Count of La Marche so humbly crying mercy, could not hold his treachery against him. He pitied him and bade him rise, and forgave him all that he had wrought ill.[17]

This dramatic encounter ended on a colourful note. 'When the Sire Geoffrey of Rançon saw the Count of La Marche, his wife and children, on their knees before the King, crying him mercy, he did call for a trestle and had his head-bands off and himself shorn all at once, before the King and the Count of La Marche and the others thereby.' He was avenged.

These stirring events were the basis for many songs and satirical ballads at the expense of the English.

> They did not stop to spin a tale,
> The English with their barley-ale;
> But all of France did dance and dine,
> For barley-ale is not worth wine.[18]

One can well imagine Blanche's satisfaction, when she heard such verses as the following repeated from mouth to mouth:

> There did the King right many deeds and true,
> As did the Counts of Artois and Poitiers,
> Who rode to bring assistance to their crew,
> On chargers noble, armed in fine array.
> God keep the King of France upon his mount!
> And also Charles, Alphonse, and Artois' Count!

One verse was devoted to the unfortunate Count of La Marche:

> There was La Marche's folly the most rife,
> Who madly dashed his forces 'gainst the King;
> Thus did he so he might beguile his wife,
> Whose rashness never willed a rasher thing.[19]

Isabella's imperious will and her husband's spinelessness were both well-known. Each, however, was destined to come to an honourable end. The year after the battle of Taillebourg they divided their lands among their children, after which Isabella entered the convent of Fontevrault. Matthew Paris gives a rather unedifying reason for such an impetuous woman's decision to end her days among enclosed nuns. According to him, Hugh had been obliged to fight a duel on Isabella's account, against a knight who had challenged him by holding out his gauntlet 'in the manner of the French', says Matthew Paris. It was then that Isabella, 'bethinking herself of so many misdeeds, hied her to the nunnery called Fontevrault, wherein she did conceal herself in a most secret cell, clad in the religious habit, finding herself even there in scant safety.'[20] But Matthew Paris is too rancorous to be taken at face-value.

Whatever may have been Isabella's real reasons for entering the convent, she was fated to end her days at that same Fontevrault where so many women before her, *femmes fatales* and passionate mistresses, had found peace. She died there in 1246, after an incredibly tumultuous life. Her tomb, with its handsome recumbent statue carved in wood, is still there, just across from Eleanor of Aquitaine's splendid sepulchre.

Her widower, Hugh, went on a crusade and died a hero's death before the walls of Damietta.

The conspiracy lost its leader and instigator when Hugh of La Marche submitted, but the hostilities could not be considered at an end. Louis had dispersed the English forces, but there were still those of the Count of Toulouse, not to mention the Kings of Aragon and Navarre, who had promised their support to the rebels but had been forestalled by Louis's promptness. Furthermore, in the summer of 1242 an epidemic of dysentery threatened to undermine the French army. Louis himself came down with it. There was serious apprehension throughout the French camp. Matthew Paris does not find the word 'despair' too strong to describe the mood. The death of Louis's father was still recent enough to weigh on the minds of all those around the King. Had the south of France cast an evil spell on the throne? One can imagine Blanche's anguish as she waited in dread, north of the Loire, fearing that the tragedy of thirteen years before, whose every detail was burned into her mind, would be repeated.

Finally a messenger came with good news. The King was recovering, he would be returning shortly to the Ile-de-France. By the end of September, amid general rejoicings and victory celebrations, Blanche's son returned to her in good health. One by one the barons in the west of France had been submitting. First William L'Archevêque, the Sire of Parthenay, in whose fortress the plot had been hatched. Then Hertold, castellan of Mirambeau, who, unable to defend his domains, went off to beg King Henry, as a faithful vassal, that he be allowed to transfer his allegiance immediately to the King of France. Henry had been lingering on in Bordeaux, but it was not long before he was obliged to admit that he was isolated. His one remaining ally was the cause of much jeering behind his back. This was the Countess of Béarn, an extraordinary woman, whom Matthew Paris describes as 'singularly monstrous and fat.' She appears to have been a creature bursting with elemental vitality, whose vast appetite at table threatened the exchequer. Still Henry lingered irresolutely on the banks of the Garonne, unwilling to admit defeat. Moreover, the news from England was not such as to hasten his return. The autumn rains had caused the Thames to overflow. Westminster Palace was knee-deep in water and they were wading about on horseback. Finally, after casting about for help of any kind, wherever he might find it, Henry yielded to the inevitable and signed a truce with the King of France, on April 23, 1243. Matthew Paris facetiously tells how, at the annual chapter-meeting of the Cistercians that year, the King of France asked for the monks' prayers, and the King of England asked for some warm woollen clothes (which was in fact the regular form in which the monks paid their subsidies to the crown).

Henry finally sailed for home in October 1243. He achieved some sort of record for *non sequiturs* by ordering a victory parade upon his return, which all the nobles of England were required to attend, with four burghers from each large town, all the clergy walking in procession, lighted candles and so on. It caused much talk in London, also in Winchester, where a similar show was put on. But the talk was not the kind Henry had intended, for his barons had long since preceded him, bringing home their own account of events. After the defeat of Taillebourg they had, one by one, asked Louis for safe-conduct through France. Louis had granted it in every case, thereby earning some reproaches from his own people. To these he replied rather jocularly, 'Let them be gone freely, so they be gone! What better consummation for me than that my country's foes be off without thought of return?' It was more than a witty remark, for France's real enemies were still within.

Count Raymond VII of Toulouse had promptly joined the conspiracy, urged on both by Trencavel and by another southern baron, Roger, Count of Foix. Having made peace with the Count of Provence, Raymond had full freedom of action. The kind of thing that had happened at Carcassonne in 1240 might happen again. There were still many heretics among Raymond's close associates who were simply waiting their chance to attempt similar raids.

On May 25, 1242, only five days after Henry landed at Royan, the Inquisition court began a circuit in Languedoc. The inquisitors were William Arnaud, a Dominican, and Stephen of Saint-Thibéry, a Franciscan (friars of that order had been associated with the Dominicans in the struggle against heresy since 1235). With them were two other Dominicans, another Franciscan named Raymond Carbonnier, a notary, two beadles (called 'apparitors'), and two other clerics. They set up shop at Avignonet, 24 miles south-east of Toulouse, in a castle of the Count of Toulouse, and began collecting the depositions of the inhabitants of the region, as they had previously done at several other places in that part of southern France, among them Laurac, Castelnaudary, Fanjeaux, and Sorèze.

The inquisitors had fallen into a trap. The man who had been given the custody of the castle of Avignonet was Raymond of Alfar, Raymond VII's seneschal and also his natural brother, the son of one of Raymond VI's mistresses. This man had resolved to do away with the Dominicans and their retinue. Once they were at Avignonet he advised Peter Roger of Mirepoix, lord of Montségur, that he held their enemies in his hands. Peter Roger was another southern baron entirely devoted to the heretics' cause; he was sheltering Bertrand Marty, an Albigensian bishop, as well as numerous other 'Perfects'. Peter Roger personally took charge of the operation. He started out with a force of forty horsemen and picked up some thirty more friends, armed with axes, on the way. The plan called for an attack on May 28, Ascension Eve. Peter Roger and some of his men remained hidden in Selve Wood, near Avignonet, where the others were to rejoin them after accomplishing their mission.

The business was quickly and dramatically dispatched. The gang broke into the castle easily. The door to the friars' chamber was knocked down with axes, which roused the victims from their sleep. They had no time to strike a single blow in self-defence. They began singing the *Te Deum* as they were slaughtered to the last man.

'Well, where's the chalice?' Peter Roger asked, when his men came back loaded with their victims' spoils. By 'chalice' he meant the skull of the chief inquisitor, William Arnaud. The murderer apologized. It was broken, he said.[21]

Needless to say, this massacre caused quite a furore. Everyone held the Count of Toulouse more or less responsible. What, people asked themselves, would have happened if Raymond's ally, Henry of England, had been victorious? After Taillebourg, however, Raymond found himself in a delicate situation. He was excommunicated. The military assistance he had hoped for was not forthcoming. The entire French clergy had voted a special five per cent tax on their own revenues in order to help Louis wage war against Raymond, 'who had caused Friars Preachers to be slaughtered'.[22] In addition, that same Count of Foix who had incited Raymond to revolt now hastened to treat with Louis, in October 1242, and even offered to fight against Raymond! An army was immediately organized, placed under the orders of the Constable, Humbert of Beaujeu, and sent against Toulouse. Raymond gave himself up for lost.

In a letter to Blanche dated October 20, 1242, in which he refers to himself as her 'cousin, loyal and true, and ready to do her homage', Raymond begged her forgiveness, addressing her as 'most serene Lady Blanche, by God's grace illustrious queen of the French', and continuing:

'After God, it is to your Serene Highness's clemency that I

may turn, I trow, with best hope. For you have long loved us with uttermost soul's grace. You love and cannot leave off loving us, forasmuch as that love for your mother, she of sweet memory, still dwells within your spirit, whereby hangs our kinship to you.'[23]

Blanche was his kinswoman and had always interceded for him, even when it meant criticism directed at herself. Raymond refers to this in his letter, mentioning 'those who speak against you as touching ourself'. His phrasing is insistent, even wheedling. 'We have a claim upon your heart,' he writes, 'not only for that we are of kin, but also by reason of our daughter [Joan of Toulouse, who was married to Blanche's son, Alphonse], who is at your court.' He begged Blanche to mediate between him and her son the King, swearing that henceforth he would behave as a faithful vassal should.

After sending his letter Raymond waited on tenterhooks to know whether Blanche would be softened once more. In allying himself with the King of England, and taking arms despite the peace he had sworn not long before, Raymond's behaviour had been on a level with that of Ferdinand of Flanders and Reynold of Boulogne. Could he now expect better treatment than they had received?

A chronicler of the time, William of Puylaurens, sums it up by saying: 'Some have chided the Lady Blanche, the King's mother, for seeming too favourably inclined to her kinsman of Toulouse. Yet it was not true nor likely that she should love him more than her own children or go contrary to their interest. Rather she did act out of prudence and discretion, meaning thereby to stablish and preserve peace in the realm.'[24]

So Raymond VII went from his residence at Penne d'Agenais, north-east of Agen, to Alzonne, west of Carcassonne, where he met the King's envoys, Humbert of Beaujeu and Ferry Pâté, the Marshal, who was often used in embassies. They signed a truce. The Count of Toulouse was summoned to Lorris, east of Orléans, to swear again before the King of

France to keep the peace of Meaux and Paris. This time he was to do so.

'Thenceforward,' writes a chronicler, 'the barons of France left off all enterprises against the King, it being manifest that the hand of God strove with him.'[25] Louis went to the main towns of the south of France and received their oaths of loyalty. He ordered Carcassonne destroyed to punish it for its rebellion; it was rebuilt along the lines of the new town-plans of the time. The castle of Montségur, still a focus of revolt, he had besieged by the seneschal of Carcassonne.* Certain small pockets of rebellion held out for some years more, ending in 1255 when the castle of Quéribus was taken by the King's troops. It had been the last asylum of the heretics and *faidits*. Before this, even Raymond Trencavel had submitted, and had gone off on crusade with the King to the Holy Land, where he fought valiantly.

* This reference to the siege of Montségur is in keeping with the importance of the incident in the 13th-century texts themselves.

VI

THE QUEEN MOTHER

Rocamadour lies half way between Brive and Cahors. Its sanctuary of Our Lady, 'which sits atop the rock', is possibly the oldest Marian shrine in France. Blanche arrived there in state on May 1, 1244, with her four sons, their wives, and her nephew Alphonse of Boulogne. It was the first time that the royal court had made the pilgrimage. There was a great turnout. The abbot of Tulle, Peter of Malemort, who had jurisdiction over Rocamadour, came to welcome Blanche and her entourage. Blanche knew Peter; he was the nephew of Élie of Malemort, Bishop of Bordeaux, who had escorted her as a little girl, all the way from Palencia in Castile to the abbey of Port-Mort in Normandy, where she had been married to the Dauphin Louis of France. Another nephew of Élie de Malemort, bearing the same name as his uncle, was now King Louis's seneschal at Limoges, 'the first seneschal of France's King since days so bygone as to be forgotten in this land.'[1] The fact in itself is sufficient indication of the growth of French influence south of the Loire, for Limoges had been part of the Plantagenet realm, as had Rocamadour. But the twofold heritage was reunited in the person of Blanche herself. In making the pilgrimage to Rocamadour she knew that she was following in the footsteps of her grandmother Eleanor of Aquitaine, and of her English grandfather, King Henry II, both of whom had come to the Blessed Virgin's shrine. They had gazed at the fresco of one of God's greatest pilgrims, St Christopher, and at that other moving painting beneath the old-fashioned semi-circular arches, depicting the Annunciation and the Visitation. It was no ordinary pilgrimage that had brought the whole court of France three hundred miles by road from the towers of Notre Dame of Paris. It was a journey of thanksgiving for the glad event that had occurred three months before, on February 25, 1244: Queen Margaret had given birth to another little Louis, the heir to the throne of France. It was her third child, the two others being daughters, of whom the elder had been named Blanche in honour of the Queen Mother. When the second daughter, Isabella, had been born, Margaret had so dreaded the King's disappointment that she had not dared send him the news herself, but had asked the Bishop of Paris, William of Auvergne, to tell him, The story goes that the Bishop accosted the King bluffly with these words: 'Rejoice, Sire! For today the throne of France has gained a king! You have a daughter, by whose marriage you shall win one realm the more!'² But now the Capetian dynasty had its own heir, and also some compensation for the bereavement that had struck recently, for little Blanche had died at the age of three. In another year Louis and Margaret were to have a second son, Philip.

There may also have been an ulterior political motive behind this royal pilgrimage, for it was no bad thing for the French court to show itself, placidly moving along these roads of southern France where peace had come only so recently. It proved that the scions of France could travel without any military escort in areas which had been the scene of bloody upheavals only two years before.

The love of pilgrimages for their own sake may also have had something to do with it. It was a time when every Christian had it more or less in mind to make the journey to the lofty cliff of Rocamadour on top of which Our Lady was enthroned. Blanche felt this urge like everyone else. She was a frustrated pilgrim. She would have liked to visit the grave of James the Apostle, at Compostela in Spain, to which the Christians of Europe had already been going in droves for over two hundred years. So many French had made the trip that their regular itinerary along the mountain paths of northern Spain was called the *camino francès*. After her coronation Blanche had watched

John of Brienne, the King of Jerusalem, take up the pilgrim's staff and turn towards Spain. When he came back from Santiago de Compostela, and also from a sojourn in Castile, he had become Blanche's kinsman by marrying her niece Berengaria, one of Berenguela's daughters. If only Blanche herself could make the same journey, visit the sanctuary and venerate the relics of the Saint, and then, on her way back to France, visit her native Castile! But what any serf in her kingdom would have been allowed to do, she could not do. The cares of state had crowded too thick and fast upon her for there to be time for such a dream.

She had once gone so far as to announce to Bishop William, her confessor, that the long-awaited pilgrimage could now take place. Everything was ready, she told him, and she had spared no expense in planning the different stages of the long journey.

The Bishop's reaction was not what she had expected.

'Lady,' said he, 'you would pour out much treasure upon the vain glories of this world, showing your magnificence in your native home. The gold might be better spent.' Blanche, taken aback, answered, 'I am open to your counsel.' 'Here is my counsel,' he went on. 'The Friars Preachers, whom we call here the Friars of St James, are some fifteen hundred *livres* in debt. Take up your pilgrim's staff and bowl and go to Saint James – I mean to the Friars' convent here in Paris. Pay them their debt. As to your vow to go a pilgrimage, I take it upon myself, before God. I will answer for you on Doomsday. Such a course is better than an excess of disbursements for needless splendour.'

Blanche had abided by this, but it had not been easy for her,[3] though it did coincide with practical considerations. The kingdom still had need of her vigilance. There were the recalcitrant barons, the turbulent University students, the increasing troubles of the townspeople, the Poitou situation, the English . . .

Despite it all, those days of May 1244 were peaceful ones.

It was as if a new leaf had been turned over. At fifty-six, Blanche was wondering if she could not now retire from the affairs of state and let Louis carry on alone. He was undoubtedly able to. She glimpsed a time of peace and rest. Why not plan to withdraw soon to the abbey of Maubuisson, which she had founded, and which was to be consecrated the next month, June 1244, two days after Midsummer Day?

A kingdom at peace! She had lived through Bouvines, La Roche-aux-Moines, Taillebourg. She had triumphed over all the enmities, the outright revolts, the insidious plots, the threats and snares. At long last an era of peace, so earnestly hoped for, seemed at hand. Among her children only Isabella and young Charles were still to be settled in life. But the princess seemed already to have made her choice, and Charles would clearly have no need of his mother in making his. At eighteen years the lad seemed to think himself cut out for the role of world conqueror. A bit more restraint might have been better for him. He was probably the most gifted musician and poet in the family. If it were not for a hard look that came into his face now and then he would have been a thoroughly delightful person. Too bad that he did not get on better with Margaret. The young Queen tended to treat him as a mere child, which Charles did not relish . . . But those were all trivial worries. Louis was fair, and firm and patient enough to settle all such bickerings, though they hurt him.

A kingdom at peace . . . If only things were as tranquil outside France as within! But the tempests seemed to lower all the more fiercely abroad for being calmed at home. In every direction there were disturbing, even terrifying prospects. It was not only England. She remained an enemy, of course, but Henry's character being what it was, one could expect the truce to last a while longer. He was more interested in collecting fine gems than in collecting an army, and he was not likely to forget his lesson of two years before. The real cause of concern lay elsewhere. The Pope and the Holy Roman Emperor were perennially at logger-heads, each hoping for the support of the King of France and his army. Four years ago the Pope had offered the crown of 'King of the Romans', which was to say the succession to the Empire, to the second son of France, Robert of Artois. Full of his dreams of flashing swords and glory, the young man would have accepted in a minute. But Blanche was dead against it.

To accept that imperial crown was to leap head first into the unknown – leap into dubious quarrels and struggles whose only outcome would be more of the same. It would have meant nothing but heartaches for France. Have done with the bastard Empire – one had only to look at the Latin Empire of the East to see what a festering sore in the body of Christendom it had become. A bloody victory had led to a still bloodier aftermath. Constantinople, far from becoming the base for the reconquest of Jerusalem which they had intended, had itself become a weak point in need of defence. It had absorbed in reinforcements and treasure what would probably have sufficed to liberate Jerusalem. Blanche was constantly being pestered by the luckless Emperor Baldwin, a childish bungler. His letters always ended with elaborate signatures, underlined with great strokes of vermilion cinnabar, as though it were Justinian himself signing. But these impressive missives were simply begging letters such as any student at the University of Paris might write to his father. Could Blanche help him pay his debts? At a time when the Empire of the East needed a sturdy warrior and wise statesman it had the misfortune to be in the hands of a nondescript little baron with no abilities at all. And a prodigal one at that. No sooner had he been crowned than he emptied the imperial exchequer. Then he came crying on the shoulders of all the kings in Europe, who had no choice but to bail him out, because that was the Pope's wish. Blanche had frequently settled his debts; her treasurer at Pontoise, Stephen of Montfort, could vouch for that. He had disbursed hundreds of *livres* to pay off Baldwin's creditors – Tuscans, most of them, long settled in Constantinople, and businessmen who knew how to look after their own interests.[4] Blanche had done more than that. She had taken in the 'children of Acre', as they were called at the French court: Baldwin's brothers-in-law through his wife, the Empress Marie, and thus Blanche's grand-nephews. In those days family ties were sacred.

Poor Baldwin was constantly pestering Blanche with re-quests for help. In a long letter recently he had set forth his own extraordinary solution to the problems of the Holy Land. In dead earnest he told how the Seljuk Sultan of Iconium ('a most mighty Sultan, and richest among the pagans, I do believe') had offered to become his ally, asking, to seal the alliance, for the hand of a Christian princess. 'Let it be one of our own kinswomen,' wrote Baldwin, going on to tell how she could keep her own faith, could bring her own chaplain and clerics with her, etc., etc. And who knows? The Sultan himself had had a Christian mother, a Greek lady. Perhaps in time he would wish to embrace the Christian faith himself. He would build churches. He would help Baldwin against his enemies in Greece and elsewhere. Could not Blanche send one of the daughters of Elizabeth of Montaigu (Baldwin's own sister) for the Sultan? The sooner the better.

Blanche had not even answered this naïve proposal. Baldwin had promised some time before to follow all her advice to the letter. She wrote to him to contain his enthusiasm for such hare-brained schemes and to give more thought to paying his creditors – so far as the imperial coffers at Constantinople would allow!

What a contrast between Baldwin's childish daydreams and the harsh realities of the Middle East situation! A few years before a very strange episode had thrown sinister light on those poorly understood lands overseas.

At first it was only a rumour of a threat to Louis's life by the agents of a Syrian sheikh to which no one paid much attention, until, startlingly, the rumours were confirmed by the appearance at the court of France of some Syrians who insisted on an interview with the King. They had come to warn him to be on his guard. Their chief, who was known as the 'Old Man of the Mountain', had indeed sent secret emissaries to murder the King, but had countermanded his own order and dispatched the men now speaking with Louis to forestall the murderers and cancel the assassination. This had happened in 1236. A year earlier Pope Gregory IX had called for another crusade to liberate the Holy Land. Perhaps the 'Old Man of the Mountain' had meant to prevent this by eliminating the young King who was the most powerful sovereign in Europe.

Whatever his motives, the orders and counter-orders of the 'Old Man of the Mountain' were to be taken seriously, as the assassination of a former King of Jerusalem, Conrad of Montferrat, had shown. One evening shortly after the retaking of Acre he had been strolling in the streets of Tyre. Two Syrians came up to him. He knew them, as they had presented themselves for Christian baptism earlier that same day. One of them held out a written petition to him, which Conrad had taken unsuspectingly. While he was reading it the other man plunged a dagger into his heart. He died on the spot, and the whole issue of Christian control over the Holy Land was raised anew. That murder clearly bore the trade-mark of its author, the 'Old Man of the Mountain', hidden away in his inaccessible eyrie of El Qadmus, thirty miles south-east of present-day Latakia.

Who was this mysterious personage? Joinville later gave a description of him, based on the report of Brother Ivo, of the Mendicant order, 'who did speak the Saracen tongue', and had had personal interviews with the terrifying sheikh. 'When the Old One rode out there went before him a crier bearing a Danish axe of long handle and the same all bristling with knives fixed in it. And he cried: 'Make way for Him who holds death to Kings between his hands!'

The Old One was in fact the chief of a Shiite sect whose members were considered monstrous heretics by other Moslems. Their founder, Hassan Sabbah, lived in the fortress of Alamout, a veritable eagle's nest perched on a cliff. There he had surrounded himself with a group of young men, most of whom he had kidnapped as children from the neighbouring villages. He had taught them a secret doctrine and had made them into mere human daggers entirely subordinate to his will. He called them his *fidawis* ('faithful') and could count on their utter obedience. King Conrad's successor, Henry of Champagne, decided when he became King of Jerusalem that it would be better to have this redoubtable sheikh as a friend than as an enemy, and had not hesitated to contact him and even visit him. The story goes that the Old One put on a special show to honour his guest. At his order, two of the *fidawis* who were mounting guard on the battlements of the highest tower simply jumped off. When the Old One asked if Henry would like to see it again, the appalled Frenchman declined. Upon bidding him farewell the Old One loaded him with gifts and whispered that if Henry had anyone he wanted assassinated he had but to say the word. The Old One and his *fidawis* would consider it a pleasure.[5] And so, from time to time, a sultan here, an emir there, guilty of having displeased the Old One, would pass from the scene. The young murderers all had a gentle, rather bewildered manner which astonished people. They would let themselves be captured, let themselves be questioned, even tortured, all with merely a vague smile. All that could be got out of them was that they were the Old One's *fidawis*, happy to die at his orders.

It was hinted that the Old One derived his power to manipulate these young men not merely by promising them heavenly bliss after death, but by building them an artificial paradise here on earth. Rumour told of enchanted gardens where his initiates drank their fill of pleasure, under soft bowers and amid gorgeous palaces full of sweet scents, of which the sweetest were carried by the ravishing houris who sidled up to them, half-veiled and eager to gratify their every desire. 'There were,' says Marco Polo, sixty years later, 'dames both ripe and tender, the loveliest in the world, knowing how to play upon all musical instruments. The Old One told his youths that those gardens were Paradise itself. He gave them drink whereby they fell asleep of mornings, and then did he have them taken into those gardens, and awaked. And being awaked they truly thought themselves in Paradise, the ladies staying with them the day long, dallying, conversing, and doing their will.' In fact the delights were tawdry, but intensified by drugs. The 'human daggers' were simply addicts.

Oderic of Pordenone, the Franciscan missionary and traveller, also describes the Old One's mystique and methods. 'Whenas the Old One did purpose to kill a man he gave his youths to drink that which made them sleep, and as they slept had them carried out of Paradise. And when they were awake he called them before him and told them that they might never more enter therein except they put such and such a man to death, the same being a lord. But if they did kill him they might enter again into Paradise and there abide, their delights to be even greater than before.'[6] The secret of the Old One's extraordinary power was hashish. His men, who became irretrievably addicted, their normal human feelings dulled, no longer feared death – whether for others or even for themselves. They were hashish-eaters, *hashishiyyin* in the Arabic, and this word, mispronounced by Europeans, became our word *assassin*. So down the centuries, drugs and murder have always been closely associated.

It was the Old One's assassins who had obediently come all the way to France under their master's orders, the first group to kill, the second to call off the killing. At that time the power of the Old One was already weakening. The reign of terror caused by the sect since its founding, 150 years earlier, was coming to an end. But no one could have predicted then, in 1236, that the Old One's fortresses at Alamout and Masyaf would soon be taken. Louis himself had not yet seen the last of the assassins. Meanwhile he sent those who had warned him back to their master loaded with gifts: five sumptuous garments for the 'Old Man of the Mountain', and two for the messengers themselves.

The real reason for the Old One's sudden change of heart in Louis's favour was not far to seek. A frightful horde surging out of northern Asia had begun devastating Moslem lands. The terror they spread round them soon reached Europe itself.

One day, says Matthew Paris, William of Auvergne, the Bishop of Paris, visited Queen Blanche and gave her a letter. She gasped as she read it. 'Where are you, my son, King Louis?' 'What's the matter, Mother?' 'Beloved son, what shall we do? Here's tidings of calamity that reach us from afar! These Tartars, in their fierce assault, do threaten us all with perdition now, ourselves and Holy Mother Church!' The chronicler shows us Blanche racked with sobs as she told her son the gist of the letter the Bishop had given her. The King comforted his mother and answered: 'Our strength and solace are in heaven. Let those whom we call Tartars come. We shall thrust them back into that Tartarus* from which they issued, or else they shall dispatch us straight to heaven, and we go to God confessing and suffering for Christ.'[7]

It was Genghis Khan and his successors, with their Golden Horde. Their exploits had begun towards the start of the 13th century, with the conquest of China. Then they passed into the Eurasian heartland, and finally reached the borders of Europe. The 'Mongol terror' had replaced the 'Saracen terror', and it threatened to devastate everyone's lands impartially, beginning with those of the Turks.

The people of Europe had at first entertained certain illusions about all this. Understandably, they had no very clear idea of events beyond the huge Moslem world of the Arabs and Turks. They had heard that the world was threatened by a strange people, and had at first thought it was that of the mysterious Prester John, a faraway legendary king who was said to be a Christian. Thus the first victory of the Mongols of Genghis Khan over the Khwarizmi shahdom, in what is now Iran, was seen as the victory of a descendant of Prester John

* In classical mythology, the lowest level of Hades.

over the Persian Empire. Little by little, however, the truth became known. A Hungarian Dominican named Julian, an indefatigable missionary whose zeal had taken him all the way to the Volga, was the first to sound the alarm regarding the true nature of this barbarous horde who intended to subjugate the entire world.[8] The first precise details to reach the court of France came from Ponce of Aubon, cavalry master of the Knights Templars, in 1241. 'The Tartars', he wrote, 'have laid waste the lands of Henry, Duke of Poland, and killed him and many of his barons, as well as six members of our Order and five hundred of our men. Three of our Order, well-known to us, escaped.' Hungary and Bohemia had also been devastated. Three Mongol armies were on the march, one into the heart of Hungary, the other through Poland, the third into Austria. 'Learn hereby that all the barons of Germany, and the King, all the clergy and religious, the monks and recent converts – all have taken the cross. The Dominicans and Franciscans, as far as Hungary, have become crusaders and now march against the Tartars. Those of our Order declare that if it is God's will that all these be vanquished, then the Tartars will have no further hindrance till they reach your own land. Learn also that they spare no one. They take no prisoners but kill all, rich and poor, great and small, save comely women whom they keep to have their will of them. They besiege neither castles nor cities, but destroy everything.'[9]

The Holy Roman Emperor himself, Frederick II, was not long in sounding the alarm. He wrote to all the princes of Christendom, beseeching them to take the cross against the Mongols. Bela IV, the King of Hungary, who himself had only escaped the pursuing Mongols by having a fleeter horse, called on the Pope to preach a crusade against the Tartars.

More was heard of this strange people. Europe learned of their armour of boiled leather, their savage appearance, their extraordinary powers of endurance – 'they do ride in one day as far as from Paris to Chartres,' Ponce of Aubon declared. A renegade Englishman, half-spy, half-interpreter, gave further details. He had been banished from England for some unknown reason and had wound up at Acre, where he had squandered his money in the gambling-dens and, after many adventures, had taken up with the Mongols and learned their language. He gave a description of them to a friend of his, a clerk of Narbonne, who promptly made it known generally.

> Their chests are hard and vigorous, their faces large and pale, their shoulders high and straight, their noses short and flat, their chins jutting and pointed, their upper jaws low-set and wide, their teeth long and scant, their eye-lids stretching from the nose to the hair on their foreheads, their eyes restless and black, their look shifty and scowling, their limbs bony and sinewy, their legs being strong but short-thighed. Notwithstanding they are of even stature with ourselves, what they lack in the legs being made up in the trunk.[10]

Suddenly the wave of terror receded. The Mongols had left Europe and gone 'God alone knows whither'. In 1245 Pope Innocent IV decided to obtain some accurate information on this mysterious people from the faraway East. He sent out four missions consisting of Mendicant Friars, both Dominicans and Franciscans. One group led by a Franciscan, John of Plan-Carpin, who was sixty years old and had been a personal friend of Francis of Assissi, managed to cross the Russian steppes and get all the way to the centre of the Mongol Empire, where they had the good luck to be present at the accession of the third Great Khan, Kuyuk, at Karakorum. On his return John of Plan-Carpin gave the Pope a very complete written report, which we still have, entitled *History of the Mongols Whom We Call Tartars*. With it the old legends about the Mongols gave way to factual information from eye-witnesses.

Meanwhile another piece of news had plunged Christendom into gloom. Jerusalem, which had been reoccupied by the Christians for a while, had now fallen into the hands of a terrible Turkish people, the Khwarizmi. No doubt this time that the Pope would exhort the King and barons to take up the cross as before. For fifty years expeditions had been attempting to relieve the Holy Land without any decisive outcome. Yet it was obvious to all that before any large-scale operation could be launched the Pope and the Holy Roman Emperor would first have to settle their interminable quarrel.

The tension was at its height when Blanche and her family reached Rocamadour on their pilgrimage. One could well wonder if Christendom itself would survive. Since about the turn of the century a number of theologians had been thinking about certain words uttered by Christ during the Passover meal in the upper room, just before his arrest:

> 'He that hath no sword, let him sell his garment and buy one. For I say unto you, that this that is written must yet be accomplished in me: "And he was reckoned among the transgressors." For the things concerning me have an end.' And they said: 'Lord, behold, here are two swords.' And he said unto them: 'It is enough.' (*Luke* xxii: 36–8)

Those two swords, it was thought, symbolized the spiritual and the temporal powers. The sword that was Peter's must remain sheathed ('Then said Jesus unto Peter: "Put up thy sword into the sheath" ' – *John* xviii: 11), but not so the sword of the Emperor, to whom temporal authority was given. The two swords, acting together, would cause justice and order to reign both in men's souls and in their worldly affairs.

But the truth was that the two swords were constantly crossing in duels between themselves, threatening both justice and order. Harmony between them had been achieved in Charlemagne's time, but only very rarely since. One such moment had been during the reign of the sainted Emperor Henry II, in the first quarter of the 11th century. The two 'swords' had clashed more and more violently during the century preceding him. The more the popes strove to get the ideal emperor, one who would give satisfaction as defender of both justice and the Church, the more obstinately did the

Blanche and her son.

The castle of Angers, rebuilt and fortified by Blanche and Louis.

The refectory of the abbey of Royaumont.

The Emperor Frederick II.

Biblioteca Apostolica Vaticana, Rome

Crusaders taking ship for the Crusades.

Bibliothèque Nationale, Pa

Archives Photographiques, Paris

The ruins of the abbey of Dammarie-les-Lys and recent excavations.

Rock crystal crozier given by Blanche to the abbey of Dammarie-les-Lys.

Musée Lambinet, Versailles

Blanche's gifts to the abbey of Maubuisson: chalice and paten
with the abbey's arms *(above);* hanap, similar to the one she
gave her son *(bottom left);* statue of the Virgin and Child
(bottom right).

Seal of the abbey of Maubuisson.

Archives Nationales, Paris

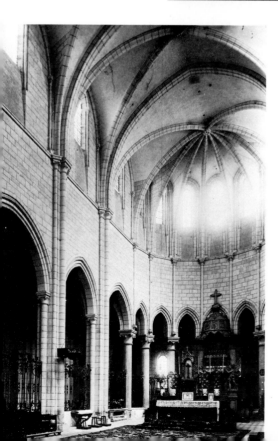

The choir of the abbey of Pontigny.

Archives Photographiques, Paris

Blanche's death and burial.

successors of Charlemagne oppose them and pursue crassly material goals. With the Hohenstaufen Frederick II the Pope's dissatisfaction reached its peak. The Patrimony of St Peter (the papal territories in Italy) had never been more overtly threatened. Frederick announced that he was going to wield just as much power as the Caesars had done. He had himself pictured draped in Roman robes, his brow crowned with laurels like those of Augustus.

As a close observer of all this, Blanche let her attitude be seen in her actions; it was the same as that shown by all the French Capetian rulers before her: polite but firm neutrality. The Holy Roman Emperors had time and again sought to extract an oath of vassalship from the burgeoning French dynasty, and each time had failed. Over two hundred years ago a mere skirmish had settled the matter, when it had looked like serious war between the Empire and the son of Hugh Capet. On August 6, 1023, the Emperor Henry II was camped at Ivois, on the right bank of the River Meuse, halfway between Rheims and Luxembourg. On the other side, at Mouzon, France's King Robert the Pious was camped. For four days the tension had mounted. Finally the Emperor had decided to cross the river, not in warlike array but simply as a visitor. 'The more thou art exalted the more must thou therefore humble thyself always.' So it was he, the Emperor, who had come to the King of France. He no longer required the vassal's oath, he simply wanted to be on good terms with this Frankish kingdom which would not accept his suzerainty.

The Emperor who had thus found a means of peaceful co-existence was a saint. The same cannot be said for his successors, though their perpetual wranglings with the Pope had kept them too busy to be able to pick a quarrel with the kings of France. They had tried it once, at Bouvines, but the little western realm, with its puny 'King of the Ile-de-France', had shown itself able to stand up to an Emperor, if not the Empire itself. Now it was the Emperor who came begging France's help, and the Pope was doing the same on the other side.

France had become a new, third force, holding the two 'swords' in balance.

The prelates and abbots were in an optimistic mood when Blanche came to the consecration of the abbey of Maubuisson, Notre-Dame-la-Royale, on June 26, 1244. A reconciliation between Pope Innocent IV and the Emperor Frederick seemed in the offing. The Genoese Count of Lavagna, Sinibaldo de' Fieschi, who had been elected Pope the year before, had the reputation of being a moderate man, possessing sound judgement. It was none too soon. During the preceding pontificate, that of Gregory IX, the conflict had been sharply exacerbated. At Gregory's death there had been an eighteen-month vacancy in the throne of St Peter, for Pope Celestine IV, elected in October 1241, had died in November. The Emperor's pressure on the cardinals was such that from November 1241 until June 1243 they had been unable to hold their conclave; he prevented it by keeping them prisoners.

Finally the negotiations had led to a détente. On Holy Thursday, 1244, in the square of St John Lateran in Rome, before an immense crowd and amid much emotion, Pope Innocent IV publicly received the oaths of fidelity of the Emperor's envoys. After years of enmity, which had caused much bloodshed in the cities of Italy, the Emperor swore to abide by the Pope's wishes in concluding the long-hoped-for peace. In his address the Pope called Frederick II 'our devoted son, a true Catholic prince'. Everything seemed to point towards the Pope's lifting the excommunication that had been laid on the Emperor.

Far from being impressed by these promising developments, however, some sceptics recalled that a similar situation had obtained during the first years of Gregory IX's pontificate. In 1230 the Pope and Emperor had even gone so far as to exchange the 'Kiss of Peace' at Anagni, 35 miles south-east of Rome – yet it had not prevented new conflicts from breaking out in 1239, with thundering new excommunications and declarations from both sides. Gregory IX had been over 90 years old on the latter occasion. Perhaps his successor, being less senile, might be less stubborn.

What was to follow proved the pessimists right. After great flurries of messages and messengers from both sides, the Pope travelled first to Città-Castellana, thirty miles north of Rome, then to Sutri, a few miles to the west, where he was to meet personally with Frederick II. To everyone's amazement, however, it was learned that the Pope had slipped out of his villa at Sutri in a disguise at night, and returned to Civitàvecchia, where a galley from Genoa was waiting to take him back to his native city, which received him in triumph. A few days later he fell ill and went to recuperate in the Cistercian abbey of St Andrew, at Sestri, just outside Genoa.

That year, 1244, Blanche and her family had been invited to be present at the general chapter-meeting of the Cistercian order. The Pope had granted a special dispensation allowing her to enter the monastery with twelve ladies-in-waiting, one of whom was her daughter Isabella. The King and his attendants had even been allowed to have meat served to them inside the monastery, which was ordinarily forbidden by the rules of the Order, except in the infirmary.

It must have been a profound joy for Blanche to be in that splendid abbey where St Bernard himself had preached, where his teachings were still faithfully handed down and his spirit taken as a model. It was a moment of special grace for her 'Cistercian' soul, walking under the flawless arches, listening to the gravely beautiful chants, watching the measured, unhurried rituals, which all corresponded to something she had been longing for more and more as the years went by: inner peace, but not a peace which excluded strong human feelings; rather, an active, loving source of strength, which she could welcome without doing violence to her feminine nature.

The monks showered honours upon her: her name and that of her son King Louis would appear henceforth in the regular masses of the Order; the birthdays of her parents, Alfonso and Eleanor of Castile, would be solemnly celebrated by all Cistercians; masses and special offices would be said for her, for her sons and their wives, on their birthdays and when they died.

But the high point of the visit was undoubtedly when the head Cistercian abbot and all the members of the chapter came in solemn procession to kneel before Blanche and to beg that she and her son would grant asylum in France to the Pope, who was being pursued by the Emperor Frederick II. (Louis had previously decided to step down on this occasion and leave the first place to his mother, knowing the Cistercian order to be specially close to her heart.) It was not the first time such a request had been addressed to a French king. In 1161 Louis VII had granted refuge to Alexander III when that Pope had to flee from the wrath of the Emperor Frederick Barbarossa.

Blanche had grown up, so to speak, with this Papacy-Empire struggle and understood it as well as anyone. She had heard much about Frederick II who, though six years her junior, had very early made a name for himself. He had become Emperor by promising to leave for the Holy Land the year after his accession (which would have meant a departure in 1221) but then had constantly put it off. He had a great admiration for everything Roman, had proclaimed himself 'the Roman Caesar forever Augustus' and declared that 'God hath stablished our Empire above all kings upon earth.' He had attempted to have Roman law and jurisprudence accepted everywhere, because of their centralizing, authoritarian tendency. He had founded a university in Naples for the sole purpose of training students in this discipline. In France it was not nearly in such favour. All in all, Frederick II was the exemplar *par excellence* of the Emperor

> Who on the earth and all abroad
> Would have himself perforce be lord.[11]

Blanche had already been asked several times by Gregory IX to step into the conflict.[12] She could scarcely find the new Pope's attitude reassuring when he declared: 'The King of

Kings hath decreed us His universal mandatary upon earth.'
It meant that Pope and Emperor were each citing God Almighty
as his justification for claiming unlimited temporal power.
Until now the French attitude had been simply to keep clear
of the whole thing – with one exception: when Frederick had
imprisoned a number of cardinals and abbots, to prevent their
holding a conclave and electing a Pope, Louis had written him
a very severe letter, threatening military action, and Frederick
had hastily released his captive cardinals.

In the present situation Louis had to make a more important
decision. His answer was what might be expected from his
piety and his devotion to the Church. He would support the
Pope and give him honourable protection from all unjust
attacks. But Louis added a condition that might be expected
from the feudal king that he was: before giving the Pope
asylum in France he must confer with his barons and counsellors.

It was certainly difficult in a squabble like that to know who
had right on his side. Why, for example, had Innocent IV
broken off the negotiations with the Emperor? Fear of a trap?
It might be, for Frederick had often shown a lack of scruple in
getting his way. But why did the Pope now wish to leave
Genoa? Was it because the Emperor was guarding the roads
leading from France into Italy, in order to cut off his enemy's
supplies? If that were so, were the Pope's material interests
taking precedence over his duty to protect the Church? When
he had been offered another personal interview with Frederick,
the Pope had replied that he had 'no longing to die a martyr
nor pine away in a dungeon's depths'. The Emperor, on the
other hand, put the blame, with some truth, on 'these clerks of
our time, who are given over to worldly things and besotted
on the world's delights, forsaking God because the abundance
of their riches doth stifle religion'. He went on to draw a disquieting inference from all this: 'It were a work of piety to
remove their guilty treasure from such as these . . .' Before a
quarrel such as this, between the two highest and mightiest

rulers in Christendom, many contemporary observers must have felt as did a certain English parish priest, who – according to Matthew Paris – told his parishioners that, not knowing which of the two should be excommunicated, the Pope or the Emperor, he excommunicated the guilty party, and absolved the innocent.

The fact remained that the King of France had no wish to take part in such a dubious quarrel in any role other than mediator. The Pope had already sounded out some of the principal Christian sovereigns: Jaime I of Aragon and Catalonia, and Henry III of England, as well as Louis IX of France. His final decision showed a good deal of political acumen. 'My children,' he declared to the Podestà of Genoa and some other notables who had come to visit him, 'I shall with Christ's help go to Lyons. I must ere I die publish to all Christians, to princes and prelates, the distress wherein faints God's Church, and the injustices heaped upon her. If I cannot go upon horseback, I shall be carried.' His fellow-citizens placed their ships at his disposal, but the previous sea-voyage had hurt his health. He went by land, sometimes on mule-back, sometimes carried in a litter, so ill that at Stella only twenty miles west of Genoa, they thought he was dying. Nevertheless he carried on: to Susa on the Franco-Italian border west of Turin, through the pass of the Grand Mont-Cenis, to Lanslebourg; along the valley of the River Arc, which winds through the Maurienne Alps, to Chambéry; and so to Lake Bourget, where he boarded a boat and sailed down the Rhône to Lyons, which he reached on December 2, 1244, after an exhausting journey of two months. Lyons was subject to the Holy Roman Emperor, but the relationship had become academic, and the county of Mâcon, just to the north, had since 1239 been directly attached to the French crown. Thus the Pope was next door to the kingdom where he knew he could find safety if he were threatened personally.

Just as the Pope was reaching Lyons the people of France were shaken by what was to them a much greater anxiety than the quarrel between the Church and the Emperor. The King was staying at the abbey of Maubuisson when a new and much more virulent attack of dysentery struck him down. He was running a high fever and the doctors had given him up for lost.

The chroniclers relate that Blanche had the relics of Christ's Passion taken to Louis's bedside, where she prayed aloud: 'Lord God! Save the kingdom of France!' Louis had already bidden those near him farewell: 'Thus it comes that I, who was most rich and most noble in this world, and exalted above all others by my treasure, my arms, and my alliances, cannot now force grim death or my illness to a truce, were it even for an hour. What then are all these worth?'[13]

One of the ladies-in-waiting became convinced that he was dead. Over the objections of another she drew the sheet over his head and opened the doors. The court had begun to file solemnly past the royal bed when a sigh was heard from under the sheet. The King was regaining consciousness. He moaned a little. The doctors were hastily summoned and found to their surprise that the man they had thought dying was recovering. They managed with great difficulty to force a few drops of warm broth through his tightened, clammy lips. Little by little his breathing became normal and life returned to the already stiffening body.

Blanche stood by as in a dream. What she had given up hoping for had happened. She had her son again. At her wish the relics were solemnly exposed in Saint-Denis on December 23, 1244. The people of Paris flocked to pray for the recovery of the King. On Christmas Day he was up again. But for Blanche that ordeal was scarcely over when another began. As soon as the King was strong enough to speak, his first announcement was that he would take the cross. When he himself told the story later to Joinville he said that his mother showed 'as much affliction thereat as had she seen him already dead'.[14]

Blanche's reaction was that of any attentive mother. She felt it was madness, after what Louis had just gone through, to risk his health again in a long, hazardous voyage, especially in a region where even the robust suffered from the climate. Louis had a fragile constitution; he was vulnerable to the heat, liable to fevers and malaria. Even the climate in the south of France had tried him. What would happen in Syria and Palestine!

Also, thinking as a queen, Blanche's common sense told her that the time was not ripe. The kingdom's affairs were precarious in a number of ways and called for the presence of the king. Her long years at the helm had inculcated in her the methodical outlook of the Capetians, as if the practical experience of her father-in-law, King Philip, had got into her blood, so that the impulsive Spanish girl, Eleanor of Aquitaine's grand-daughter, had become as cool-headed as those around her.

It is possible that still another thought was in Blanche's mind. She was sixteen when the crusaders had been sidetracked by their Venetian imbroglio and had wound up, instead of liberating Jerusalem, besieging and taking Constantinople and then having to defend it. Recalling the day-by-day accounts as the messengers reached the court of France, and the ill effects the fiasco had had on all Christendom, Blanche may have wondered if there were not some other way to honour the Holy Land than the way of violence, the endless struggles that had gone on now for a century and a half.

The Emperor Frederick II had thought himself very clever in gaining Jerusalem for the Christians without shedding a drop of blood. He had begun by declaring himself *ex officio* the head of the new Latin kingdoms in the East, a bit of sleight-of-hand by which he chalked up everyone else's past efforts to his own credit. Then he had negotiated with the sultans for free access to the Holy City for the Christians. It had been another fiasco; his diplomatic victories had not lasted ten years. The sultans had proved themselves craftier than he by laying down as a condition that the walls of Jerusalem be levelled. The result had been that in this same year 1244 an incursion of Khwarizmi Turks had once again wrested the Holy City, now totally defenceless, from the hands of the Christians.

Only one man had thought of a new approach: Francis of Assisi. Though Blanche best understood the monastic way of life as practised by the Cistercians, she had been keenly interested in the career of this wealthy Italian burgher who had left his father's counting-house and the world of business to espouse total poverty. When he had been elevated to sainthood in 1228, two years after his death, all Christendom had rejoiced. That was the year that the monks of the Mont-Saint-Michel had finished their cloisters, with their 227 little columns as if suspended in the sky, and almost the first thing they had done upon its completion was to put a statue of Francis of Assisi in the place of honour.

As every Christian at least dreamed of doing, Brother Francis had made the voyage to the Holy Land. But he had done more than that. He had gone to the crusaders' camp at Damietta. At that time the gateway to Islam was through Egypt. To reach Jerusalem it was necessary to battle in the delta of the Nile and on the banks of the Red Sea. When St Francis arrived in 1219 the Christians had been besieging Damietta for two years. The struggle had become bitter and no more prisoners were being taken. The Sultan of Egypt had promised a gold bezant for every Christian's head brought to him.

One day the turbaned watchers on the ramparts of Damietta spied two extraordinary figures. They were barefoot, clad in long robes of coarse homespun, girt at the waist with hempen cords; their hair blowing in the wind. And they were singing.

For two months nothing had been heard in that place but the whistling of the arrows, the rumbling of the Greek fire, and the screams of the wounded. Here now came these two, their hymns pealing to the sky, seemingly oblivious of all that. The Saracen archers on the battlements were so taken aback that they relaxed their drawn bows without loosing the shafts. Reaching the gates, Brother Francis cried: 'I am a Christian! Take me to your master!' Francis was a man who disarmed hate and turned aside anger. The fascinated guards let him and his companion in and took them before the Sultan. They stayed as his guests for several days. Brother Francis and the Sultan had many long heart-to-heart talks, each of them being a man in search of God. On bidding them farewell the Sultan wished to give them 'many fine gifts and treasures', but the man of God declined. He cared nothing for the world's goods and declared that God provided for the poor. The chronicler tells how the two men were then carefully escorted back towards the Christian army, and how the Sultan's last words to Francis were: 'Pray for me, that God may deign to discover to me that faith and law which please Him most.'[15]

That had been twenty-five years ago. Now the spiritual heirs of St Francis were found throughout Europe, and even in the Middle East. Called 'Cordeliers' from the knotted cord they wore round the waist, they helped to spread the Christmas custom of venerating the effigy of the Christ-Child, the 'Santo Bambino' as Brother Francis had called him, in his crib as he had been at Bethlehem. Sometimes in the Christian East the preaching of one of the Mendicants whom Brother Francis had scattered over the highways of the world would make converts even among the Saracens. In Europe countless Christian laymen, organized in what was called the Third Order, joined in some of the activities, particularly the prayers, of the full-fledged friars of St Francis. Louis and Margaret loved these 'sons of Francis' and helped them in every way they could. Margaret habitually went to a Franciscan friar for confession.

It is conceivable that Blanche may have been wondering if the time had come to follow more in the footsteps of Brother Francis than in those of the crusaders.* In order to do that, however, she must first set her own house in order, beginning in France itself. She must settle the bickerings, contain the overweening ambitions, moderate the greed of the usurers, those

---

* It must be emphasized that this is the author's own conjecture, unsupported by documentary evidence. None the less it seems plausible in the light of Blanche's general attitude, which was doggedly hostile – surprisingly so – to her son's plans for a crusade.

blood-suckers of the people, and assure justice to all. It would be necessary to begin with the King's officials themselves, who too often overstepped their authority. The King and Blanche had received countless complaints about their extortionary methods. Many of them were so far away that it was impossible to supervise them properly. They were using their authority to mete out injustice and feather their own nests at the expense of the people. For one careful and conscientious bailiff there were ten unjust and rapacious ones.

Matthew Paris tells how Blanche enlisted the Bishop of Paris, William of Auvergne, to help her dissuade Louis from going on his crusade. It led to a dramatic scene, with almost comic overtones.

'Sire, bethink you that when you took the cross, vowing so harshly and unconscionably, you were then ill and, to say all, your understanding was bereft. Your mind was vacant; you were not your own master. Wherefore the words you did then speak were without weight and authority. The Pope will readily grant us dispensation for this oath, being advised of the dire state of the realm and your faint health. See here on the one side the redoubted might of the schismatical Frederick; here on the other side the costly snares of the King of England; there the traitorous ruses of Poitou, for all you have but lately subdued it; and the threatening obstinacy of the Albigenses. Germany is in turmoil. Italy has no peace. The access to the Holy Land is uncertain; one can hardly say if they would receive you there. Behind your back would be the unrelenting hatred between the Pope and Frederick, still implacable, to which you would abandon us.'

Then Blanche added her own plea, deliberately exaggerating her forebodings: 'Well-beloved son, hearken to your closest friends' counsels, grant their pleas, and heed not your sole prudency. Remember the virtue it is, and pleasing to God, to heed your mother and agree with her judgements. Stay – the Holy Land shall not be the more ill for it. We shall dispatch thither more armies from France than if you went yourself. God is not grudging or stubborn. Your late illness is dispensation enough, when you were deprived of reason, your senses idle, yourself almost dead, in any case your spirit wandering . . .'

The King answered: 'Thus, you would have it, I took the cross because I'd lost my wits. So be it. I yield me to your counsels and your wishes. I shall put down the cross. I do resign my cross to you.' And putting his hand to his shoulder he tore away the emblem that had been sewn there. 'My lord Bishop, here is the cross that I had taken up. I deliver it unto you with my good will.' Then, as those present, scarcely able to believe their eyes, were breaking into congratulations and huzzas of joy, the King's countenance and voice changed, and he went on: 'Friends, you will allow I have my wits about me now. My will is free and nothing impaired. So now I would my cross be restored to me. He that is all-knowing be my witness, that I will not touch a bite till I shall have got it back again.'[16]

From then on the 'journey oversea' was the chief preoccupation of the court of France. The preparations were undertaken systematically. No political alarums and excursions – frequent enough during those years – were allowed to deflect the main purpose. Nor were personal matters such as the birth of Philip, the royal couple's second son, in 1245, or that of little John, three years later.

John lived only a few days and was buried in the family crypt at Royaumont, next to his little sister Blanche. The children's effigies can still be seen on the two tombs, which are encased in gilded and enamelled copper plates. These fortunately escaped the scrap-metal drives during the civil wars and the French Revolution. The likenesses are beautifully framed in medallions decorated with enamel foliatures done in delicate colours. The two childish silhouettes, with their coats of arms, stand out against a fine-grained background: John with his feet upon a lion; Blanche with hers resting upon a greyhound. With two of his children now buried at Royaumont, the King's favourite abbey had become a kind of private Saint-Denis, the repository of Louis and Margaret's personal bereavements.

The main point to be settled in the King's departure plans was the port of embarcation. The land route, used a hundred years before by his great-grandfather Louis VII, was now out of the question. Despite the risk of shipwreck, the sea was by far the more practical and less costly route, all the more so for important recent improvements in the art of navigation. Whereas before, ships had had to keep close to the coast, they could now sail off on the high seas without fear of losing their way, thanks to the clever device known as the 'compass', consisting of a magnetized needle, which, when sheathed in a straw and allowed to float in a bowl of water, would always line itself up in a north-south axis. No one knows who first brought this marvellous instrument to Europe some time around 1200, but it was an engineer in Louis IX's army, Peter Maricourt, known as 'Peregrinus' ('The Pilgrim'), who in 1269 first wrote a detailed description of the invention, in a letter from Italy (where he was helping to besiege a city) to a friend back in France.

Sailors were also starting to use two-masted vessels, with bowsprits, which greatly increased their speed. Manœuvrability was also much improved by the use of a new kind of rudder, which enabled a ship to be brought about as readily as a knight turns his horse. There were also maps, traced on parchment, which helped the mariner to locate the dangers along the coast and the ports of call. Now the heavy vessels leaving the ports of Montpellier, Barcelona, Genoa, and Marseilles every year were able to carry up to a thousand pilgrims in addition to the cargo.

Louis would leave by sea, but he was determined not to have to make use of a port located on foreign territory, such as that of Marseilles, Genoa or Pisa, the last two in the Holy Roman Empire. The Italian ports were all more or less involved in the struggle between the Pope and the Emperor. If he used one of them he was liable to get involved himself, which was precisely what he intended to avoid. As for Venice, it was too far away, and furthermore everyone knew what kind of price the Venetians were liable to ask in payment for their services!

So the King of France, having no port, would make a port. There was nothing remarkable in that at a time when new towns were springing up all over France. The problem was finding the right place. Finally a somewhat reluctant decision was made in favour of a place which the fishermen called Aigues-Mortes. It is a sandy hillock in the midst of the marshes of the Rhône delta. Its advantage to Louis was that, as part of the seneschalsy of Beaucaire, it was the only point at which his domains touched the Mediterranean. Only a few monks lived there, cultivating their vineyards in the sandy soil. After some bargaining with the abbot of Psalmodi a port was built a little way inland, with a channel leading to the sea. Soon a tower, called the Tower of Constance, started going up in the midst of wagons full of stones, wooden beams and lime. Planners laid out the street-grid of the town-to-be: parallel carriage-ways lined up one way, with cross-streets at right angles to them, creating a network round the main square in the centre, in which the church of Notre-Dame-du-Sablon was built.

According to custom the King drew up a charter for the burghers of the new town.

We, Louis, by the grace of God King of the French, hereby make known to all now present and to come, that we have herewith granted to the people of our town of Aigues-Mortes the following freedoms and privileges; to wit:
– That the dwellers in this place shall be exempt and free of all taxes, levies, and tallage . . .
– That they shall never be required to make payment of money in place of the military chevauchée, and that the

latter shall, from year's end to year's end, be no more than forty days only . . .
– That they shall be forever free of all tolls, whether on land or sea . . .
– That the commonalty of the town may have at least four councillors . . . and that the men of this place shall be free to choose their councillors, even without the consent of our court . . ., etc.
Done at Paris in this month of May of the year 1246.

Though resigned, Blanche watched all this without enthusiasm. She no longer took a very active part in the affairs of the kingdom. The ledgers of these years show more and more clearly the distinction between her personal expenditures and those of the court.

Louis had decided to use the island of Cyprus for his supply-base. Year after year, in the proper season, he stocked grain and wine. The grain piled up in silos and the wine in casks. According to the tales of the time they became small mountains which one could sight on the coast from afar. Cyprus was ruled by one of the Lusignan family, a kinsman of the Counts of La Marche. He was well-disposed towards the crusaders and might be expected to join them when the fighting began. Louis, as was his habit, was also having a number of war-machines built by his artillery master, Jocelyn of Cournault.

If one can believe Matthew Paris, Louis used a subterfuge to induce his barons to join him in taking the cross. It occurred at his Christmas court in the year 1245, at which Blanche was present.

As we have seen, it was traditional at the Christmas gatherings for kings and great lords to give garments to their vassals. The story goes that that year Louis had more than the usual number purchased. On each of the costly capes, lined with fine vair, he caused to be sewn secretly during the night a small orphrey cross. The capes were given out late at night on Christmas Eve, the King requesting those who received them to put them on before dawn for mass. So it happened that each of the barons, going to church in the small hours, noted that the man next to him was wearing a crusader's cross on his shoulder. The story concludes that each of them, discovering that he himself had become a crusader unawares, had the tact to fall in with the pious stratagem and join with the King whom they called 'huntsman of pilgrims and fisher of men'.

Though she took little part in the preparations for the crusade, Blanche went in person with her son to help him at his meeting with Pope Innocent IV at Cluny.

For his establishment at Lyons the Pope had elected to settle in the monastery of Saint-Just, to the north of the old town and some distance removed from the River Saône. It was a place then described as 'fortified, mighty, and most noble'. Its position on top of a steep hill was easily defendable, as were its ramparts, and it looked to be a fairly safe residence even if the Emperor himself should arrive in Lyons. The town could not complain of the Pope's sojourn there. He contributed generously to the rebuilding of the Cathedral of St John and to the construction of the bridge of La Guillotière over the Rhône. Also the tradesmen of Lyons were pleased with the increased commercial activity brought about by the presence of the Papal court, and the townsfolk in general benefited from the establishment of a school of theology and law, in 1245.

The Pope's first move on settling in Lyons had been to call a council. He opened it with a speech that was one long cry of anguish. He called upon the whole world to witness the 'five wounds' in the body of Christendom: the need to reform the clergy; the need to recapture Jerusalem from the Saracens; the need to defend the Latin Empire of Constantinople; the menace of the Tartar advance in Hungary; and the persecution of the Church by Frederick II.

It was this last 'wound' which seemed to be the most urgent in the Pope's mind, and the one which he wished to remedy immediately. The council opened on June 28, 1245, and ended on July 17 with a new excommunication of the Emperor – his third so far. The assembled bishops were treated to the spectacle of Frederick's devoted representative, the jurist Thaddeus of Suessa, beating his breast and uttering loud lamentations. He was Frederick's man to the bitter end and could not understand how such a harsh sentence could be meted out to his master after his own able and persuasive pleading.

A few months later the King of France set out for Burgundy. Frederick had protested to all the princes of Christendom against the decisions of the Council of Lyons, and Louis had agreed to attempt a reconciliation. The meeting was scheduled for November 30, 1245, St Andrew's Day, in the abbey of Cluny.

The royal party that drew up under the high walls and seven towers of the abbey church of Cluny had a strikingly warlike appearance. 'In the van rode an hundred armed crossbowmen, on steeds richly caparisoned. Thereafter of knights an hundred others with sparkling hauberks, bearing round shields and targes, the coursers as the men clad in whole mail. Thereafter again a third body of an hundred men armed at all points, their swords drawn. Fourthly rode the King amid the glorious knighthood of his realm, in numbers truly not to be believed.' The King had clearly intended this martial display to suggest prudence to Frederick, who, as it happened, was just then off waging fierce war against the rebelling Lombards, with many hangings and mutilations.

This St Andrew's Day meeting was one of the great moments in the history of the abbey of Cluny. Its church was the largest in Christendom, and remained so until the rebuilding of St Peter's in Rome two centuries later. The monastery buildings were on a comparable scale. The chroniclers of the time note that both visitors, the Pope and the King of France, together with their enormous retinues, were lodged and fed without the ordinary routine of the monks in residence being in any way disturbed. They carried on in their own dormitories and re-fectories, and held their chapter-meeting, as if what had descended on them were no more than the usual crowd of pilgrims. Yet the Pope had with him twelve cardinals, the patriarchs of Antioch and Constantinople, eighteen archbishops and numerous abbots from other abbeys, all gathered at Cluny for the occasion. The King was attended by his whole family, Blanche first and foremost, for she was to take an active part in the discussions. There were also the King's brother Robert, his sister Isabella, and perhaps his two other brothers Alphonse and Charles. In any case the Emperor of Constantinople, Baldwin, was there, with several noblemen of his entourage, including the Duke of Burgundy, the Count of Dampierre, the Sires of Bourbon and of Beaujeu, and others. It all added up to an extraordinary gathering at the St Andrew's Day mass, which was celebrated by the Pope himself. The annals of the period note that it was the first occasion on which the 'cardinal's hat' was used. In accordance with a decision taken at the recent Council of Lyons, the twelve cardinals wore the red hat whose colour signified their readiness to risk their lives and to shed their blood on behalf of the faith and the Church. Frederick's treatment of their colleagues four years earlier, when he imprisoned them and prevented their holding the conclave to elect a new Pope, gave more than academic meaning to the red colour of the hats. Moreover, several of the prelates present had taken the cross along with the King of France, among them one of the cardinals, Odo of Châteauroux, the papal legate for the Holy Land, as well as the Bishops of Clermont and Langres, Hugh of La Tour and Hugh of Rochecorbon. These two, who went with Louis to the fighting in the Holy Land, were destined not to return.

For a whole week now the discussions were held, with only three persons participating: The Pope, King Louis and Blanche. What was said and decided among them was never made known. But we may suppose, as did Matthew Paris, that they talked about the need to restore harmony between the Empire and the Papacy, and 'the means to an honourable peace, forasmuch as the King was firmly resolved to be off to Jerusalem with many other noblemen of France, the same being already marked with the cross as much for loyalty to the King as to God. Wherefore they could not set off by sea or by way of the Emperor's lands unless the Church be wholly at peace and all Christendom of one mind for it.'

The talks undoubtedly dealt also with the marriage plans of the King's younger brother, Charles of Anjou, and Beatrice of Provence, youngest of Raymond-Bérenger's four daughters. Her father had just died, leaving a will in which he named Beatrice his heiress. The girl had been besieged by a number of ardent suitors. Among them Jaime I, King of Aragon and Catalonia, nicknamed 'The Conqueror'. Jaime had set out to conquer Beatrice's heart for his son Pedro by besieging her city of Aix with armed forces. 'Whenas the King was departing he did send a large body of his men to free by the sword the Lady Beatrice, youngest sister of Margaret of France, the same being besieged by the King of Aragon with his army at war . . . impudently meaning thereby, it was said, to wed her to his son.'

It was a brisk campaign. Charles of Anjou himself led the French forces. On the way down he met an envoy of Raymond VII of Toulouse. When Raymond had learned of the death of his old enemy Raymond-Bérenger he had immediately repudiated his wife, Margaret of La Marche, the daughter of his ally, the Count of Lusignan. The lady had not been too upset by this, for their marriage had never been consummated. An annulment of the marriage had been granted by the Pope on September 25, whereupon Raymond had evidently thought he could acquire by marriage that tempting county of Provence that he had not been able to take by force of arms, even with the help of the Holy Roman Emperor. 'He had sent a messenger to the Queen Mother of France, to beg that it might please her to bring to pass that which had hitherto been treated of between himself and the lady's father. The same messenger did meet upon the way the Lord Charles, likewise hastening to plight his troth with her.' It became a question of whose spurs were the sharper. They turned out to be Charles's, and seven weeks later, on January 31, 1246, the wedding took place at Paris. Charles of Anjou became the Count of Provence.

He was an insatiably ambitious young man. Among other things he does not seem to have thanked his mother Blanche as adequately as she deserved. He complained that the festivities attendant upon his wedding were not so lavish as those for Louis's wedding at Sens. 'I am the son of a king and queen,' he is supposed to have said, 'and he was not' (by which he meant that when his brother Louis was born, in 1214, Philip Augustus was still King of France, while when he, Charles, was born in 1226, Louis VIII and Blanche were on the throne). We have the story only from Matthew Paris's acid pen, and it may not be true. Still, there may not have been time enough to organize a wedding as brilliant as usual. King Louis had only left Burgundy towards the middle of December. On the 8th, the Feast of the Conception of the Blessed Virgin, he, with Blanche and his brothers, was present at the dedication of the Church of St Peter of Mâcon, which the Pope personally consecrated.

However, if Charles was only half-satisfied with the outcome of the race for Beatrice's hand and dowry, there were others who did not hide their complete dissatisfaction. Jaime's and Raymond of Toulouse's feelings may be imagined. But in addition Henry III of England and his brother Richard of Cornwall, both of them also sons-in-law of the departed Raymond-Bérenger, found it quite out of order that he should have left the heritage of Provence to his youngest daughter who now brought it to a son of France. Oddly enough, Queen Margaret herself was the most annoyed of all. She had never liked her young brother-in-law Charles; now, doubly allied to him, she began to despise him. Their enmity created a painful atmosphere at court, where until now all had been harmony. Margaret went so far as to declare openly that she preferred her English relatives to her French ones.

For Blanche, however, this redoubled alliance with Provence was everything she had dreamed of. Now those regions which had been the scene of such bloody struggles during her husband's reign were sure to be peaceful. Her efforts in bringing about the alliance had been seconded by the Pope, who had perceived in it a means of both scoring off the Emperor and gaining the protection of the powerful King of France.

At Pentecost, 1246, Charles's knighthood was celebrated at the castle of Melun, this time with all the splendour that his heart desired. It was then that he began to be styled Charles of Anjou, since the two holdings of Maine and Anjou, left to him by his father's will, were officially handed over to him at that time. He was to lose no time in showing his talents as administrator in his wife's domains – also his heavy-handedness in meting out justice.

Whenas Charles, being made Count of Provence, betook himself to those lands, he set about doing justice, and did punish pilfering, hang thieves, and rid the highways of robbers [says a foreign observer]. The better to do so he contrived to hold personally all the castles in the land, so as to leave the rogues no refuge, for hitherto those holding the castles were wont to befriend and shelter the miscreants, keeping them and giving them all the succour they might.

There were administrative problems in the French royal domains also, and there is reason to believe that Blanche continued to take an interest in such matters. In January 1247 the King dispatched certain letters patent. He had named investigators whose mission was 'to set down in writing, and to examine in the manner we have prescribed, such complaints as may be brought against ourself or our ancestors, as likewise allegations touching upon the injustices, extortions and all other faults of which our bailiffs, provosts, foresters, sergeants, and their assistants might have been guilty since our reign began.'

It was a quite remarkable innovation, whose importance can scarcely be overestimated. Till then, when kings had sent personal representatives and seneschals to oversee the management of local affairs, their job was essentially to look after the royal interests by supervising the subordinate agents on the spot. This was not the case with the investigations ordered in 1247. The 'lords commissioners' were to deal directly with the people. They were neither high prelates nor mighty barons, but rather Mendicant Friars – Dominicans and Franciscans – already in close touch with the common people. They were known as the 'friars who do look after the restitutions'. Their job was to make the King's own agents, whenever they had abused their power, disgorge.

It hardly needs saying that these investigations constituted an entirely new departure. Through them Blanche's son earned his renown as a justice-giving king, a true friend of the poor and lowly, for this friendship was seen not only to consist in alms-giving, but in royal decrees, in practical measures designed to let the poor be heard, to listen to those to whom the high and mighty would not listen. It was a milestone in the history of government administration.

The investigators wrote down a huge number of facts, often very trivial ones. Some of these reports, traced on their parchment scrolls, have come down to us. They give us details of the innumerable little daily dramas of people with names like 'Will Drink-water', 'Stephen Snotty-nose', 'Ivo Ass's shadow', 'Stephen Fire-pot', and so on, it being a time when there were few regular family names, but many nicknames.

The investigators were particularly attentive to the grievances arising from the wars and civil disturbances which had affected certain regions during the preceding thirty years, specially Normandy and the south of France. Many complaints were heard from those whose lands had been seized because they had been in England at the time of the siege of Bellême. Such confiscations had often been carried out indiscriminately. For instance, one William the Seneschal, from Authieux-sur-Calonne, north of Lisieux, had been deprived of a property in Normandy which brought in thirty *sous* a year because he had gone off to England to claim his wife's dowry, for which he had had the King's permission. The preparations for invading England, thirty years before, had left bitter memories in Artois. Some things had been commandeered and never paid for. Thus, Walter Hanikaigne recalled that his mother Margaret had been obliged to surrender some leather goods and the sum of 47 *livres*, none of which had ever been made good. Yet Margaret Hanikaigne was from Tournai and had remained faithful to King Philip of France. Walter Pavio complained that when the Lord Louis had gone over to England he had proclaimed up and down the land that any merchant who sent grain, wine, or other provisions by boat to England, to supply his army, would be repaid double the amount if the merchandise were captured by the English. Walter Pavio had sent a boat loaded with grain to help Louis, but the English had seized it on the high seas, along with many other ships out of Gravelines. Walter Pavio's servants had been killed and he himself had lost 500 *livres* in the affair, while his fellow-merchants lost 3000 *livres*. All of them claimed compensation.

It was the same story in Languedoc, the Albigensian lands, and the seneschalsies of Beaucaire and Carcassonne, where there had been many extortions. Some people had been dispossessed during the siege of Carcassonne, such as Reine and her sister, the daughters of Ermengarde of Cavenac, who lost their paternal heritage when the town was destroyed. The King's seneschal had compensated everyone but them, they said. At Tourbes, south-west of Montpellier, there were peasants who had been required to pay taxes at the very moment they were setting out to fight for the King at the bridge over the River Vidourle.

It was a veritable Pandora's box of grievances including many very trivial ones. Maria La Saunière complained of losing a blanket and a pillow. Simon, a poor Jew of Arles, said that his brown cloak lined with rabbit's fur had been taken. Through it all, however, one can discern the important events taking place. At Arras William Le Vieux and his sons had had their five well-harnessed horses requisitioned and only one horse had been returned, without its harness. Peter Serda and his eleven companions, from Roullens, west of Carcassonne, had been ordered by Theobald of Corbeil, an officer of the King, to go to the siege of Montségur for one night, 'to cast stones with the mangonel'; each of them had been promised twelve pence for it, which had never been paid. Peter Bordas, of Villemagne, had been accused of heresy and put in prison because he had sheltered – though forced to it despite himself, he claimed – a renegade from Toulouse with his wife, one Stephen Massa. David, a Jew of Béziers, had been despoiled by the Seneschal William of Ormes of a small farmhouse he owned outside Béziers; he asked that it be restored to his children. Many petty lords complained that they had been dispossessed because they had taken up arms against the King at the time of Trencavel's revolt. Pons, the castellan of Villalbe, near Carcassonne, had had four oxen taken from him in the middle of the market-place just after he had bought them, on the pretext that he had them from *faidits*, renegades. Isarn Guiffred, of Couffoulens, east of Carcassonne, had put his grain in safety at Leuc, near by, during the fighting, but when he came to fetch it away after peace was declared he was told that it was the 'King's spoils of war'.

All the petty miscellaneous wrongs and alleged wrongs of the period were written down in the investigators' parchment scrolls: trees felled without the owners' permission, like those at Pézenas, north-east of Béziers, used to build war-machines; wandering cows seized, like those of one Isabelle Chaucebure, because they had been found grazing in an enclosed wood; assaults and brawls; moral offences, like that involving Martin Frottecouenne, who had been imprisoned by two villagers of Beaufort-en-Vallée, east of Angers, because a girl accused him of raping her; even those two boys in a village in Normandy who had given a drubbing to their father's concubine.

The striking thing in all these affairs, from the most serious to the most trivial, is how carefully the little people were heard.

Anyone – serf, Jew – could come and complain, and his grievance was duly recorded. Even those who had till now been afraid to voice their complaints, and those to whom the King's agents had refused to listen – all were now given a hearing. Everyone was aware that a new situation had arisen. The deposition of one Raymond Bernard, carpenter and boat-builder at Roullens, is significant. He came to complain that the town bailiff had fleeced him of the revenues of his fields and vineyards. When he was asked why he had not complained before, he replied: 'Then I was young, feeble and poor, and never once did that blameful bailiff or his successors deign to hear me.' For the first time justice was siding with the little people; it was seeking them out, letting them have their say.

Without disparaging her son's well-known reputation as a giver of justice, we may wonder to what extent all this was Blanche's doing. There is certainly a 'maternal' quality to such investigations. Blanche's concern for the little people was noted by her contemporaries: 'She did take care that the common people be not trodden down by the rich, and gave even-handed justice.' We sense something indefinably feminine in her approach. It is the same thing that made her say at the siege of the castle of Bellême: 'These good folk are cold. Above all they must be warmed.'

It must also be pointed out that in 1247 these investigations were undertaken very thoroughly in Blanche's personal estates of Hesdin, Bapaume, and Lens, those which had comprised her dowry until 1237. It was Blanche who gave the order, when she was at Caen, to pay thirty *livres* long due to Robert of Champeaux. In some instances she intervened to have prisoners' sentences shortened. She also did so to compel Colin of Lorris, a soldier of the King, to pay back to Peter Potet of Loudun the 600 *sous* he owed him. The plaintiffs very often linked her name to that of the King, appealing 'to the King who now reigns and to his most beloved mother'. It seems clear that in this business of justice to the little people, as in all the other affairs of state, we can make no distinction between King Louis's purposes and those of Blanche.*

Finally, it was quite in the mood of the time to wish to restore ill-gotten gains and repair all injustices before leaving on a crusade. To do so helped one to get ready for the crusade. On the eve of his departure Joinville acted within his own modest domains as the King had done in all of France. He called his men together and said: 'My lords, I am off oversea and know not whether I shall return again. So now do you come forward. If I have done to any of you aught that was not just, I will redress it to each in turn, as was always my wont, who shall lay his cause before my counsellors.' He added, according to his own account: 'And thereupon, lest my presence sway any, I left the council and did maintain all that was therein concluded, without debate.'

With every passing day the departure of the great pilgrimage drew closer. At one point it seemed that it might be postponed. The Emperor Frederick II claimed he was coming to Lyons. He had summoned his vassals and ordered them to be at Chambéry in arms, three weeks after Pentecost, 1247. One can imagine the flurry this caused in the Pope's entourage. The King, Blanche, and their family were at Pontigny at the time, north-east of Auxerre, where they had gone to take part in what was for them a ceremony fraught with meaning. Edmund Rich of Abingdon, the Archbishop of Canterbury from 1233 till his death in 1240, had just been canonized by Pope Innocent IV. Now his mortal remains were to be solemnly laid to final rest in the minster of Pontigny.**

* It is most significant that a querulous seneschal, Peter of Athies, when pressed to do justice in the King's name, burst out angrily: 'What would you? Out with it quickly! I should gladly give a hundred silver marks that I might hear no more of the King, nor of the Queen!'
** When Pope Gregory IX's legate, Cardinal Otho, had arrived in England in 1237 at Henry III's request, Edmund found himself thwarted and over-ruled at every turn. Finally in protest, he had gone into voluntary exile at Pontigny in the summer of 1240, and had died at the monastery of Soisy, halfway between Paris and Troyes, that November.

A few days before this, messengers brought Frederick II the news that if he were to cross the Alps he would be met by King Louis of France, with the King's mother Blanche and his three brothers. Already the King's vassals and knights were gathering on the banks of the Rhône and of the Saône. Frederick decided not to put it to the test. On June 17, 1247, Pope Innocent IV sent multiple letters to Louis, Blanche, and Louis's brothers full of his gratitude: ' "Let the heavens rejoice, and let the earth be glad!" '

The Minstrel of Rheims has left us a description of the parting of Blanche and her sons that is moving in its simplicity.

Whenas the King had his way made ready, he took his staff and baldric at Notre-Dame-de-Paris, and there the Bishop sang him Mass. Then he came out, unhosed and barefoot, himself, the Queen, his brothers and their ladies. And all the monks and people of Paris bore them company till Saint-Denis, weeping and wailing amain. There did the King bid them farewell and send them back to Paris, himself also weeping no little in taking leave of them.

But the Queen, his mother, went on and journeyed with him three days despite him. Then said the King: 'Mother most sweet, by that allegiance that you owe to me, I bid you return henceforth. I leave my three children for your wards, Louis, Philip, and Isabelle. I leave this realm of France to you to govern it. Truly I know that they well guarded, and it well governed, be.' Then, weeping, the Queen did answer him: 'Fairest son, how can my heart suffer that we be sundered? Truly, if it break not atwain it be harder than stone, for never was son to mother better than you to me.' Then swooning she fell, and the King did lift her again and kiss her, and weeping took his way. And the King's brothers and their ladies took their leave of her and wept. And she did swoon anew and lay long senseless. When she recovered she said: 'Sweet son and fair, I shall see you nevermore, my

251

heart hath told me.' And she spake true, for she was dead ere he returned.

We can picture how Blanche must have cast a long last look on those four sons, each so different from the others, yet each embodying some trait of her husband, or herself. 'Two among the brothers were very mild and meek, soft of body and little apt to arms; these were Louis and Alphonse. The other two, Robert and Charles, were men of undaunted mettle, strong and robustious, skilled in the manage of arms and most warlike.' All four were in fact excellent knights when it came to fighting, but the chronicler rightly discerned the underlying traits in each: Robert and Charles impetuous; Louis and Alphonse milder and more restrained. But Robert, for all his impulsiveness, was tender-hearted, and Louis secretly loved him the best. So Joinville tells it, at any rate, drawing upon what the King confided to him much later. But Louis himself was the crowd's favourite, as he was his mother's. 'The King was tall and delicate, rather slender, but of a seemly stature. He had an angel's face and gracious bearing,' says Salimbene, an Italian Franciscan who saw the royal pilgrimage procession go by in Sens. He describes it as follows:

> The King came to the Friars Minor Church, not in regal pomp but clad as a pilgrim, his scrip and baldric at his neck . . . He came not on horseback but afoot, his brothers the three Counts following in the same manner and with like humility. The King did not cumber himself with a train of noblemen, but rather heeded the prayers and approbation of the poor. One might in truth have taken him more for a monk than a knight in arms, and this because of his heart's devotion. He went into the Friars' church, bent his knee most piously, and prayed before the altar. When he came out again he stopped a moment at the door, myself being nigh . . . When we were assembled in the chapter the King began to speak, commending him, his brothers, the Queen his mother, and all his suit, and he did claim the Friars'

prayers and suffrages. Certain of the French Friars, who were nigh to me, were touched at the heart with pious devotion and did weep without retention.

The good monk was rather difficult to please where facial beauty and expression were concerned. He found that the French women, those at Sens anyway, all looked like serving-girls. But he had nothing but admiration when describing King Louis.

It was at L'Hôpital, on the outskirts of the thriving town of Corbeil, eighteen miles south of Paris, that they parted. Alphonse remained with his mother; he was to stay another year in France before joining his brothers in the Holy Land. It was a bright June day. Blanche and Alphonse must have watched the procession ride down the hill towards the valleys of the Seine and the Essonne. The horses' hoofbeats blended with the deafening roar of the water-wheels beneath the bridges. The sun glinted on the spire of the large church of Notre-Dame, and on those of Saint-Spire, Saint-Étienne, and the little chapel of the commandery of Saint-Jean-en-l'Ile. With all their banners flying, the knights and men-at-arms wound up the further hill as the motley file stretched out along the road.

Many barons of northern France were with the King. They were to be joined by many more from the south. Soon those faithful vassals whose loyalty had never wavered were riding side by side with others who, only a few short years before, had seemed implacable enemies: the Count of Brittany, Peter Mauclerc, and southern barons such as Trencavel of Béziers and Oliver of Termes. It was eloquent proof that concord and peace had really come to France.

Blanche dried her tears. Once more she must forget her own grief, master her own feelings. She was the Queen. She gave an order, and the escort wheeled about and started back to Paris.

VII

'LIKE A LILY'

Notre Dame's two towers, like two arms upraised in prayer, were finished. The north tower, perhaps for being a copy of the other, seemed a little heavier, a little less delicate. One should never do exactly the same thing twice; the second time will always lack the boldness of discovery.

But Notre Dame was beautiful. Her façade displayed colours as dazzling as those of an illuminated manuscript. Her massive underpinnings rose up to the airy grace of her tiny columns. Her new neighbour across the way, the Sainte-Chapelle, by the Palace, saluted her with its fragile spire, and, with her, overtopped the twelve parish belfries around them.

The people of Paris were proud of Notre Dame. They loved to gaze at the great triple portal with the apostles marching on eternally, to identify the twenty-four kings of Judah lined up on the high gallery, and point out, among the blessed souls in the central tympanum beneath over-arching flights of angels, the handsome Negro with his ecstatic smile.

Notre Dame's beauty was complete, the stone-masons' yard about her was gone. The work had lasted eighty years and involved many worries for Bishop Maurice of Sully and his predecessors. A man's lifetime was not too much to ask to raise a cathedral big enough to hold almost all the faithful of the diocese of Paris. But now the masons and lead-workers were returning and setting up their tool-sheds. The architect in charge, John of Chelles, a past master in the field, was at work on his plans in the draughtsman's booth. The glassmakers were coating their long tables with chalk in which to trace the lacy networks of stained-glass windows. The cathedral was not finished after all. It had been decided to enlarge the transept and let in the light through a huge rose-window of blue, a mighty labour of the glazier's art to be dedicated to Our Lady. The job was not yet done. The work went on, as life goes on, never complete, always more vibrant with challenge.

For Blanche also the work went on. Her job as Queen was not yet done. The King, off on his far pilgrimage, had left her the care of the kingdom, just as Philip, sixty years before, had left his kingdom in his mother's care. His rival, Richard Lionheart, had also left his realm in the care of his mother, Eleanor of Aquitaine. Blanche, little by little, had stood aside and let Louis govern France, but she had never entirely stopped helping. Louis had approved of her being 'she who deals with all the kingdom's business.'[1] She would have liked to go into quiet seclusion in some monastery, as had the Countess of Mâcon, for instance, who had turned over the suzerainty of her county to the King and retired to Maubuisson. But it could not be. Blanche must pick up the reins and plunge back into active life. The King could not have left on his crusade if she had not been willing to do this. But he had gone off in complete confidence, knowing that his kingdom was in good hands.

So Blanche, at sixty, was back in harness again. Clearly she could face the world with less apprehension than she had twenty-five years before. She knew the politics of Europe as she knew the palm of her hand. But her joy in life was gone, gone with that colourful army that had formed up and left despite everything she could do to prevent it. Now she must show her love for her beloved eldest son, the handsome knight with dreaming eyes whom her heart told her she would never see again, by standing in for him, and stand in she would. It would not be the first time she had had to summon up 'a man's valour within a woman's heart'.

Her son Alphonse had stayed with her, delaying his departure for several months. The truce with England would shortly be over, and then what would King Henry do? For a while it had been hoped that he would take the cross also. He had not, though a few Englishmen had crossed the Channel to swell the ranks of the departing army; among them William de Longespée (or Longsword), the Earl of Salisbury, who had accompanied Richard, Earl of Cornwall, to the Holy Land in 1240. Would there be war with England yet again? If so, the Count of Poitiers was on hand. At twenty-eight he was quite able to lead a military campaign. He would also have the job later of escorting the wife of Robert of Artois to the Holy Land. She was pregnant and had stayed in France to have her baby. But after that she meant to go off crusading at her husband's side, just as her sisters-in-law had done.

Blanche must now be a mother to the children of Louis and Margaret: Isabella (later the Queen of Navarre); little Louis, the heir, who was only four and a half; and Philip, three years old. The children lived most of the time in the Louvre, whose castellan was responsible for them. Once more it was Blanche's job to oversee the training of a king.

Her own daughter Isabella was with her, helping her in countless ways. She was a striking young woman of twenty-three, 'the noblest dame who ever was on earth; most gracious was she, and of radiant beauty.' She resembled Louis and was so blonde that her maids said the hairs left in the comb when they had attended her were like gold threads. They saved those blonde hairs and treasured them almost as they would have the relics of a saint, for Isabella was virtually worshipped by everyone around her. Blanche had never needed to be stern with her, even as a child. Rather, she had watched with secret wonder, as she had with Louis, her daughter growing up. Isabella's only fault was an ascetic tendency which Blanche considered excessive. She had to watch that Isabella be always dressed in keeping with her station in life, and not neglect the adornments proper to a princess. Isabella's whole life was an inner one. She was later to confide to her sister-nuns that she 'did as truly yield her heart to Our Lord when decked with rich ornaments upon her head and body as when she wore the nun's habit.'[2] Blanche felt that she fasted too much. Since childhood Isabella had voluntarily deprived herself, so much so that Blanche had had to promise her she could give more alms to the poor if she would eat more. It did not do much good, for Isabella was constitutionally far from robust. At the age of twenty her health became a matter of grave concern to all around her, as had her father's and brother's. Blanche had left her at Saint-Germain-en-Laye with her sister-in-law Margaret and gone off elsewhere to attend to state matters. Suddenly both she and the King had been summoned by Margaret to come to Isabella, who seemed to be dying. She pulled through, however, and lived till 1270 (the year that Louis also died) having founded in the meantime in 1252, the convent of the Clarisses at Longchamp, outside Paris, where she died. Her biographer, Sister Agnes of Harcourt, the third abbess of that convent, summed up her life and personality as follows: 'She was a mirror of innocence, a model of penitence, a rose of patience, a lily of chastity, a fountain of mercy.'

It was a strange era. The priests, those officially dedicated to God, seemed all too often to forget, amid their creature comforts, that Christ had told them: 'Whosoever he be of you that forsaketh not all that he hath, he cannot be my disciple.' (*Luke* xiv: 33) The laymen, on the other hand, seemed to be trying to outdo each other in their saintly ardour. Deep within, Blanche must have been comparing her daughter to those other princesses, such as Elizabeth of Hungary, Hedwig of Silesia, and Agnes of Bohemia, who, despite their radiant beauty and high rank, had chosen the celestial Spouse above the pleasures and favours of the world. They had often led lives of such heroic asceticism, such unrelenting self-imposed privations that Blanche, for all her own piety, felt it was too much. Yet they had perhaps in that way made up for the failings of others, priests included. Perhaps, amid the world's vanities, the way of true holiness must involve just such an excess of voluntary privation.

Isabella seemed to have dedicated her life to study and meditation. She took part in the court entertainments only when she was actually forced to, and preferred to relax by embroidering church ornaments. She was an only girl among several brothers. She could have led a splendid life. The Holy Roman Emperor had asked for her hand for his son Conrad, but she had elected instead to serve only 'the perdurable Spouse in perfect virginity'. Blanche had respected her wish.

For the time being the main worry was, as usual, England. Shortly before Louis's departure Henry III had renewed his claim to the old Plantagenet possessions. He had demanded the return of Normandy and the west of France and had even gained the support of the Emperor, Frederick II, who had married his sister Isabella. Theoretically the domains of the King of France were inviolable during his absence, as were the belongings of any crusader. The Pope had recently stepped into the picture to recall this fact. But this had not stopped Henry from calling up his knights. They had been summoned to London and told to be ready to sail from Portsmouth on September 15, 1248.

Blanche was not over-impressed. Better than anyone else, she knew her English cousin. He was a trifler, a man of fits and starts; his resolves were so many flashes in the pan. His English barons were getting to be weary of it. Blanche was not surprised when, on September 20, another Englishman came calling on her. It was Simon de Montfort, Henry's brother-in-law, who was becoming more and more the strong man of England. He sought Blanche out at Lorris and proposed that the truce be prolonged until December 27. This was agreed to. Another prolongation was then made, and then another. Thus it went, from truce to truce, until Louis's return. Henry had forbidden the crusading English barons to sail with Louis. They began to wonder how much longer they must postpone their pledged departure in order to let their King give vent to his ancient grudge. Had not the Pope said that the needs of the Holy Land must come before private quarrels?

Not that the Pope seemed in any great hurry to set an

example. This created a dangerous handicap for the crusaders themselves, when one considers how much help the Emperor could have given them. Blanche received regular messengers from the departing French army. When he had reached Lyons the King had talked with the Pope but had been unable to win any concession from his stubborn resolve. The excommunication laid on Frederick II would not be raised, even temporarily. Then Blanche had received a reassuring letter from the Pope, promising that he intended to watch over France's safety during the King's absence.

Louis and his army had gone down the valley of the Rhône, still full of grim memories of the siege of Avignon. At the people's request he had meted out justice on his way. He had ordered the destruction of the castle of La Roche-de-Glun, north of Valence, whose owner, a robber baron named Roger of Clérieu, was addicted to plundering travellers and imposing exorbitant tolls. As they drew near to Avignon some of the barons urged the King to avenge the wrongs done in former times to his father. Louis would have none of it: 'I did not take the cross that I might work vengeance on my father's offenders, nor yet my mother's nor mine own. I have left France that I may avenge Our Lord.' Here and there a few skirmishes and brawls did take place, in Avignon and later in Marseilles, where the shipowners were accused of taking advantage of the situation in order to enrich themselves at the pilgrims' expense. But it was nothing serious and nothing the King could not quell.

Raymond of Toulouse came to meet Louis at Aigues-Mortes. He excused himself for not sailing for the Holy Land with Louis's party, but said he planned to leave next year without fail. The new town was beginning to fill up with a motley population. There were people from Provence, both the coastal areas and the hinterland, as well as people from Languedoc, and even some Catalans and Genoese The Tower of Constance was still rising, straight and white under the Mediterranean sun. From it, on August 25, 1248, the watchers waved farewell to the royal bark *Montjoie*, surrounded by the white sails of attendant ships, and dancing on the waves till the wind took her out of sight of her native land.

Neither the King nor the mighty barons who had thus set sail had balked at forsaking their worldly possessions, whereas the Pope would suffer no peace or truce with the Emperor and brazenly paraded his love of the world's goods. The year before, Louis had personally protested against the pontiff's financial demands and his practice of doling out ecclesiastical benefices on decidedly non-spiritual grounds. The Pope had been accused of giving Church preferments to his nephews and to personal friends who had done him a good turn. Louis had spoken out very sharply: 'This Roman Church, unmindful of her pristine simpleness, lies stifled with her treasure, the which doth prick her heart on to avarice and its attendant train . . . The King will not suffer the churches of his realm to be thus fleeced. . . . It has come to such a pass that our bishops can no longer provide their clergy and the learned men within their deaneries . . .'[3]

Yet that same Innocent IV, though guilty of much, could also be far-sighted and high-minded. He warned of the Mongol menace at the opening of the Council of Lyons. He showed great initiative in sending out embassies of Dominicans and Franciscans to those very Mongols, at a time when everyone thought they were utter savages. He also showed his tolerance and fair-mindedness in a papal bull sent to all the bishops of France and Germany, ordering them to treat Jews kindly.

There had been a bad business the year before at Valréas, north of Avignon, in the maquisate of Provence, a fief of the Empire which had just become the property of the Count of Toulouse.* Meilla, a little girl of two, had disappeared on Tuesday in Holy Week, March 26, 1247. A few days later her body was found in a ditch. The fact that the murder had

---

* The distinction must be made between the county of Provence properly so called, and the marquisate of Provence, which was later called the Comtat-Venaissin.

occurred during Holy Week was enough to make everyone
think that the Jews had done it. Wasn't it said to be their
custom to perform the ritual sacrifice of a child for their
Passover? The inquiry led to the arrest of three Jews of Valréas
who, after seven days of torture, confessed to the murder. Six
other Jews were also interrogated, one of them, despite the
torture, denied any guilt to the bitter end. The townsfolk had
become very overwrought and had chased out all the Jews,
killing several of them in the process.

Pope Innocent IV was furious. In two successive bulls
addressed to the Archbishop of Vienne he gave the order to
release the prisoners and indemnify the Jewish community.
'We condemn whatever Christian cruelty covets Jewish goods;
thirsts after Jewish blood, strips, maims, and murders without
judgement. It is to mistake the gentleness of the Catholic faith,
which gives the Jews leave to live by its side and orders that
they be suffered to perform their own holy offices.'[4] Not long
after, on July 7, 1247, another bull went out, this time to all
the bishops of France and Germany, ordering them to show
the same tolerance.

This incident undoubtedly reminded Blanche of the time,
exactly seven years earlier, when she had felt personally called
upon to act in a similar manner. She had very deliberately
taken all the Jews of Paris under her protection. It was at the
time of the great debate on the Talmud. A Jew of La Rochelle,
Nicholas Donin, had become a Christian convert. But even
before that, while still a member of the Jewish community, he
had cast doubt on the validity of the Talmud. He had been
ostracized by his fellow-Jews for this in 1225, eleven years
before his conversion. He had remained obsessed by the Talmud
question and in 1238 had gone to Rome, where he had persuaded Pope Gregory IX to issue an encyclical ordering all
copies of the Talmud to be confiscated. This had led to the
idea of a public debate. Blanche herself had taken up the idea
and had arranged with Rabbi Yehiel, head of the Paris Talmudic
school, for it to start on June 25, 1240. It should be noted that

at that time, as in the past, there were still frequent dialogues between Christians and Jews on Biblical questions, though they were beginning to be less frequent. In 1200 the Bishop of Paris had forbidden Christian laymen to discuss religious matters with the Jews, feeling that they were not always qualified to defend their faith competently. This prohibition had later been reiterated by the Pope. By about 1300 almost all dialogue between Christians and Jews was to come to an end.

Blanche, however, came from a country where the Jews were very numerous and entirely free. She had jumped at the chance of hearing a fine 'dispute' (in the students' terminology) between the outstanding experts on both sides of the question, and she herself presided over the debate. The Jewish community had designated four rabbis: Yehiel; Moses of Coucy; Judah, son of David of Melun; and Samuel, son of Solomon. Each had brought a copy of the Talmud, which the abbot of Cluny, Peter the Venerable, had had translated into French a century earlier, at a time when religious feelings had been much more relaxed.

Rabbi Yehiel had been reluctant to open the debate, which was held in the Palace itself. 'You cannot shield us from the people's fury,' he said to one of the King's counsellors. Blanche herself had answered this indignantly: 'Say not so to me. I mean to shield you, and all your people. None shall dare trouble you. Whoso should attempt it shall be guilty of a capital offence. As for that,' she added, 'we bethink us of the protection granted you by pontifical decree.'

Blanche personally intervened several more times, as the debate proceeded. Nicholas Donin attempted to force his former coreligionists to speak under oath, but they refused because it was forbidden by their Law. Rabbi Yehiel turned to the Queen: 'I beseech you, Lady. In my whole life I have never sworn an oath. I cannot do so now.' Blanche upheld him. 'If thus an oath cost him so much and he hath never sworn it, leave it so. On several occasions the dialogue became a direct exchange between her and the rabbis. When fair play called for it she even took their side, and vigorously. It was to be an unforgettable experience for her, in its every detail. Mention was made in the text of the Talmud of a Jew called Jesus, but the rabbis insisted that it was not the Jesus of the Christian gospels – which was precisely what their opponents were trying to force them to admit. Blanche became exasperated and stepped in again: 'Whence this determination to make your own selves odious?' She pointed to Rabbi Yehiel: 'He minds that his ancestors spoke not in their time 'gainst Him Whom you honour. It touches not Him. Would you tear from this man's lips that very thing that is hateful to you? Have you no shame?' Rabbi Yehiel was encouraged by this outburst in his favour, and dared to remark that there were many persons in France named Louis at that time, but only one of them was King. Finally Blanche asked him point-blank: 'I would you told me the truth touching the faith of your religion: is the Jesus there in question the same whom we Christians adore, or another?' 'It was not in the minds of our ancestors to speak of the one whom you adore . . . These words were not written in his regard.' At that, Blanche declared the discussion closed.[5]

That did not end the debate, however. A number of important prelates were involved, including Walter Cornut, Archbishop of Sens; William of Auvergne, Bishop of Paris; and Odo of Châteauroux, the Chancellor of the University of Paris, among others. They continued their investigations for two years. Finally, in 1242, they gave their verdict: the Talmud was condemned. Twenty-four wagonloads of copies of the Talmud – all those in Paris – were taken to the Place de Grève (now the Place de L'Hôtel-de-Ville), where they were burned. A rabbi who happened to be on his way through Paris at the time, Meir of Rothenburg, Bavaria, composed an elegy on the occasion which from that time on the Jews always recited on the anniversary of the destruction of the Temple.

The Jews themselves, at any rate, including the Talmudists,

continued to enjoy the Queen's protection. Rabbi Yehiel later opened a school in Palestine and died at Acre 44 years later, in 1286. Blanche was powerless to stop the growing public feeling against the Jews, who were accused of continuing the practice of usury despite the ordinance of 1230. But if the truth were known, there were Christian burghers who had nothing to learn from the Jews in that respect. Those of Cahors, in particular, like the Lombards in northern Italy, made a speciality of collecting interest on money loaned; so did those of La Rochelle, Poitiers, Saint-Jean-d'Angély, Niort, Saintes, and Saint-Maixent; and they may not have been averse to ridding themselves of competitors in this field. In 1249 they sent a deputation to Count Alphonse of Poitiers, just as he was leaving for the crusade, asking him to drive the Jews out of their towns. The Count took no notice of the request.

To his excellent and most dear mother Blanche, by the grace of God illustrious Queen of France: Robert, of Artois the Count, her devoted son: greeting . . . Knowing how greatly you will rejoice at our good fortune, and that of our followers, and at all the stately triumphs to Christian folk befallen, when you shall be truly advised thereof, may your Royal Excellence herewith learn that our most dear brother the King, the Queen and her sister, and ourself by God's grace, are in good health of body, for the which we mind to have your own earnest prayers to thank. Our most dear brother, the Count of Anjou, still feels his quartan ague, though it be lately less violent. And may Your Highness learn further that our most dear brother and Lord, together with those barons and pilgrims that did spend the winter at Cyprus, boarded their ships on Ascension Day, in the evening, in the port of Limassol, meaning to sail against the foes of our Christian faith.

Thus began the letter in which Robert of Artois described to his mother how the Seventh Crusade got off to a flying start and triumphed initially at Damietta in the Nile delta. It was

full of heart-warming details for Blanche: how the arrival of
the crusader fleet was met by a huge army of Turkish horsemen
and foot soldiers massed on the shore; what battle-plan was
decided upon by the royal council, how the crusaders had had
to leave their big ships, which could not make land because of
the shallow sandy bottom, and go ashore in the boats; how the
papal legate had gone in the King's own boat; how the whole
Christian army, armed cap-à-pie, had with one impulse leapt
into the sea up to their necks and waded ashore; and how the
defending Turks had had to yield ground foot by foot before
the ardour of the Christian onslaught, finally shutting themselves up inside the city walls.

> God Almighty delivered that city unto us without a blow
> struck, all defended as it was both by river and also ramparts
> and strong towers, on the morning after the octave of
> Trinity, towards the hour of Tierce, the Saracen infidels
> having abandoned it and being fled of their own accord, the
> which was done by the pure gift of God and the generosity
> of the Almighty Lord. Know also that the Saracens left
> that city full of victuals and viands in great plenty, also
> engines of war and all manner of goods.

Robert closed with a rapid review of the King's plans. The
Nile was then at its height, submerging much of the land. The
army would wait till it fell, so as not to endanger the Christian
pilgrims. He added 'Know: that the Countess of Anjou did
bear at Cyprus a most fair and well-knit son, which she hath
put to nurse and left there.'[6] The letter was dated St John's
Eve, June 23, 1249. The surrender of Damietta, which it
related, had taken place on June 6.

Shortly after this great news reached the court of France
Alphonse of Poitiers set sail from Aigues-Mortes in his turn,
one year to the very day after his brother the King. He used a
rented Genoese ship, which also carried Joan of Toulouse, his
wife, as well as Robert's wife, the Countess of Artois. The
remaining levy of crusaders sailed with them, the entire

arrière-ban of vassals called up by the King in exercise of his feudal prerogative. Blanche had personally provided Alphonse with 4400 Parisian *livres*, pending reception of 6000 *livres* owed by the clergy. For the provisioning of the troops she had made up her mind to ask the help of the Holy Roman Emperor. He had answered promptly with a letter of unimpeachable courtesy. The Queen knew his sentiments, he said. He would have been only too glad to take part personally in the expedition, but the Pope, by excommunicating him, had thus deprived the crusaders of the support that he, the Emperor, had been so eager to lend them. He also would very much have liked to help with the provisions, but prices in Sicily had gone up incredibly in the past two years. None the less, he neither could nor would turn a deaf ear to Blanche's request. He was immediately drawing from his own granaries a thousand pack-loads of wheat, and as much barley, which he was sending to the Count of Poitiers along with fifty sound war-horses. Naturally, also, he freely granted the Count permission to buy whatever he might need in Sicily and elsewhere, for himself and his people.

Shortly before Alphonse and Joan sailed, Raymond of Toulouse arrived in Aigues-Mortes. Was he at last to go off crusading himself? Well, not quite yet. But this time, he solemnly declared, his departure really was imminent. For twenty years now, since taking the cross at the time of his absolution at Notre Dame de Paris, in 1229, Raymond VII had been skilfully spinning out the game of the crusader without a crusade – more skilfully than his ally Frederick II, for whenever Raymond realized that he was about to be excommunicated he had managed to wriggle out of it in the nick of time. It was thanks to Blanche, actually; she had always interceded for him with the Pope. More than ten years before, Gregory IX had let it be known that he expected Raymond to carry out his vow within a year. Louis and Blanche had pleaded for him, and the Pope had granted more time. But Raymond had used the time to attack Count Raymond-Bérenger of Provence.

The Pope had lost all patience and ordered him to sail at once. Yet – still by Louis's and Blanche's intercession – he had said that he need spend only three years in the Holy Land, instead of the five that Raymond had committed himself to.

But just then the important events leading to Louis's brilliant victory at Taillebourg Bridge had taken place. These were followed, as we have seen, by the spectacular pardon granted to Raymond, still through the intercession of Blanche, whom they began to accuse of favouritism towards her cousin. Shortly thereafter Raymond had persuaded his former enemy Raymond-Bérenger to promise him the hand of his daughter Beatrice. Raymond would thus have married his way to the ownership of the county of Provence after vainly trying to fight his way to it. But Blanche was watching. For all her affection for the Count of Toulouse, she did not intend to let him extend his sway to the east of the Rhône. He must content himself with the marquisate of Provence (Comtat-Venaissin today). Blanche was adamant on this score, and she had gone to the Pope about it. In addition, Beatrice's three elder sisters had all pleaded with her not to wed the Count of Toulouse.

So Raymond, ousted from the County of Provence, had gone off on pilgrimage to St James of Compostela, and the story has it that while he was in Spain he fell in love with a 'foreign lady' but she refused to marry him. All this would have seemed to make it the appropriate time to carry out his crusader's oath, especially since the King of France was getting ready to sail. This was Pope Innocent IV's reasoning in 1247. He promised Raymond the sum of 2000 marks if he would go now – the money to be paid upon his arrival in the Holy Land, the Pope prudently added.

Raymond again renewed his promise to sail. This time he really seemed to mean it. Encouragement was showered on him from all sides. King Louis promised him 20,000 Parisian *livres*; the Pope wrote a letter of recommendation for him to the Patriarch of Jerusalem and to the Knights Templars; all the imprisoned heretics in Raymond's domains were promised amnesty if they would leave on the crusade with the Count. All eyes turned towards Raymond of Toulouse and great things were expected. Aware of all this, Raymond chose that moment – April 26, 1249 – to give a demonstration of his religious zeal. At Berlaigues, near Agen, he had eighty heretics burned at the stake – a greater number, scholars have pointed out, than all those burned by the Dominican Bernard Guy during a long career as inquisitor.

Still Raymond of Toulouse did not sail for the Holy Land. This time, however, he finally had a valid excuse. He sickened and died at Millau, to the north-west of Montpellier, on September 27, 1249, at the age of 53. He had returned from a visit to his daughter Joan and son-in-law Alphonse of Poitiers less than a month before.

His will, written four days before he died, is a moving document. In it he calls himself, as he had had the habit of doing during his last years, 'Count of Toulouse, Marquess of Provence, son of the deceased Queen Joan' (by which he meant Henry II Plantagenet's third daughter by Eleanor of Aquitaine, who became Queen Joan of Sicily, sometimes also called Joan of Fontevrault). Raymond had never known his mother, but he seems to have brooded a good deal about her during his last years. 'We will our sepulchre to be in the convent of Fontevrault,' he wrote, 'where rest Henry of England, our grandsire; our royal uncle Richard; and Queen Joan, our mother. We would be laid at the feet of the aforesaid, our mother.' He bequeathed 5000 'easterling'* marks to the Fontevrault convent – a large sum, and with it all his gold

* The term 'easterling' (d'esterlins), referring to certain coinages, is found often in the Anglo-French and Latin of the 13th century, and was later thought to refer to the 'East', meaning money minted in the Hanseatic League towns. It was once believed to have been the etymological origin of the word 'sterling'. But the Oxford English Dictionary doubts this, finding rather the origin of 'sterling' in the little star found on the new Norman pennies, or in the starling (the bird) seen on some coins minted under Edward the Confessor.

and silver plate, his rings and gems. He also gave all his herds of cattle to the Cistercians. Among his bequests were 100 *livres* for the enclosed nuns of Prouille (near Carcassonne), the first convent founded by Brother Dominic. Clearly, also, his failure to keep his crusader's oath had been tormenting Raymond. Two days before he died he added a codicil to the will, designed to get the matter off his conscience. He said that if he should recover from his illness he would personally keep his vow to go to the Holy Land. If not, he laid it upon his heiress Joan to send fifty well-accoutred soldiers to the Holy Land for an entire year, at her expense.[7]

As Alphonse of Poitiers had sailed shortly before Raymond's death, it was up to his mother Blanche to claim the heritage of Toulouse in her son's name. This was a delicate business because it meant taking possession of a much-disputed domain in the absence of the real claimant, and doing it promptly. Both Alphonse and Louis were counting on her. 'When I was come to seek out My Lady,' Alphonse's chancellor Philip wrote him shortly after his departure, 'I told her how you did stop at the port, and the day and hour of your taking ship, and the dear expenses you were then put to. I beseeched her in your behalf that she would perform your business as being your mother, forasmuch as you repose all your confidence in her, and your entire expectation. And she did make me answer thereto, that thus she would most willingly.'[8]

The oaths of fealty and acts of homage took place at the Château-Narbonnais in Toulouse on December 1, 1249. Blanche was not able to go herself, but sent her representatives, the brothers Guy and Harvey of Chevreuse, along with Alphonse's trusted chancellor Philip, who was the treasurer of the abbey of Saint-Hilaire in Poitiers. These men were to receive, in Count Alphonse's name, the oaths and homage of the Languedoc barons. After the reading of the representatives' credentials the first of the barons, Count Bernard of Comminges, stepped forward. 'I, Bernard,' he declaimed, 'of Comminges the Count, will be true to the Sire Alphonse, Count of Toulouse and of Poitiers, Marquess of Provence, and to the Lady Joan his spouse, daughter of Sire Raymond, deceased, and will with my entire strength, in good faith, save their lives and limbs, their seigneury and right, and those of whomso holds lands in their name, saving the right of the Sire King of France and his inheritors, according to the conditions of the peace concluded at Paris between the Sire King of France and the Sire Raymond, Count of Toulouse. So help me God and this Holy Writ beneath my hand!'

The other barons then came forward and took the same oath. After them it was the burghers of Toulouse, with wording that safe-guarded their franchises: 'I hereby declare, protest, and intend that we, myself and all other citizens and burghers of Toulouse, shall on this oath's account lose none of our customs and freedoms . . .' Finally the King's bailiff designated by 'the Lady Blanche, illustrious Queen of the French', came in his turn to swear to maintain the burghers' special rights.

The ceremony was repeated on December 12 in the cloister of Moissac, south-east of Agen, and then again in the principal towns of the county: Millau, Peirusse, etc. At Agen, however, Blanche's envoys met with a refusal. The aldermen assembled in the church of Saint-Étienne protested that the oath would be contrary to the peace previously sealed in Paris and contrary to Count Raymond's will and the rights of Joan of Toulouse. The Queen's envoys took no action, contenting themselves with recording the protest. But the question had been raised. Was it the start of fresh disorders in the south of France?

In the following February, 1250, a letter was sent by the aldermen and the University of the towns of Agen and Condon to 'their most excellent Lady Blanche, by the Grace of God Queen of the French'. They had reconsidered and had thought of a phrasing by which they could take the oath. And they wished long life to the Queen and a prompt homecoming, safe and sound, to the King and his brothers.[9]

It was the final conclusion of a conflict whose beginning went back to the time when Blanche was only twenty years old and the crusade against the Albigensians had just been launched. Who could have known then that one day a scion of France would be the immediate suzerain of all those lands situated at the other end of the country? With the letters attesting to the fealty of the southern barons in her possession, Blanche must have had a tremendous feeling of relief. She little guessed that at the same moment, on the far-off shores of Egypt, events were taking place that would break her heart and plunge all Christendom into mourning.

At first it was merely idle tales at which one shrugged. Matthew Paris even says that those who spread them were given short shrift and hanged high. What they said was sacrilegious and defeatist rubbish, liable to discourage persons planning to sail off and join the crusaders. But letters came soon enough from the East that confirmed it. The worst had happened. The splendid Christian army had been annihilated. The victors of Damietta lay dead on the banks of the Nile or else – scarcely better – languished in Saracen jails, awaiting death from one moment to the next. 'France entire was into anguish and confusion cast. Clerks and knights alike cried woe and comfort would take none.' A kind of universal bereavement spread across the land. There were no more ballads, no more dancing, no more colourful finery. The grief involved everyone, 'all joy now turned to woe.'[10]

Despite her strength of character Blanche was shaken and, for a time, overwhelmed. Her son Robert was dead at El Mansura. Her other children were prisoners of the Sultan. The Christian forces were humiliated and dispersed, and France itself was full of the lamentations of bereaved families. As more details came in the horrors of the crusaders' ordeal grew blacker and blacker. Louis himself was stricken with the dysentery that was epidemic in his army. He was so ill that his cook Isambart was obliged to carry him about bodily, and had cut a back flap in his breeches, for his bowels were a torrent. When the retreat had been sounded he had been judged to be in so desperate a condition that they had left him behind in a house. Outside it one of the barons, Gaucher of Châtillon, kept chasing away the Saracens, 'like flies', while within a burgheress of Paris, one of those crusading women of whom there were many, held up the King's head, expecting him to die at any moment. Then came the surrender and the humiliating sight of the King in chains, guarded by a eunuch called Sabih in the pay of the Sultan.

Still, there were countless heroic moments in the story, as when the King had refused to be evacuated with the other sick, who were being put aboard boats and taken back towards Damietta. His brother Charles, hoping to get the King to spare himself, had pointed out that he was so ill he would slow down the rear-guard if he insisted on staying with them. Louis had replied, 'Count of Anjou, do you rid yourself of me if I cumber you. For my part, I shall never rid myself of my people!' So he had stayed with the army amid all its perils, a prey to the Saracen arrows as well as to his illness.

Some said also that the Sultan of Egypt had been given advance information of the movements of the King's armies by a spy of the Emperor Frederick II, disguised as a merchant. In Florence the Ghibellines had celebrated Louis's surrender with bonfires and feasting . . .

Finally it was learned that on May 8, 1250, the King and his brothers and chief barons had been freed and allowed to board ship for Acre. Once in Syria he would be able to marshal his forces and decide what course was best.

Blanche got a grip on herself. A plan was taking shape to send help to the crusaders. Even the King of England had taken the cross on March 6 and seemed inclined to carry out his vow. Urged by Blanche, the Pope wrote to him: "Tis no more fitful succour but a general reinforcement that is needed in the Holy Land,' and called on him to sail in August of that year. A few days later Henry III spontaneously suggested a sixteen-year prolongation of the truce between France and England. Until then Blanche's letters to Louis had constantly stressed the dangers that Henry's behaviour might lead to. Now she could at least heave a sigh of relief on that score. But what she hoped for most was that Louis would follow her advice and return to France, now that disaster had literally wiped out his army. She was bitterly disappointed when she learned that he intended to stay on in the Holy Land for the purpose of freeing the rank-and-file Christians still held in Egyptian jails, and to re-build the forts in Syria and Palestine. However, he was sending back his brothers Alphonse and Charles in an attempt to muster reinforcements. They were to sail for France in August with their wives.

Others besides Blanche were upset by the turn of events. After the first shock of grief and consternation a wave of unrest swept over France. Everywhere the events in the Holy Land were the main topic of conversation. From one town market-place to the next those bringing news were surrounded by anxious throngs, who then held animated discussions on the street-corners, on the church steps, and at the fairs. They were sometimes vehement discussions. How had such a disaster been possible? The saintliest man in Christendom had gone off to fight the good fight, and he was precisely the one who had suffered the crusaders' worst defeat in the Holy Land! Why had Providence allowed it? Why had Christ deserted his very own soldiers? When the clergy scolded the townsfolk for such blasphemies they were answered with insults. Wasn't it the preaching of these same priests that had paved the way for such a massacre of decent folk? They could preach all right, but they didn't untie their purse-strings! Everyone knew the trouble Queen Blanche had had in collecting the tithes due from the clergy to help King Louis. And what about the Pope? Why didn't he excommunicate the King of England, who never so much as budged to help King Louis? For that matter, why didn't the Pope make peace with Emperor Frederick, who might then himself leave for the Holy Land? The mutterings became querulous, then violent, and discontent grew into disorder. Small riots broke out here and there,

mainly between the clergy and townspeople. The whole
country began to feel the pressure. Above all, the young
people were eager to do something. Why not rise up and band
together, as they had done thirty-eight years before, at the call
of Peter the Hermit? What were the priests and barons waiting
for – why didn't they rush to bring help to King Louis? If
everyone got together and went to Egypt in one great united
throng the Sultan would have to yield to superior might and
surrender his prisoners! Why, the new army of Christ could
go on from there and deliver Jerusalem! The call to arms
sounded and bands formed everywhere, in the towns and in
the country. The shepherd lads left their flocks; the apprentices
left their smithies and mills and shops. Groups of excited boys
and girls started moving along the roads, singing hymns. They
decked themselves in motley rags and let their hair fly in the
wind. They carried banners. They begged their food and slept
in barns. Wherever they went they raised a hullabaloo, and
the stodgy good folk watched the shaggy mobs go by and
asked whose children they were and where they were off to.
The only answer was a shrug and the word: 'Shepherds!'
Parents were well-advised to watch their children, for many
who did not awoke the next morning to find that they had
run away from home and been herded off down the road by
the 'Shepherds'.

The movement became a tidal wave in the north of France.
The 'Shepherds' travelled in hundreds, then in thousands.
They had found a leader, their own latter-day Peter the Hermit.

He was a strange man, pale, thin, and ascetic, with a fanatic
gleam in his eye. He was old, too, sixty at least, with a long
white beard and the look of a wizard or a desert prophet. The
Blessed Virgin had appeared to him in person, he declared, and
commanded him to lead the 'Shepherds' on a crusade. Furthermore she had given him a letter, actual written instructions,
which he held at all times in his left hand, tightly clutched.
He was clearly a well-educated man. He spoke several languages
not only fluently but with what was described as irresis-

tible eloquence. They called him 'The Master of Hungary',

At his call the 'Shepherds' began to organize. He grouped
them into bands, naming a chief for each. They carried his
banner: an image of a lamb bearing a standard with a cross.
They flocked to him from everywhere, especially from Picardy,
where he had preached, but also from Flanders, Brabant,
Hainault, Lorraine, Burgundy. Under his guidance, they felt
a sense of mission, though to an observer they must have seemed
a mere rabble, armed with whatever came to hand: axes,
cutlasses, old swords, crooked scythes, cudgels. Amiens, the
first town they went through, gave them a good welcome. The
'Shepherds' were wined and dined, and the burghers clustered
about the 'Master of Hungary', whom they took to be a new
prophet, another Francis of Assisi for sure. For that matter, the
friars of St Francis, as well as those of St Dominic, were considered to have degenerated. Here was the man to bring the
true evangelical spirit back to the crowds again, and hopefully
to the clergy too, who were so glutted with their wealth. From
then on, when a friar of one of the established Mendicant
orders tried to appeal to the crowds for alms, he was spat upon.

The 'Shepherds' grew more and more numerous. Undoubtedly a good many young scamps and girls of easy virtue
joined their ranks, only too glad of the windfall which allowed
them to pass through crowds unnoticed and feed off the good-
natured burghers. It began to be said that the personal lives of
these new crusaders were far from irreproachable. The 'Master
of Hungary' married and unmarried them to suit their fancies,
and the pregnant girls were legion.

The 'Shepherds' had turned towards Paris. Blanche's advisers
urged her to have them dispersed. Enough was enough, and it
was high time to put a stop to such goings-on; the vagabond
children should be returned to their parents and the apprentices
to their masters. It was turning into an uprising. Blanche
hesitated, however. She had a deep-seated sympathy for these
youngsters, and did not hide it. How could one be angry with
them for displaying the generous feelings of which the clergy

were incapable. Furthermore, these 'Shepherds' stirred a memory from her youth which still moved her deeply.

It was the winter of 1211–12; she had been barely twenty at the time. Then also the children had risen up with the idea of crossing the sea and doing what the high and mighty had clearly been unable to do: recapture the tomb of Christ. It had started near Liège, she remembered. Later a little shepherd lad near Vendôme, Stephen of Cloyes, had had supernatural revelations, and a pilgrim who had shared his bread with him had told him to go to the King of France. He had attempted to do so, walking to Saint-Denis and Paris with a multitude of children and adolescents traipsing behind him. They had been joined by a similar group, which had formed in almost exactly the same way round a boy called Nicholas of Cologne. The throng of children had grown like a rolling snowball as they wended their way towards the ports on the Mediterranean. Pope Innocent III, whose one fixed purpose was the recovery of the Holy Land, had remarked gloomily: 'The children put us to shame. Whilst we here sleep they press on to deliver our Lord's tomb.'

Their story had a grim ending. Some shipowners of Marseilles, and also some Italians, having agreed to carry them oversea, had shamelessly handed them over to the Muslim slave-traders. A few had managed to escape and told the story of their luckless odyssey. It was said that more than 700 of them had remained slaves of the Saracens.[11]

Naturally the 'Shepherds' must at all costs be prevented from ending up like that, but could one not hope for a bit more efficiency on the part of their 'Master'? In any case he must be heard before his youngsters were dispersed, as Blanche's advisers urged.

There was a danger, however: the students of the Latin Quarter. Blanche had never quite got over her resentment of them, and the continual disturbances they caused. They had clamoured for their liberties, and now they had them. The royal sergeants-at-arms were not even allowed to intervene when they caused a riot. And now they were quarrelling among themselves. During the great strike of 1229–31 some of the Mendicant friars of the convent of St James had opened their own school and begun to teach. When the regular masters of the University returned to Paris they claimed that the friars were poaching on their preserves, and took steps to have them forbidden to teach. The students, naturally, were divided on the issue, some taking one side, some the other, and now it was simply one row after another. What effect would the arrival of the 'Shepherds' have on all this? Would the students give them a hearty welcome and perhaps even swell their ranks? Or, as was more likely, would they pick a quarrel with them on some pretext or other? It seemed pointless to risk it.

The 'Shepherds' (whose numbers some scholars have estimated at 60,000) were allowed to roam freely about Paris. But when some of them wished to cross the Petit-Pont, leading to the Left Bank, they found the way stoutly barricaded and defended by a cordon of soldiers. At about the same time Blanche was in Maubuisson, talking with the 'Master of Hungary'. The fellow intrigued her. He answered her questions with a perplexing blend of arrogance and piety. His intention of going to the Holy Land seemed sincere, and for Blanche going to the Holy Land meant bringing help to her son. She loaded the 'Master of Hungary' with gifts and dismissed him.

This so encouraged him that from then on he acted as though he could count on the Queen's support whatever he did. He began to show himself for what he was: a coward, but a brazen one. He took to preaching in the church of St Eustache, dressed up as a bishop with crozier and mitre and surrounded by his 'Shepherds', who had begun to act as if they were in conquered territory. They went after the clerics, particularly the Mendicant friars, drubbing and looting them pretty much as they pleased. When they finally departed from Paris they left a harvest of wreckage behind them.

Their 'Master' had understood by that time that no town was large enough to lodge and feed his horde. He divided them into several separate armies, each of which went off in its own direction, zestfully looting and ransacking what lay in its path as the fancy took it. In Rouen they laid siege to the Archbishop's palace. At Orléans, a university town, there was the inevitable flare-up with the students which Blanche had managed to avoid in Paris. The whole scope of operations was escalating; in the fracas with the Orléans students there had been some killed and wounded. At Tours the 'Shepherds' attacked the Dominican and Franciscan convents and started desecrating the churches. In Bourges it was the Jews they went after, surging into the synagogues and tearing up the books of the Law.

By this time the people of France had had enough. The royal troops, assisted by town militias, began hunting down and dispersing the 'Shepherds'. The 'Master of Hungary' was killed not far from Bourges, between Morthomiers and Villeneuve-sur-Cher. Matthew Paris writes that the youngsters were hunted down 'like mad dogs'. Some gangs managed to reach the valley of the Rhône, and others headed towards Guienne, where the Earl of Leicester, Simon de Montfort, was governing the province in the name of King Henry III, his brother-in-law. He dispersed them by his own efficient methods. Some of the 'Shepherds' even landed in England, where they started preaching. But Henry had no intention of allowing his English youngsters to join them; he gave orders to the port authorities to ship them back to France without delay. In the end a few of the 'Shepherds' became reasonable. They relinquished the crosses they had awarded themselves, received others from the hands of the clergy, and actually went to the Holy Land. Matthew Paris states that the 'Master of Hungary's' private scheme had been to take his cue from the Marseilles and Genoese ship-owners during the Children's Crusade, and sell his 'Shepherds' for slaves in Saracen ports oversea.[12]

The care that remained uppermost in Blanche's mind was

her son's position in the Holy Land and the help he urgently needed and which she had been unable to supply. A ship she had fitted out with the help of Alphonse and Charles, at great expense, and which sailed full of money and reinforcements, had gone down with all hands. It is said that when Louis learned of this fresh disaster he simply quoted St Paul: 'Who shall separate us from the love of Christ? Shall tribulation, or distress, or persecution, or famine, or nakedness, or peril, or sword?' (*Romans* viii: 35). Even the infidels admired Louis's fortitude.

He was having his share of tribulations in finishing the tasks he had set himself in Syria and Palestine. He wanted to strengthen the Christian positions, rebuild the forts and walls, ransom the prisoners in the hands of the Saracens, and above all to stop the squabbling among the crusading barons. He and those of his barons still with him were short of funds and were obliged to go to the local money-lenders, Italian merchants mostly, who definitely meant to make a profit from their services. On September 27, 1251, Louis wrote to Blanche from his camp near Caesarea: 'We are herewith sending to Your Highness, with our other letters, by these same messengers, the letters of certain barons and knights at our side, touching the loans that were made them, for that the same letters be delivered to the creditors, and no harm or damage ensue from their delay.'[13] So it was Blanche who personally saw to it that the debts of the barons oversea were honoured. They were usually paid at the fairs in Champagne, which had become the geographically logical meeting-place in Europe of creditors and debtors, merchants and money-changers, all of whom practised some degree of usury. The custom of meeting at the fairs in Champagne went back to the time of the First Crusade, at the end of the 11th century. There are promissory notes of that period in the French National Archives, bearing some of the greatest names of France. We find that William of Dampierre, heir of Flanders, received a loan from a merchant of Montpellier, which was to be repaid at the Lagny fair; Ralph of

Coucy promised to pay back 3500 *livres tournois* to the merchants of Siena on the same occasion; Érard of Chassenay was to pay a debt at the Bar fair; Guichard of Beaujeu, Gaucher of Châtillon, the hero who gave his life defending the bed-ridden King Louis during the retreat from El Mansura, had similar commitments. In addition there were loans granted by the Knights Templars, who, with their commanderies both in Europe and the Holy Land, were the ideal intermediaries for crusaders who needed to borrow money.[14]

King Louis went on doggedly doing the job he had set out to do. His letters came quite regularly. There had been some developments favourable to the Christians. The Sultans of Egypt and Aleppo had quarrelled, with the result that the pressure on Palestine had slackened a bit. The tiny Christian kingdom was caught like a nut in a huge vice whenever the sultans on each side were on good terms, or when there was only one sultan of both Egypt and Syria, as in Saladin's time towards the end of the 12th century. But usually the enmity between Egypt and Syria led one or other of them to propose an alliance with the Christians. 'Could we but receive some succour today,' Louis wrote to Alphonse on August 11, 1251, 'we might conclude a good and serviceable truce with the one or the other, if not with both.'

The army was resting at Caesarea, Louis wrote. Neither the Saracens nor the Bedouins had attacked recently. The road to Acre was open. Pirates sometimes raided the Christians' galleys, but sometimes also they were caught, which ensured the freedom of the seas for a while. Louis was methodically carrying out the rebuilding of the Christian strongholds; at times he even lent a hand personally with the menial labour. He ended the letter as follows: 'Have a care to advise us in all matters touching our most dear Lady and Mother. Send us news of you, and of our very dear and true Charles, Count of Anjou and Provence, and our dear sister. Do you tell us what's all the talk in our lands, the same each time you dispatch us messengers.'[15]

The situation in Europe itself was changing rapidly when Louis wrote. The death of the Emperor Frederick II on December 13, 1250, was like a huge reprieve for the Pope. Frederick left the Holy Roman Empire in an undeniably muddled state, particularly in the cities of Italy, which had been perennially switching their allegiances from Pope to Emperor and Emperor to Pope. Now that he was rid of the man whom he had called 'Christ's foe, the serpent Frederick', Pope Innocent IV prepared to return at once to Rome. On Holy Thursday, April 13, 1251, a great open-air ceremony was held in Lyons, as the Pope bade farewell to the people among whom he had found refuge for six years. The man whom Innocent had named as the new Holy Roman Emperor, William of Holland, held his stirrup for him as he mounted his horse. Blanche had written offering her services for his journey, but the Pope had immediately answered that she must not tax her strength merely to come to Lyons to bid him farewell. He was not eager to meet the queen, who would inevitably have asked, with all her well-known determination, that he find help for the crusaders in the Holy Land.

It was true, however, that under such terrible stress Blanche's health was beginning to weaken in that spring of 1251. She could still summon up all her energy, however, when it was called for. The full force of her anger burst out when she learned shortly thereafter that the Pope was preaching a new crusade – this one against Conrad IV, the dead emperor's son! Blanche furiously, openly, proclaimed throughout France that she would seize the lands and chattels of anyone who took the cross to help the Pope fight his personal enemy. 'Those who would battle for the Pope shall feed upon the Pope's cost, and they shall depart forever!' Matthew Paris, at any rate, vouches for the fact that that is what she said.

The ordinary running of the kingdom would have sufficed to absorb Blanche's energy. She kept an eye on everything. She continued to deal personally with whatever difficulties cropped up, particularly in the south of France, in towns such

as Avignon and Arles which had recently been under Frederick
II's suzerainty, and Marseilles, which was revolting against the
rule of Charles of Anjou. In the north trouble had broken out
in Flanders, where the heirs of Countess Johanna were quarrelling but had agreed to accept the arbitration of the King of
France. But the chief new problems resulted from the death
of Joan of Boulogne, the daughter of Philip Hurepel. Blanche
had at once seized the county in the King's name, thereby
earning the reproaches of Alphonse and Charles, each of whom
felt it should be his. Blanche had listened to the advice of her
council and then given a ruling that showed her watchful as
always, and anxious, like a good *materfamilias*, to safeguard the
rights of each member of a household: 'Whatever is, past
question, the King's own, we maintain for him. Whatever
clearly is the Countess Mathilda's we restore to her. Whatever
is in doubt we mean to hold in the custody of our most dear
son Louis, but with proviso and exception that whatever from
this succession shall fall to our other sons Alphonse and
Charles, the same being come to petition us, we hereby preserve
for them.'[16] Thus the King would settle the matter when he
returned; they could all trust his sense of justice. Until then
not an inch of the land that was rightfully under their elder
brother's jurisdiction would be handed over to Alphonse or
Charles. 'There is but one King in France.'

Relations with England had improved. Blanche had been at
great pains to get on good terms with this most perennially
dangerous of her neighbours. Richard of Cornwall had passed
through France the year before, on his way back to England
from Rome. Blanche had received him with great pomp and
had lavished gifts on him. Richard had gone to Pontigny to
pay his respects at the tomb of Edmund of Canterbury, who
had been canonized a few years before. It was a graceful
gesture. Edmund, like Thomas Becket before him, had been
driven from England by the reigning king, and had found
refuge – and died in exile – in the same town where Thomas
had been welcomed by the King of France. Blanche had been

to the ceremonies at Pontigny in honour of Edmund's canonization and she cherished fond memories of the saintly man. The
prayer that she uttered publicly at the time has come down to
us: 'Most holy confessor, who didst deign in time past to bless
me and my children, when I besought thee during the exile
thou didst come to spend with us in France, pray now to our
Heavenly Father that He might confirm by his grace what He
has wrought in us, and maintain this realm of France in its
peaceable and triumphant strength.'[17]

The two countries continued on good terms after Richard's
visit. Henry III corresponded several times with Blanche. The
altercations which arose occasionally on the borders of the
English possessions in Guienne and Gascony were settled
amicably. Oddly enough, there was even a rumour that
Blanche meant to give back to the King of England a part of
the lands taken from him by conquest, to ensure peace. This is
what Matthew Paris says, adding that Blanche was merely
going by Louis's own wishes in the matter. But the idea at once
elicited 'monstrous murmurings and grumblings' from the
French barons. The rumour can be understood in the light of
what was to follow.[18]

All this made Blanche fervently wish for Louis's return.
She felt her strength ebbing. She was painfully aware of the
many surging ambitions that must be held in check, the many
wrongs that must be righted, or prevented from happening.
Much goes awry when a king is absent from his kingdom. The
year 1252 started badly, with an unusually warm March
followed by fierce winds in April and May. The flowers which
had blossomed too soon, withered. The crops were ruined by
early-morning frosts. It was as if nature herself were in anguish,
or in mourning.

A little earlier, in August 1251, Blanche had once more given
a public demonstration of her energy. It was destined to be her
last official act. For some months the Paris chapter had been
bickering with the serfs on its lands in Orly and Châtenay.
The serfs' protests had to do with tallage, an arbitrary tax

levied on them according to estimates of their harvests. Sixteen peasants had been arrested, then released in June in return for their promise that they would return to the chapter prison on August 28 if the quarrel was not yet over. The Paris provosts had become involved. One of them, Warner of Verberie, had gone to Orly but had been unable to persuade the serfs to pay a tallage which they insisted was greater than that allowed by local custom. The matter had often been debated in the chapter, and the proposed tallage had its supporters and its foes. Among its enemies, surprisingly, was the papal legate himself, Odo of Châteauroux, but he was off crusading with King Louis. The whole question had already arisen at the time of the King's illness, and Louis had been at odds with the chapter about it.

When Blanche learned that the canons, not content with imprisoning their serfs, were also starving them, she at once proposed her own good offices to mediate the dispute. Let the serfs be released on bail and she would personally investigate the matter so that the proper amount of tallage could be decided once and for all. The canons' answer was that the Queen should mind her own business. They became furious and, not content with the men, they threw the Orly women and children into prison too. The poor wretches were piled one on top of another in the cramped cell in the midsummer heat. When Blanche was told of this she flew into a rage as fierce as any of her career.

The old Queen summoned the castellan of the Louvre Palace with his men-at-arms. She herself took the head of the column. The chapter was only a hundred yards or so from the Palace. The townsfolk of Paris were treated to the spectacle of their sovereign marching along with all her old dash and vigour, surrounded by crossbowmen and soldiers with maces. The news of the expedition leapt from mouth to mouth and reached the chapter-house ahead of her: those overfed canons would have an angry queen to deal with. When she arrived the cloister was virtually deserted. Blanche ordered the trembling porter to hand over the keys of the cellar and dungeon, and she started down the stone steps, with a firm tread. The dungeon was inside the cellar. Blanche seized a cudgel from one of her soldiers and personally dealt the first blow on the cellar door. Then one of the crossbowmen, William of Senlis, set about bursting it open, after which he and the other soldiers smashed the door of the dungeon with their maces. Blanche herself greeted the men, women and children who came stumbling out into the light from where they had lain 'in great distress of the heat they had had one of the other, such that there were several dead of it,' the chroniclers assert.[19] The Queen took them under her protection and cared for them until they were able to get back to Orly on their own.

Once more Blanche had been moved by a maternal reaction towards those who looked to her for help because they could not help themselves. Regardless of right and wrong, the main thing was to end the scandal of locking up men and women in a cell where they could not even live.

Blanche began by impounding the canons' revenues. Then she ordered an investigation, since it was only justice to determine whether the Orly serfs did or did not owe the tallage claimed by their chapter. Interestingly, the investigation showed that the chapter did have a right to the tallage claimed; it had been established by ancient precedents. The affair ended with the emancipation of the serfs in consideration of their payment of an annuity to the chapter. This question of emancipating serfs was very much on Blanche's mind. Some time before she had had the serfs of Wissous (south of Paris) freed from their bondage, and shortly before her death she ratified the emancipation of a large number who were dependent on the abbey of Saint-Maur-des-Fossés, just to the east of Paris, including some who worked in Paris itself, and others in La Varenne and Chennevières.

It was a grim year. One ordeal followed another until finally Blanche no longer had the strength to endure them. First it was the death of Berenguela's son, King Ferdinand III of

Castile, on May 30, 1252. Though she had never met him, Blanche loved her nephew as she loved everything to do with her family in Castile, especially everyone connected with Berenguela, whom she cherished. Ferdinand's subjects had been devoted to him, as were Louis's to their King. Amid the many jostling races and religions of his native Castile, Ferdinand had been a model king, meting out strict justice to all, be they Jews, Muslims, or Christians. He himself had chosen the title 'King of the three faiths'. Castile at that time was a remarkable haven of peaceful coexistence. The Inquisition had not yet started there, and it would in any event have been pointless, for although there were several different religions in close contact with one another, there were no heretics, strictly speaking. When Ferdinand III had heard of the disastrous defeat of Louis's crusaders in Egypt he had himself taken the cross. Blanche had been very grateful for the gesture, but illness and then death had prevented the keeping of the vow.

Scarcely had the news of Ferdinand's death come when another blow fell. Alphonse of Poitiers was stricken with partial paralysis. He and his wife were very happy, but unfortunately, childless. For a time his life was feared for, but he improved, though the attack left him with impaired eyesight. The following year he sent two of his retainers to describe his case to a Jewish doctor in Aragon. Just how effective this diagnosis by proxy was is not known, but Alphonse ended up almost completely cured. His first act, when his health was restored, was to take the cross again.

Blanche had only one wish, one hope: that her son would return. She felt she had come to the end of her strength. The retirement that she had yearned for so long seemed now like an inalienable right. The two abbeys she had founded, Notre-Dame-du-Lys (also called Sainte-Marie-Royale) near Melun, and Notre-Dame-la-Royale at Maubuisson, seemed more and more the obvious sanctuaries for which her whole being cried out. She had given herself up, body and soul, to the running of the kingdom. It had been her calling – at first forced on her by circumstances, later freely accepted. Now it had become too much for her. She was utterly exhausted, and aware that she could carry on no longer. Someone else must come, or rather, come back. Indeed, perhaps her own death would hasten his return . . .

In November 1252, at Melun, she had to take to her bed. They fussed over her. The Bishop of Paris, Reynold of Corbeil, hastened to her side. When he had given her the Eucharist he listened to her last wish: she wanted to wear the habit of the enclosed Cistercian nuns. The Bishop supposed she was voicing a pious custom of the times, that of being buried in the dress of one of the religious orders. But that was not what Blanche meant. She actually wanted to become a nun then and there, and remain one until her death, even if she recovered from her present illness. It was a free act of renunciation. She meant to resign the royal power and enter a convent.[20] From that moment on she considered herself under the authority of the Mother Superior of the convent of Maubuisson.

But the end was approaching. Blanche asked to be laid on a simple straw pallet, on which a sheet had been spread. The priests and religious clustered silently about her. She had already received the last sacraments. She felt death coming. What more did they want? As if to give the signal and add the final touch to the ritual of her own departure from this world, Blanche herself broke into the prayer of the moment of death, called in the liturgy the 'recommendation of the soul': '*Subvenite, sancti Dei* . . . Help me, ye saints of God; fly hither, ye angels of the Lord; receive my soul and bear it before the All-high. . . .' Her lips moved through five or six of the verses. Then those near her sang on alone.

It was three o'clock in the afternoon of either November 26 or 27, 1252. They dressed Blanche in her royal robes, but on her head was placed her Cistercian nun's veil, and on it her crown. Her body was placed on a litter and carried by her sons and the barons of her entourage from Melun to Paris, and then to the abbey of Saint-Denis. The clergy and the people held her wake one whole night. The *Great Chronicles of France* stress the people's grief: 'At her death the common people sorrowed much, for she had ever a care that they be not fleeced by the rich, and did well defend the right.'[21] The common people kept watch over the queen they loved, in the choir of the splendid abbey church, recently restored, which now glowed with innumerable tapers.

After the mass and office for the dead on the morning of November 29, the procession wound its way to the abbey of Maubuisson, where a further service was held before Blanche's body was laid in the abbey vault.

'She left the realm of France inconsolable,' says Matthew Paris, himself obviously moved – for once – by the intense grief caused by the Queen's death.[22]

Her gravestone was an enamelled copper plate like those of the small children she had lost. It remained in place until the French Revolution, when it was melted down for scrap metal.

Messengers were sent oversea to bring word to the papal legate, Odo of Châteauroux, who was to inform Louis and Margaret. It was the season of Advent. The whole of France awaited the return of the King.

EPILOGUE

Queen Margaret sat alone at her window. From the royal apartments she looked down on the Palace courtyard and the city of Paris. More and more it was the official royal residence, the place from which the King set out on journeys through his realm, and the place to which he returned. The lower arcades had been built recently. Their busy murmur came faintly to Margaret's ear: the calls of the servants and kitchen-people, among them a few enterprising merchants who had been allowed to set up their shops within the Palace precinct. Those lower levels hummed with increasing activity, with the shouts of the soldiers keeping garrison, and with the crowd of litigants come to lay their suits before the King's officers or even the King himself. Louis was a great builder, and under his impetus the Palace had been enlarged. It had grown to be the hub of the realm, both a hive of humanity and a stoutly defended fortress. Towards the setting sun the Bonbec tower rose almost directly from the Seine to guard the new 'Little Palace' which he had built, its walls – rising literally out of the water – adjoining the Sainte-Chapelle, where the King spent many long hours in prayer.

Sitting apart, above the bustle, Margaret reflected. Ten years had gone by since her doughty mother-in-law had died, since that day when the papal legate had come to her and Louis at their residence in Sidon,* on the coast of Palestine, with the news of Blanche's death. Ten very busy years during which much had happened within France and without. And still Blanche's memory was as fresh in the hearts of the people as

* Called Sayete, Saiette, Saete, etc., in the chronicles.

if she had died only yesterday. Ten years during which Louis
and Margaret had not once gone out of the Palace but what
they had met someone who spoke to them of Queen Blanche,
and told how, on a certain day, he had seen her do such-and-
such a thing, or how, on another, she had favoured him with a
smile, or rendered justice on his behalf, or conferred a dowry
on some girl he knew, so that she might get married. Ten years
during which King Louis had not once reached an important
decision without first asking himself what his mother would
have done in the same case. Blanche's spirit seemed to be all
about them, as present in the realm of France as if she had never
died. The people recited litanies of her name: 'Blanche the
prudent; Blanche the valiant; France's good Queen; she who
ruled so wisely and so well; she who so well preserved the
realm whilst her son was oversea; she who never while she
lived did know the people's spite nor blame . . .'[1]

Margaret may have been a bit ruffled by this continued
veneration of her mother-in-law, but hers was too generous a
nature to be embittered by it. In her own daily life she had
learned to dismiss mere personal grudges from her mind. She
did not question the dead Queen Mother's worth; within her
heart she concurred when people sang Blanche's praises.
Moreover, the example set by Blanche had not been wasted
on Margaret; in many things she took her as her model.

Margaret was no longer the 'Young Queen'; she was now
the only queen in France. She had turned forty. If she could not
look back over her own life with a sense of vast achievement,
she could look back without shame. She had earned her fair
place in the gallery of France's queens; she could stand com-
parison with any that had gone before her. That is, with any
except Blanche.

Whenever she caught herself doubting her own merit,
Margaret would call up her memories of the Holy Land. She
had come through ordeals that Blanche had never known.
Would Blanche have done better in her place? No, Margaret
could honestly tell herself that she had played her role as well

as any queen could, that her 'Lady' had matched Louis's 'Knight'. She remembered those disastrous days with the army at Damietta. Her husband had been far up-river, at El Mansura. She had been with child, on the point of giving birth. Then they had come with the horrifying news: the King was gravely ill; the defeated army had capitulated; the victorious Saracens were almost upon them. How long would the walls of Damietta hold? Everyone about her was terrified, but she, in addition, must go to childbed. Each time she managed to snatch a few hours' sleep she dreamed of Saracens bursting into her room to cut her throat, and woke up screaming for help. She had begged an old knight who had remained in Damietta, a man of eighty, to sleep next to her bed. He held her hand, and each time she was alarmed he would comfort her: 'Fear not, Lady, for I am nigh.'

When attack had seemed imminent, she had sent everyone out of her room and stayed alone with the venerable knight. She had kneeled before him and begged a favour of him. Though taken aback he had quickly sworn to do whatever she asked. She had solemnly enjoined him: 'I bid you, Knight, by that faith you have ever given me that should the Saracens possess the town you strike off my head e'er they lay hold on me.' She preferred death to one of those seraglios where so many Christian women and girls had ended their unhappy days, forced to deny their faith and to prostitute their souls as well as their bodies.

The old knight had not been startled by her request: 'Lady, I'll do't, be sure of it. I had already bethought myself I should kill you sooner than let them take you.'

The next day she had given birth to a son who had been christened John and nicknamed 'Tristan' because of the sad circumstances under which he was born. But that was not to be the end of her job. On the very same day, they came to inform her that all the merchants still lingering in Damietta were going to desert the city. Only the women and children of the crusaders who were dead or prisoners further up the

Nile would be left. She sent word to the merchants asking them to meet her the next morning at dawn, and, pulling herself together, she appealed first to the merchants' pity, for the town of Damietta was the only tangible thing she could hope to offer the Saracens as a pledge for the life of the King and his companions. 'For the love of God,' she pleaded, 'do not quit this place. If you pity me not, nor those whose hope is in this town, at least take pity on this tender babe here at my breast. At least wait until I am afoot again, that I may look to the business.'

The merchants were those same men from Pisa, Genoa, and other Italian and Mediterranean towns from whom the crusaders were borrowing in order to feed and equip the Christian army. They exchanged glances among themselves and then turned to Margaret: 'How shall we do, Lady? We shall starve if we stay here!'

Margaret reflected. There was no hope in trying to awaken their pity. She was dealing with merchants. She must talk to them in the only language they understood. The solution came to her in a flash. 'Myself shall purchase all that's in this place, victuals and supplies. From this day you shall be as in the King's service. Your expenses are upon his cost, and the royal exchequer.'

It worked. After a brief consultation among themselves the merchants returned to Margaret and, to her intense relief, announced their agreement. Damietta would not lack for defenders. She at once gave orders to buy up all the supplies in the town – more than 360,000 *livres*' worth; a staggering sum, but the King's life depended on it. Thus Damietta was able to hold on and become a feasible pledge for the ransoming of the crusaders. It was not yet time for Margaret's churching (forty days after the birth of a boy, according to *Leviticus* xii) when she had to leave Damietta with her little John Tristan and sail to Acre, along with her attendants and ladies-in-waiting. Several months later she was at last able to rejoin the King. And everyone in France, England, and all over

Europe, had said: without Queen Margaret's courage the army would have died.

So why did she still not feel Queen Blanche's equal? She too was a successful wife and mother, with everything a woman needs to be happy. Two years before she had given birth to little Agnes, the royal couple's eleventh child. Of the eleven, eight were still alive, including John Tristan and two others, a brother and a sister, also born in the East. As to her husband, could she ask for a better? In addition to their mutual unstinting love, there was that special admiration that she, like everyone else, felt for Louis as for someone unique, someone akin to the heroes of legend. Her intuition told her that one day his image would be in the stained-glass windows of churches, and on the altars, along with the blessed Dominic and Francis of Assisi. For that matter he was already referred to as the King who was a saint – by the common people mainly, for the bourgeois and the barons were afraid of him. She knew his heart better than anyone, and knew that he had yielded it wholly to God. She admired him despite his uneven temper. He had his mother's impulsiveness, sometimes even her violence. He was not merely a saintly man – he was a *saint*, with all the burning intensity that makes a saint the man he is. But she knew also that he could always be trusted. When he lost his temper, it was because his sense of justice had been outraged. No one, neither baron nor kinsman, ever got the better of that evenhanded justice of his, dealt out serenely, but inflexibly. The Sire of Coucy had found it out, when he had had three young lads hanged in his forest. Even the fiery Charles of Anjou (whom Margaret detested) had had to yield to his elder brother's will.

Louis was the perfect husband. Margaret knew that so long as she kept within the bounds of justice his heart belonged to her, after God. He had proved it more than once. It was at her urging that he had finally agreed to leave the Holy Land. Back in Europe, he had not wanted to go ashore at Hyères (near Toulon), saying that he would only set foot on the soil of his own kingdom. He had hesitated two days, thinking to sail on to Aigues-Mortes. But the ships had had a frightful crossing and could not be asked to go further. Everything had happened to them: storms, running aground on a sand-bank off Cyprus, even a fire at sea. The blaze had started at night in Margaret's own cabin, through a maid's carelessness. The Queen had leapt out of bed stark naked, bundled up the flaming sheets and blankets, and thrown them overboard. They had watched them burn for a long time, drifting away on the dark water. To set to sea again when the shores of her native Provence were at hand had seemed unthinkable to Margaret. It would have been tempting fate. Her personal plea, taken to the King by his close friend Joinville, the faithful seneschal of Champagne, had finally won the day.

There was more than that to Margaret's credit. On his return to France Louis had determined to renounce his temporal responsibilities and become a monk. He was seriously considering joining the Cistercians of the abbey of Royaumont, of whom he was very fond, or else the Franciscans. Margaret had managed to dissuade him, vividly pointing out all the dangers to France that his abdication would bring. Their heir, little Prince Louis, whose memory made her weep bitterly, was only ten at the time. He would have fallen into the barons' hands just as Louis IX himself had almost done at the beginning of his reign, but for Queen Blanche. What most counted, however, was that by becoming a monk Louis would be shirking his responsibilities. For her clinching argument Margaret had brought in all their children and stood them before him. The King had said nothing, but in his heart the tide had turned. When she remembered that moment Margaret felt a special, private satisfaction: Blanche had not been able to talk her son out of his crusade . . .

Even in politics Margaret had brought the King round to her own views. She had got him to sign a really serious peace treaty with her brother-in-law Henry III of England which returned some conquered lands to Henry, in order, said

Margaret, 'to bring love 'twixt my children and his, who are their cousins-german'. And through whom had it come about that the scions of France and the scions of England were first cousins? Through herself, Margaret the Queen.

A happy woman, yes . . . but somehow still unfulfilled. What more did she need to leave her mark on history? Her mother-in-law had treated her simply as someone for the King to go to bed with and bear his children. For some time now Margaret had been considering a way of getting even. The idea had come shortly after the loss of young Prince Louis, whose death had affected both Louis and Margaret deeply. It had been a disaster for the hopes of the kingdom, for the Prince had been the embodiment of all that could be hoped for in a king-to-be. He had been just like his father, with qualities if anything even more promising, a thoroughly noble youth – dead at sixteen.

It had been an irreparable loss. Philip, the brother next in line, was far from showing the same promise. True he was a handsome lad, well-knit and handy with the lance. But he was muddle-headed and irresolute. There was something in him of his uncle Robert of Artois, a kind of reckless bravery; and also something of his uncle Charles of Anjou's restless ambition out of all proportion to his means of gratifying it. Margaret, an attentive mother, had carefully noted these things. Was there not something she should do about it? A role for her rather like Blanche's role in times past?

In the spring of 1263 the King of France learned of a shocking vow which Queen Margaret had wrung from their heir. Louis was dumbfounded. Margaret had made Prince Philip swear on the Bible that until the age of thirty he would remain in her 'bail', which is to say in her custody, under her surveillance; and would heed no one's advice against her wishes.

But Philip's misgivings had grown as he realized that his mother meant to keep him in a state of artificial minority until he was thirty. In violation of one of the oath's very provisions, he had gone to his father and told him everything. Since then he had lived in constant remorse, not knowing which was worse; to have made such a rash vow, or to have broken it. Louis reassured his son. To set his conscience completely at rest he sent messengers at once to Pope Urban IV, a Frenchman. On July 6 the response, a document duly sealed with lead[2] at the pontifical chancellery, released the young man from his unconsidered promise. Louis wisely did not hold it against his wife, and Margaret yielded to the inevitable. There had been many queens of France. There would be many more. There could be only one Queen Blanche.

NOTES AND SOURCES

NOTES AND SOURCES

Chapter I: A FOURSOME OF QUEENS

1 See *Magna vitas. Hugonis. The Life of S. Hugh of Lincoln* published by Decima L. Douie and Hugh Farmer (2 vols., London and New York, 1961); Vol. 2, pp. 156 and 142

2 Cf. R. Bezzola: *Les origines et la formation de la littérature courtoise en Occident*, Part III, 2: p. 343

3 William Le Breton: *La Philippide*, Book VI, 28

4 *Chronique de Jean d'Oxford* cited by Élie Berger: *Blanche de Castille* (1895), p. 10

5 *Lettres* of Étienne de Tournai, published by Desilve (1893); p. 367

6 Jean Maillard: *Un roi-trouvère au XIIIᵉ siècle*. Vol, 18 of *Musicological Studies and Documents*, American Institute of Musicology, 1967.

7 Roger de Wendover, vol. 1, p. 316

8 *Chronique de L'Anonyme de Béthune*, in *Rec. des Hist. de France*, XXIV, 2, p. 760

9 *Histoire des ducs de Normandie*, published by F. Michel; p. 93

10 *Ibid.*, pp. 94–5

11 *Histoire de Guillaume le Maréchal*, published by P. Meyer; III, p. 164

12 *Ibid.*, pp. 167–70

13 These accounts were published in Brussels: *Usage des fiefs*, II (1750), pp. 157 and 174 *et seq.*

14 Villehardouin: *Histoire de la conquête*, published by Faral, pp. 90 and 128; and a letter of Innocent III cited in Fliche and Martin: *Histoire de l'Église*, X, p. 71

Chapter II: BLANCHE'S HERITAGE

1 William Le Breton: *Chronique*, published by Delaborde, No. 149, p. 226

2 Cf. Delisle: *Premier registre de Ph.-Aug.* (Paris, 1883), p. 93
3 *Histoire des ducs de Normandie*, pp. 119–20
4 William Le Breton: *La Philippide*, Book XII, 835 *et seq.*
5 *Histoire des ducs de Normandie*, p. 105
6 *Ibid.*, p. 121
7 William Le Breton: *La Philippide*, Book IX, 569–70
8 *Histoire des ducs de Normandie*, p. 126
9 Published in *Rec. des Hist. de France*, XIX, pp. 254–5
10 Published in *Layettes du Trésor des chartes*, II, Nos. 1813–21, pp. 97–9
11 William Le Breton: *La Philippide*, Book II, 87–149
12 William Le Breton: *Chronique*, No. 203, pp. 296–7
13 *Ibid.*, No. 202, p. 295
14 Guillaume Guiart: *Branche des royaux lignages*, p. 280
15 *Chronique de L'Anonyme de Béthune*, in *Rec. des Hist. de France*, XXIV, 2, p. 763
16 Cf. Petit-Dutaillis: *Louis VIII*, p. 52
17 *Chanson de la croisade albigeoise*, cited in Petit-Dutaillis: *Louis VIII*, p. 194
18 Roger de Wendover: *Flores Historiarum*, published by Hewlett: II, 135–6
19 *Histoire des ducs de Normandie, op. cit.*, pp. 160–1
20 Roger de Wendover: *Flores Historiarum*, II, p. 176
21 *Histoire des ducs de Normandie*, p. 164
22 Roger de Wendover, *Flores Historiarum*, II, 177
23 *Ibid.*, 178–80
24 *Histoire des ducs de Normandie*, p. 167
25 Letter cited in the *Chronique* of Hoveden (published by Stubbs), IV, p. 190
26 *Histoire des ducs de Normandie*, pp. 169–70
27 *Histoire de Guillaume le Maréchal*, III, p. 212
28 *Ibid*, pp. 213–14
29 Cited in Petit-Dutaillis: *Louis VIII*, p. 136
30 *Ibid.*, p. 140
31 Matthew Paris: *Chronique*, III, 25–6
32 *Récits d'un ménestrel de Reims*, Nos. 301–2
33 This and preceding citations from *Histoire des ducs de Normandie*, pp. 198–202

Chapter III: THE REALM OF THE FLEUR-DE-LIS

1 See *Annuaire-bulletin de la soc. de l'Hist. de France*, 1885, p. 132
2 Conon de Lausanne, cited in Petit-Dutaillis, *op. cit.*, p. 216
3 *Ibid.*, p. 114
4 Étienne de Bourbon: *Anecdotes*, published by Lecoy de la Marche, No. 323, pp. 271-2
5 Nicolas de Bray, cited in Petit-Dutaillis, *op. cit.*, p. 223
6 Unpublished manuscript, No. 870 in the Mazarine Library; the subject of a study in *Hist. litt. de la France*, XXX, 325-9
7 *Ornatus mulierum*, a 13th-century Anglo-Norman text, published by P. Ruelle (Brussels University Press, 1967)
8 *Histoire des ducs de Normandie*, p. 206
9 *Grandes Chroniques de France*, VII, p. 11
10 The texts cited are from *Grandes Chroniques de France*, VII, pp. 17-18
11 *Chanson de la croisade albigeoise*, published by Martin-Chabot, III, pp. 290-1; lines 91-104
12 *Historia albigensis*, published by Guébin and Lyon, III, p. 14
13 *Grandes Chroniques de France*, VII, p. 9
14 See the study of Simon de Montfort in *Cahiers de Fangeaux*, 4, p. 283
15 *Annales* of Dunstable and Roger de Wendover, cited in Petit-Dutaillis, *op. cit.*, p. 295
16 *Grandes Chroniques de France*, VII, pp. 23-4
17 Robert Saincereau or de Sancerre, in *Rec. des Hist. de France*, XXIII, p. 124-31

Chapter IV: CHECK TO THE QUEEN

1 It is inaccurate to speak of Blanche's 'regency' or of Louis IX's 'majority'. On this subject see F. Olivier-Martin: *Études sur les régences*
2 *Grandes Chroniques de France*, VII, p. 38-40
3 Joinville: *Histoire de Saint Louis*, chap. 16
4 Cited in Élie Berger, *Blanche de Castille*, p. 108
5 French National Archives: *Layettes du Trésor des chartes*, Supplement II, No. 1979 7 to 1979 33

6 See Élie Berger, *op. cit.*, pp. 123–5

7 *Grandes Chroniques de France*, VII, pp. 43–4

8 *Récits d'un ménestrel de Reims*, Nos. 348–351

9 Cf. Élie Berger, *op. cit.*, pp. 157–8

10 Roger de Wendover, *Flores Historiarum*, II, p. 347

11 Published in *Histoire de Languedoc*, VIII, 893

12 The original of the treaty of 1229 is preserved in the French National Archives, J. 305 No. 60; and published in *Layettes du Trésor des chartes*, II, No. 1992

13 Matthew Paris: *Chronica majora*, III, p. 166, *et seq.*

14 *Récits d'un ménestrel de Reims*, Nos. 187–8

15 Étienne de Bourbon: *Anecdotes, op. cit.*, No. 513, p. 443

16 Geoffrey of Beaulieu's account is found in Duchesne, *Historiae Francorum Scriptores*, vol. V, pp. 445–6

17 Guillaume de Saint-Pathus, pp. 13–18

18 *Ibid.*, pp. 88 and 71

19 French National Archives, J. 427 No 11 *bis*; and published in *Layettes du Trésor des chartes*, 11, No. 2083

20 *Grandes Chroniques de France*, VII, pp. 66 *et seq.*

Chapter V: THE TWO QUEENS

1 Philippe Mouskès: *Chronique rimée*, lines 28,692 *et seq.*

2 *Grandes Chroniques de France*, VII, pp. 64–5

3 Aubry de Trois-Fontaines, in *Rec. des Hist. de France*, XXI, p. 619

4 These accounts have been published in *Rec. des Hist. de France*, XXI, pp. 220–60, the total amount being mentioned on p. 248, See also XXII, pp. 579–622

5 We are indebted for this theory to Rita Lejeune, the eminent authority on Romance languages. See her article in *Le Siècle de Saint Louis* (Paris, Hachette, 1970). Chap. XVIII, *La courtoisie et la littérature au temps de Blanche de Castille et de Louis IX*, pp. 181–96

6 *Le Dictié d'Urbain*, cited in the Introduction to the edition of Philippe Mouskès, II, note on p. 225

7 The letter is preserved in the French National Archives, J. 1030, No. 73. It was displayed in the 1970 exhibition: *La France de Saint Louis*, as No. 115 in the catalogue. See the article by Douët

d'Arcq: *Le Siège de Carcassonne en 1240*, in *Bibliothèque de l'École des Chartes*, 2nd series II, 1845–6, pp. 363–79

8 See Dossat on the subject of the Inquisition, in chap. XXV of *Le Siècle de Saint Louis* (Note 5 above), pp. 259–66

9 Blanche's letter has been published by Bourquelot in *Revue des Sociétés savantes*, 4th series, V, p. 447 (1867)

10 The bull of Gregory IX is in the French National Archives and was published by Teulet: *Layettes*, II, No. 2514, 339–40

11 The letter of the La Rochelle spy is preserved in the French National Archives, and has been published by L. Delisle, in *Bibliothèque de l'École des Chartes* 1856, pp. 513–55

12 The letters of Bishop William of Beaumont and the Angers chapter were published by Teulet in *Layettes*, II, 22nd Sept. 1232

13 Citations taken from *Grandes Chroniques de France*, VII, pp. 87–9

14 *Ibid.*, pp. 90–1

15 See the story in Joinville (p. 74 of the edition of the 'Club des Libraires de France')

16 Matthew Paris: *Chronica majora*, IV, 211

17 *Grandes Chroniques de France*, VII, pp. 99–100. See the details of the fighting in Bémont: *La Campagne de Poitou 1242–3: Taillebourg et Saintes*, from *Annales du Midi*, V (Toulouse, 1893)

18 Philippe Mouskès: *Chronique rimée*, lines 31,110–31,114

19 The song on the Taillebourg battle was composed shortly after the event and preserved in a manuscript in the library of Modena, Italy. It has been published by A. Thomas in *Annales du Midi*, July 1892, pp. 362–70

20 Matthew Paris: *Chronica majora*, IV, 253

21 Cf. Y. Dossat: *L'Inquisition toulousaine*, in particular pp. 145–51 and 273

22 Matthew Paris: *Chronica majora*, IV, 226

23 The letter is preserved in the French National Archives, Toulouse repository, V, J. 309, No. 20. It has been published by Teulet in *Layettes*, II, pp. 482–3

24 Guillaume de Puylaurens, p. 305 in Guizot's edition

25 Guillaume de Nangis, in *Rec. des Hist. de France*, XX, p. 550

Chapter VI: THE QUEEN MOTHER

1 See *Grande Chronique de Limoges*, in *Rec. des Hist. de France* XXI, p. 766

2 Étienne de Bourbon: *Anecdotes*, note on p. 388

3 *Ibid.*, note on p. 389

4 Many letters on this matter have been preserved in the French National Archives. Cf. Teulet: *Layettes*, II Nos. 2577 and 2729 (from Pope Gregory IX); III, Nos. 3604, 3740, 3741, etc. (from Empress Mary of Constantinople); III, Nos. 3772–3774 (from Blanche, reimbursing Mary's creditors), and others

5 See R. Grousset: *L'Épopée des Croisades*, pp. 284–6; and Guillaume de Nangis in *Rec. des Hist. de France*, XX, 325

6 Citations taken from the texts published by Bouthoul: *Le Grand Maître des Assassins*, pp. 166–7

7 Matthew Paris: *Chronica majora*, IV, p. 111

8 See chap. XXII, dealing with the Middle East and Far East, in *Le Siècle de Saint Louis* (Paris, Hachette, 1970), pp. 230–7

9 Ponce of Aubon's letter to Louis IX was cited in H. Wallon: *Saint Louis et son temps*, 2 vols. (1876), I, note on pp. 153–4

10 Matthew Paris: *Chronica majora*, IV, p. 275

11 Philippe Mouskès: *Chronique rimée*, lines 31,022–31,023

12 Pope Gregory IX's letter has been published in *Layettes* II, No. 2836

13 Étienne de Bourbon: *Anecdotes*, No. 58, p. 63

14 See A. Dimier: *Saint Louis et Cîteaux*, note to p. 94. Cf. also Matthew Paris's account, cited in Élie Berger, *op. cit.*, p. 356

15 *Chronique de Jean Eleemosyna*. Cf. my works: *Les Croisés* p. 243; and *Les Croisades* (in the series 'Il y a toujours un reporter'), p. 246

16 Matthew Paris: *Chronica majora*, V, pp. 3–5

Chapter VII: 'LIKE A LILY'

1 Cf. Matthew Paris: *Chronica*, III, p. 196

2 From the biography of Isabella by the abbess of Longchamp, Agnès d'Harcourt; published by Du Cange after his text of Joinville (1668), pp. 169–70

3 Fliche and Martin: *Histoire de l'Église*, X, pp. 261, *et seq.*

4 Élie Berger: *Saint Louis et Innocent IV*, pp, 309–10

5 Rabbi Yehiel's account of the *Disputatio* has been published by J. C. Wagenseil: *Tela ignea Satane* (Altdorf, 1681, 2 vols. 4to) II, 2nd Part. It was amusing to note, at the time of the celebration of St Louis's 700th anniversary year, in 1970, how a section of the press was at pains to call him a 'Jew-burner'. It was the Talmud that was burned, not the Talmudists.

6 The letter was published by A. Foulet in *Lettres françaises du XIIIe siècle*, in *Classiques française du Moyen Age* (Paris 1924), No. 43, pp. 16–18

7 Raymond VII's will was published in *Layettes* III, No. 3802; the codicil being No. 3803; pp. 78–9

8 Cited in Élie Berger: *Blanche de Castille*, p. 375

9 The originals were published in *Layettes*, III, No. 3829, pp. 87 *et seq.*

10 Matthew Paris: *Chronica majora*, V, pp. 169–70

11 The latest and most complete work on the Children's Crusade is that of Zacour in *History of the Crusades* (University of Pennsylvania Press), II, pp. 325–42

12 Matthew Paris: *Chronica*, V, p. 239. According to some chroniclers, the 'Master of Hungary' may have been a runaway Cistercian monk by the name of Jacques. Cf. A. Dimier: *Saint Louis et Cîteaux*, pp. 209–10

13 The letter is published in *Layettes*, III, No. 3960, p. 142

14 A whole series of such letters are preserved in the French National Archives. Cf. *Layettes*, III, Nos. 3769 *et seq.*, pp. 68 *et seq.*

15 See *Layettes*, III, No. 3956

16 *Layettes*, III, No. 3978

17 See Shirley: *Royal and Historical Letters*, II

18 Matthew Paris: *Chronica*, IV, p. 631

19 *Grandes Chroniques de France*, VII, p. 168–9

20 A. Dimier: *op. cit.*, p. 95

21 *Grandes Chroniques de France*, VII, p. 167

22 Matthew Paris: *Chronica*, V, pp. 311–12 and 354

Epilogue

1 *Chronique anonyme*, published in *Rec. des. Hist. de France*, XXI, 116
2 The original is preserved in the French National Archives, J. 711, No. 301

INDEX

PRINCIPAL SOURCES

Abbreviations

CHFMA   *Les classiques de l'Histoire de France au Moyen Age*
SHF   *Société de l'Histoire de France*
RHF   *Recueil des Historiens de la France*
SATF   *Société des Anciens Textes français*

Chanson de la croisade albigeoise, ed. E. Martin-Chabot, Paris 1957, 3 vols. CHFMA No. 24
Chronique rimée de Saint-Magloire, RHF, XXII, p. 83 *et seq.*
Comptes de dépenses (Blanche de Castille, Saint Louis), RHF, XXII and XXIII
Enquêtes faites sur l'ordre de Saint Louis, RHF, XXIV
Grandes Chroniques de France, ed. J. Viard, Paris 1932, SHF No. 120
Guillaume Guiart, *La Branche des royaux lignages*, ed. Buchon, Paris 1828
Guillaume de Puylaurens, ed. Beyssier. *G. de P. et sa chronique*, University of Paris, Bulletin de la Faculté des Lettres, XVIII, 1904, pp. 85-175
Guillaume de Saint-Pathus, Queen Margaret's confessor, *Vie de Saint Louis.* Pubd. H.-F. Delaborde, Paris 1899. Coll. de textes pour servir à l'étude et à l'enseignement de l'Histoire, No. 25
Guillaume le Breton, ed. Delaborde, 1882, 2 vols. SHF
Guillaume le Maréchal, ed. P. Meyer, 1891, 3 vols. SHF
Histoire des ducs de Normandie, ed. F. Michel, 1840, SHF
Layettes du Trésor des Chartes, Vols. I and II ed. Teulet, Vol. III ed. J. de Laborde, Paris 1863-75
Magna Vita Sancti Hugonis. The Life of St Hugh of Lincoln, ed. Decima L. Douie and Hugh Farmer, London-New York 1961, 2 vols.
Matthew Paris, *Chronica majora*, ed. H. R. Luard, 1872-84. 7 vols. Rolls Series No. 57
Ménestrel de Reims (Récits d'un), ed. N. de Wailly, 1876, SHF
Mouskès, Philippe, *Chronique rimée*, ed. de Reiffenberg. Coll. de chroniques belges, Brussels, 1836-8, 2 vols.
Brai (Nicolas de), *Gesta Ludovici VIII*, RHF XVII
Vaux-de-Cernay (Pierre de), *Historia albigensis*, ed. Guébin and Lyon, Paris 1926, SHF

Shirley, W. W., *Royal and other Historical Letters illustrative of the Reign of Henry III*, Rolls Series No. 27

Theobald of Champagne, *Chansons*, ed. Wallensköld, Paris 1925, SATF

Villehardouin, *La Conquête de Constantinople*, ed. E. Faral, 1938, CHFMA No. 18

WORKS CONSULTED

Berger, Élie, *Histoire de Blanche de Castille reine de France*. Paris 1895. Bibl. des Écoles franç. d'Athènes et de Rome, fasc. 70

Petit-Dutaillis, Ch., *Étude sur la vie et le règne de Louis VIII (1187-1226)*. Paris 1894. Bibl. de l'École des Hautes-Études, fasc. 101

Siècle (Le) de Saint Louis. Hachette 1970. Collective vol. covering every aspect of the reign in 35 chapters, each by a specialist on the aspect concerned

Le Nain de Tillemont, *Vie de Saint Louis*. Pubd. J. de Gaulle, Paris 1847-51, 6 vols. SHF

Berger, É., *Saint Louis et Innocent IV*, Paris 1893

Bloch, M., *La France sous les derniers Capétiens, 1223-1328*. Paris, Cahiers des Annales ESC, 1958

Bémont, Ch., *La campagne de Poitou, 1242-3. Taillebourg et Saintes*. Toulouse 1893

Bezzola, R., *Les origines et la formation de la tradition courtoise en Occident*, 5 vols., Paris 1946-63

Boissonnade, P., *Quomodo comites Engolismenses erga reges Angliae et Franciae se gesserint et comitatus Engolismae atque Marchiae regno Francorum adjuncti fuerint, 1152-1328*. Angoulême 1893

Boutarde, E., *Marguerite de Provence, femme de Saint Louis. Son caractère, son rôle politique*, in *Rev. des questions historiques*, 1867, III, pp. 417-58

Cahiers de Fanjeaux, esp. Vol. 3, *Cathares en Languedoc*, 1968, and Vol. 4, *Paix de Dieu et guerre sainte en Languedoc au XIIIe siècle*, 1969

Dimier, Fr. Anselme, *Saint Louis et Cîteaux*, Paris 1954

Dossat, Yves, *Les crises de l'Inquisition toulousaine au XIIIe siècle, 1233-73*, Bordeaux 1959

Olivier-Martin, F., *Étude sur les régences. I. Les régences et la majorité des rois sous les Capétiens directs et les premiers Valois*, Paris 1931

Thouzellier, Ch., *Catharisme et valdéisme en Languedoc à la fin du XIIe et au début du XIIIe siècle*, P.U. 1966